The Political Ideas of St. Thomas Aquinas

Representative Selections

Edited with an Introduction by
DINO BIGONGIARI

THE FREE PRESS
New York   London   Toronto   Sydney   Singapore

THE FREE PRESS
A Division of Simon & Schuster Inc.
1230 Avenue of the Americas
New York, NY 10020

First Free Press Paperback Edition 1997

ISBN: 0-684-83641-6

Manufactured in the United States of America

10   9   8   7   6   5   4   3   2

CONTENTS

THE SUMMA THEOLOGICA, I-II

THE SUMMA THEOLOGICA, II-II

ON KINGSHIP

APPENDIX

INTRODUCTION *

I. THE STATE AS A NATURAL ORDER

A STATE according to St. Thomas is a part of the universal empire of which God is the maker and ruler. Its laws are, or can be made to be, particular determinations of this empire's eternal code; and the authority which enforces these laws is a power whose origin is also in God. Its goal and justification is to offer to man satisfactory material conditions of life as a basis for a moral and intellectual education which, in turn, must be such as to lend itself to the spiritual edification of the Christian man. For "God . . . instructs us by means of His law and assists us by His grace." [1]

St. Thomas follows the Aristotelian doctrine that makes of man a "political animal," but he modifies it in accordance with the exigencies of his Christian philosophy. The fact that man operates, not by instinct, but by reason makes social organization indispensable. This interdependence of reason and sociability is explained by St. Thomas as follows: by endowing man with reason and at the same time depriving him of instinct and of an available ready-made supply of the necessities of life, God decreed that man should be a political animal. For to the beasts nature furnishes food, body covering, weapons of defense and offense (claws, fangs, horns, etc.), means for survival through flight (rapid wings and quick feet), etc. But all this, and much more, man must produce for himself under the direction of reason. What lower animals perform spontaneously and instinctively (i.e., by the exercise of the "estimative" faculty) man achieves as a result of rational processes.

* The Introduction that follows is made up of extracts from a book of the editor (not yet published) on the political philosophy of St. Thomas. There is, therefore, no attempt at exhaustiveness or organic consistency. The aim was to facilitate the understanding of the selections from the *Summa* and the *De Regimine Principum* here included, by giving a detailed discussion of certain important topics and by introducing material from works of St. Thomas other than those above mentioned. [1] *S.* I-II, Q. 90, pp. 3 ff.

Beasts, without instruction, devoid of experience, deprived of mod-
els, know immediately what to do and how to act: the newly born
lamb at the mere sight of a wolf runs for safety; birds hatched
from eggs that have been removed from the nest, when the time
comes, build a nest identical to the one from which they came and
which they never saw; ailing animals instinctively pick out the
herbs that will cure their illnesses. Man, however, is born with a
common vague notion in place of this precise and particularized
instinct. To that general notion he applies reason and thus is able
to take care of himself. He, too, discovers the herbs that cure his
diseases, but as the result of a process of reasoning:

Man . . . has a natural knowledge of the things which are essential for his life only in a general fashion, inasmuch as he is able
to attain knowledge of the particular things necessary for human
life by reasoning from natural principles.[2]

But for this there is need of collaborative efforts, and a division
of labor is unavoidable.[3] Again in the words of St. Thomas:

It is not possible for one man to arrive at a knowledge of all these
things by his own individual reason. It is therefore necessary for
man to live in a multitude so that each one may assist his fellows,
and different men may be occupied in seeking, by their reason, to
make different discoveries—one, for example, in medicine, one in
this and another in that.[4]

This social process implies collaboration not merely of the members of one generation and of one nation, but of all men at all
times. Each coming generation which thrives on what its predeces-
sors bequeathed to it in turn leaves to posterity an intellectual
culture perfected by its own contributions. As our author says:

It seems natural to human reason to advance gradually from the
imperfect to the perfect. Hence, in speculative sciences, we see
that the teaching of the early philosophers was imperfect, and that
it was afterward perfected by those who succeeded them. So also
in practical matters. Discursive rationality implies progress.[5]

[2] *R.P.* (*On Kingship*) I, § 6, p. 176.   [3] Cf. Avicenna, *De anima* v. 1.
[4] *R.P. loc. cit.* The things which our mind discovers by this process St.
Thomas calls "adinventiones" (*S.* II-II, Q. 55, A. 2).
[5] *S.* I-II, Q. 97, A. 1, pp. 78 ff.

That man was intended to collaborate rationally is proved by the fact that he alone is endowed with the capacity to speak. Speech is the specific communication of rational beings. Lower animals convey to each other only emotions or feelings—fear, desire, hunger, etc.; for such communication all that is needed is sound, e.g., braying or roaring. But man uses words, which are the outward manifestation of concepts, that is, products of a conceiving reason.[6]

The naturally ordained distribution of tasks is described thus: "One man works for many, and many work for one." A political community is made up of artisans, farmers, soldiers, statesmen, etc. These constituents must do their work with competence, which means that they must be appropriately endowed and properly trained. A state, therefore, can function only if nature produces some men who are physically strong, others who are intellectually keen, and still others who are fearless. St. Thomas, on the authority of Aristotle, assures us that such men will always be forthcoming. Being indispensable to the state, they will be furnished by nature, since the state is "by nature," and "nature is never found lacking in what is necessary." The diversification of capacities essential to social collaboration is the unfailing gift of nature.[7]

In St. Thomas, however, the stress is placed on the fact that this "naturality" is but the execution of a decree of providence. Nature is a secondary cause and only an instrument. In his own words,

One man does not suffice to perform all those acts demanded by society, and therefore it is necessary that different persons be occupied in different pursuits. The diversification of men for diverse tasks is the result, primarily, of divine providence, which details the various compartments of man's life in such a way that nothing necessary to human existence is ever lacking; secondarily, this diversification proceeds from natural causes which bring it about that different men are born with aptitudes and tendencies for the different functions and the various ways of living.[8]

---

[6] Cf. *Ibid.*, A. 3, and *In Pol.* i. 1.

[7] Seneca had said: "God gave man two things which transformed him from a dependent into a master: reason and sociability" (*De benef.* iv. 18). St. Thomas says: "reason through sociability."

[8] *Quodl.* vii. 17; cf. *C.G.* iii. 132 and *C.I.* v. 27.

Man cannot satisfy his instinct for social life with the resources offered by the home, nor by those available in an estate, nor even by those furnished by a village. These are not capable of providing the economic basis for "being," nor the educative one for "well-being." For man's nature, over and above mere subsistence, longs for knowledge and virtue. ("All men by nature desire to know"; and "the desire for virtue is inborn in man.")

Because of these shortcomings, the above-named communities must be integrated into a larger and fuller body. Such is the self-sufficient group which St. Thomas (after Aristotle) calls the "perfect community." It is the city-state (*polis*), the *civitas*, or better still the *provincia*, and best of all the kingdom.

The difference between the perfect community and the others is not, as Plato thought, one of mere quantity; it is qualitative, as St. Thomas, following Aristotle, teaches. The perfect community is the goal toward which the other natural associations strive and in which they find their fulfillment. And that is one of the reasons why the state is "natural." For the Christian this naturally instituted process of moral edification which controls and regulates the production of economic goods is in turn subordinate to a third and higher interest: man's spiritual welfare, or the enjoyment of God, for the attainment of which the bonds of political society are indeed necessary but in no way sufficient.

The promotion of the appropriate conditions of life in both the economic and the cultural sphere is, then, the purpose of the state. Herein lies the common good of man and his highest worldly end. As such it sets in motion our actions and should control our individual aspirations. Its demands justify the employment of all the varied means that are required for its attainment. Reason tells us what these subordinate tasks, these indispensable occupations are; nature furnishes the appropriate workers for them; authority must see to it that the right man is put in the right place. When this is done, we say that "order" has been introduced, which means that multiplicity has been reduced to unity, and that, consequently, action is possible within the sphere affected by the desire for the common end. "Society is obviously nothing else than the unification of men for the purpose of performing some one thing in common," says St. Thomas.[9]

The divine intention is primarily directed to the order and then to the components unified in it and by it. As St. Thomas says, "If we remove order from created things, we remove the best they have. For though the individual beings are good in themselves, joined, they rise to the highest goodness because of the order of the universe." [10] Evil, on the authority of St. Augustine, is a condition that obtains when *order* is removed. An angel is superior to a stone. But a universe of angels and stones is better than one made solely of angels.[11] (Or, as one might say, a violin is better than a banjo. Yet an orchestra, with all sorts of instruments including the banjo, is preferable to an ensemble composed solely of violins.) The reason for this is "that the perfection of the universe is obtained essentially through a diversification of natures, which natures, so diversified, fill the various ranks of goodness; it is not obtained through the plurification of the individuals in any of these given natures." [12] The Angelic Doctor goes so far as to say:

A universe in which there was no evil would not be of so great goodness as our actual one; and this for the reason that there would not be in this assumed universe so many different good natures as there are in this present one, which contains both good natures free from evil as well as some conjoined with evil; and it is better to have the combination of both rather than to have one only.[13]

II. PUBLIC POWER

1. *The Ruler*

Order, then, comes into existence when a multiplicity of individuals are brought together and so arranged that by their united efforts a common end may be attained. But the "ordering" toward an end implies the action of a commanding authority. "In

---

[9] *C.I.* iii. [10] *C.G.* iii. 69. [11] I *Sent.* 44.1.2.6.
[12] *Ibid.,* 44.1.2.5. [13] *Ibid.,* 44.1.2.6.

every multitude there must be some governing power," according to St. Thomas:

For where there are many men together and each one is looking after his own interest, the multitude would be broken up and scattered unless there were also an agency to take care of what appertains to the common weal. . . . Indeed it is reasonable that this should happen, for what is proper and what is common are not identical. Things differ by what is proper to each; they are united by what they have in common. But diversity of effects is due to diversity of causes. Consequently, there must exist something which impels toward the particular good of each individual. Wherefore also in all things that are ordained toward one end, one thing is found to rule the rest.[1]

This applies pre-eminently to the order on whose existence all others depend, viz., the state, which Aristotle taught rests on the necessary relationship of "ruler and ruled." St. Augustine, too, as St. Thomas reminds us, had taught that men greedy for worldly goods were about to exterminate one another in their bloody competitions when by divine mercy it was permitted that "concord be established by means of a regime of *commanding* and *obeying*." [2] Today we still hear: "Obedience is the tie of human societies." [3]

That this subordination to authority is in accord with the intentions of nature is shown by the fact that some men are born with a capacity for ruling, while others are endowed with aptitudes for performing tasks under the direction of a commanding power. "Among men an order is found to exist, inasmuch as those who are superior by intellect are by nature rulers." [4] And the authority of St. Augustine is again adduced: "Ruling power is given by nature to the best." [5] This relationship of ruler and ruled is not the result of the Fall. It would have existed in the state of innocence.[6] Of course, the common goal aimed at by the ruler in the state of innocence would have been different from the actual one; the element of coercion would have been absent. "There would have been no need for protection, there being no hostility either internal or foreign, and no need of correcting transgressions, all

---

[1] *R.P.* I, §§ 8-9, pp. 176-7.   [2] *De civ. Dei* xix. 17.
[3] Prevost-Paradol, *La France Nouvelle*, Ch. 4.   [4] *C.G.* iii. 81.
[5] *Contra Iulianum* iv. 61.   [6] *S.* I, Q. 92, Aa. 1, 2; Q. 96, Aa. 3, 4.

men desiring the real good." [7] The ruler would not have been expected to guarantee conditions for material subsistence (*esse*) nor for moral betterment (*bene esse*). The only use for a ruler would have been "to guide in active life and in the field of studies according as one was wiser and intellectually more enlightened than another." [8]

Because of the Fall this spontaneous adherence to Order could not be maintained. The regime of *concupiscentia*, the *lex fomitis*, made coercion necessary. The authority over spontaneously obedient men was replaced by a power of making laws and of compelling observance through penalties: loss of property, liberty, life. This dread power imposes itself not only because of necessity but also and above all because it is authorized by God. Political power is divinely instituted. St. Paul proclaims this: "All power comes from God." [9] His divine commission, which transforms what would otherwise be brute force into just power, creates the *public person* [10] with unique attributes; to it belongs the exercise of the *publica, suprema potestas*.[11] No one else may inflict major punishment on a human being. The words of St. Augustine admonish us: "He who, without being authorized by the governing power, kills a malefactor shall be adjudged to be a murderer, and this all the more because he did not hesitate to usurp a power that God had not given him." This text was incorporated in the canon law.[12]

The doctrine of the divine origin of power must not be interpreted to mean that St. Thomas looked upon the state as existing in virtue of divine law. The state is an organization that rests on human law. "Dominium," he says, "was introduced by *ius gentium*, which is a human law." [13] Power comes from God, but the various political formations which are made possible by the exercise of this power are the result of natural law, for the state is natural. St. Thomas here says that it is by *ius gentium*, giving to this word the

[7] II *Sent.* 44.1.3.　　　[8] *Ibid.*　　　[9] Rom. xiii. 1.

[10] For public power and public person, cf. *S.* II-II, Q. 65, A. 1.

[11] For *plenaria potestas* of the sovereign, cf. *S.* II-II, Q. 67, A. 4

[12] Can. *quicumque percusserit*, causa 23, qu. 8.

[13] Cf. *S.* II-II, Q. 12, A. 2. That dominion here has to do with political control and not with the rights of a master over his slave is made clear by the context of the passage (*subditis fidelibus*, etc.).

sense which it has elsewhere, viz., of a rational elaboration of the principles of natural law, valid for all humanity and not too far removed from the original proposition.[14]

What St. Thomas means when he speaks of this divine origin of power may be clarified by the following. There are, he says, three factors involved in power: first, the manner of acquisition; secondly, the use to which it is put; thirdly, the mode or *form*.[15] This last one is always blameless. *Formally,* we are told, all power is good and comes from God, for it consists of a certain order connecting someone who rules with someone who is subject to this rule.[16] Therefore, when we speak absolutely and unrestrictedly, we say that power, as such, is good, because a thing in its unrestricted absoluteness is judged on the basis of what is *formal* in it.[17] But if we proceed to examine what relationships may affect this absolute goodness, we discover that they proceed from one or the other of the remaining two factors: either the "manner of acquisition" or "the use to which power is put." This "manner" (the origin) may be bad (and therefore not divine) in two ways: either because of the unworthiness of the ruler or because of the illicit practices (violence, simony, etc.) resorted to in the acquisition of it.[18] The latter vitiates the competence of the ruler so completely that "his power under these circumstances should be disowned as soon as the opportunity for so doing presents itself."[19] The former does not justify disobedience, "for inasmuch as power *formally* is always from God and creates the obligation of obedience, subjects are held to obey rulers even though unworthy." As for the third factor, St. Thomas teaches that the abuse of power is twofold: first, if a command is given "contrary to that for which power was instituted, as when a ruler enjoins practices destructive of those very virtues for the upholding of which power was ordained."[20] Here disobedience is obligatory. Secondly, if a com-

---

[14] Cf. *S.* I-II, Q. 94, A. 5 *ad* 3, pp. 52 f.
[15] II *Sent.* 44.1.2; 44.2.2.   [16] *Ibid.*
[17] That is: a man, absolutely speaking, because of his form (the rational soul) is a reasoning animal, which does not mean that he is exempt from irrationality.
[18] II *Sent., loc. cit.*   [19] *Ibid.*   [20] *Ibid.*

mand transcends the sphere of a given authority, in which case neither obedience nor disobedience is required.

Power is given by God to the ruler in order that he may realize justice on earth. In fact, we find that in the Middle Ages people looked upon the king as the person entrusted with "the maintenance of order and peace through justice." [21]

As custodian of justice, the ruler is or may be the legislator, the executor of the law, or the supreme judge.

a) The extent of the legislative power of the ruler depends naturally on the nature of the political regime. St. Thomas considers the case of "a free multitude which can legislate for itself" in contrast to one which is not free to do so. In the first instance the people (*multitudo*) as a whole may make laws or they may authorize the sovereign to do so, in which case the latter "has the power of legislating only in so far as he bears the person of the multitude." [22] This representative role of the legislative sovereign may be set forth thus: commands which are essential to the political order are not actions of the sovereign will on the *will* of the subjects; they are directed to their *reason* and therefore take the form of rational propositions. These propositions properly formulated are what we call laws and as such are necessary for the "ordering" to the common good. But the ordering of anything toward the common good belongs· either to the whole people or to someone who is the vicegerent of the whole people (*gerentis vicem totius multitudinis*).[23] The ruler is "vicegerent." But when the definition is narrowed down to the more precise legislative terminology, we find that the representative aspect of the legislating prince is attenuated. Instead of being a *vicegerent*, we find that the ruler acts as *guardian* of the community. Says St. Thomas: "The making of a law belongs either to the whole people or to a public person who has care (*curam habet*) of the whole people." [24] The representative character of the legislator is further obscured in

[21] Cf. Luchaire's statement that monarchy rested on the belief "that God instituted kingship so that rulers might render justice to men and establish peace, which is their first and most essential duty." *Histoire des Institutions Monarchiques de la France sous les premiers Capétiens.* I. 40 (Paris, 1883).

[22] *S.* I-II, Q. 97, A. 3 *ad* 3, p. 83.

[23] *Ibid.,* Q. 90, A. 3, pp. 7-8.   [24] *Ibid.*

the article that follows (A. 4), where no mention is found of alternate possibilities, law being made to proceed solely from the one who is in charge of the community. And, finally, in the first article of the following Question (91) even the references to the *cura* are omitted, and law is defined as a "dictate of practical reason emanating from the ruler who governs a perfect community."

This definition is the one to which St. Thomas normally resorted, so that its formulation cannot be considered merely casual. It is essential to human law, he tells us, that "it be framed by that one who governs the community" (*a gubernante civitatis*).[25]

b) The ruler is not only the lawmaker; he is also and above all the judge, the supreme judicial authority.

The person who delivers a judicial sentence interprets the wording of the law by applying this wording to a particular case. But both the interpretation of the law (which is the judicial act) and the making of it pertain to the same person. Therefore just as a law can be made only by a power which is public, so a judicial sentence must be rendered by public authority.[26]

The significance of the judicial function of the ruler was extended to other phases of jurisdiction:

Judicial orders are not only those which refer to litigations, but also all those that pertain to social relations (*ad ordinationem hominum ad invicem*), which matter is under the control of the ruler in his quality of supreme judge.[27]

It was as judge, then, that the ruler exercised that unique and sacred function which might necessitate the destruction of life, limb, and property and the deprivation of liberty whenever such action was deemed necessary to uphold *justice*. That which for a private person is murder, theft, or extortion becomes in certain circumstances a praiseworthy act when performed by one who, ruling a perfect community, is vested with a public power which, being "perfect," is "plenary."[28]

c) The ruler, who is under the obligation to protect the common

---

[25] *S.* I-II, Q. 95, A. 4, pp. 62-64.
[26] *S.* II-II, Q. 60, A. 6; cf. Q. 67, A. 1.
[27] *S.* I-II, Q. 104, A. 1.
[28] Cf. *S.* II-II, Q. 65, A. 2; Q. 66, A. 8, pp. 139-41; Q. 67, A. 4.

good from the assaults of a foreign enemy, has the right and duty
to resort to the necessary measures of war. The nature of his power
authorizes the destruction of life and property, provided the war
is just.[29] An offensive war is just when three conditions are com-
plied with. First, it must be declared by the sovereign. Private
persons may not wage war, and this for two reasons. In the first
place, war is resorted to only when there is no higher authority
to which the contestants may submit their conflicting claims. In
the case of private persons this does not obtain, for there is over
them a superior authority qualified to judge their controversies.
Secondly, war demands the levying of a multitude of men, and
this can be done only by one who is in charge of the multitude,
hence by no private individual.[30]

The second condition is a just *cause*. Those who are attacked
must, because of some fault of their own, have deserved the aggression. St. Thomas here restates the argument endorsed by St. Augustine:

A just war is usually defined as one by which a wrong is righted,
viz., when a state or a nation is attacked because it neglected to
punish some crimes committed by one of its members or when it
failed to make restitution of something that had been unjustly
seized.[31]

The third condition is the maintenance of righteous intentions
on the part of those who have declared war, viz., that the purpose
of war is to lay the foundations of a better and more lasting peace.
For it may well be that a war has a just cause according to the
above definition and that it has been declared and is being waged
by the supreme political power, which was the other condition
set, yet it is made iniquitous by the evil intentions entertained by
the attacking power. What these evil intentions are St. Thomas
tells us in the words of St. Augustine:

They are a desire to harm the enemy more than the conduct of
hostilities demands, a spirit of revenge, implacability, recourse to
destructive practices that fit beasts better than men, and finally
lust of supremacy.[32]

---

[29] Cf. *Ibid.*, Q. 66, A. 8.   [30] Cf. *S.* I-II, Q. 40, A. 1.
[31] *Quaestio in Heptateuchon*, 10.   [32] *Contra Faust.* xxii. 70.

d) It is true, then, that the ruler of a state which is a *perfect community* has a perfect (complete) power of coercion, and therefore he may inflict irreparable penalties, such as death and mutilation. But neither the slave master nor the *pater familias*, for the protection of the estate or of the household, can avail himself of the prerogative of public power. The power over slaves and the power over family are determined on the basis of *ius dominativum* and *ius paternum*, respectively, both of which are subordinate to the *ius politicum* by which public power operates. A sentence of death and or confiscation issuing from these subordinate powers is, therefore, plain murder and theft.

A father or a master in charge of a family or of an estate, which are imperfect communities, has an imperfect coercive power. He may inflict lighter penalties which do not carry with them an irreparable harm, such as, for example, whipping.[33]

Also:

And just as one may by public power be lawfully deprived of life because of major crimes, so he is liable because of minor crimes to be deprived of limb. This, however, a private person may not do, not even with the consent of the possessor of the limb, because of the harm that thereby results to the community.[34]

e) The political order is, then, the rule of justice. The prince is expected to govern by laws, and these laws must be just; that is, they cannot be the arbitrary expression of a will, either individual or collective, but rather the rational deduction from principles of justice imparted by God to man; the nature of their content conditions their validity. In view of this, how does St. Thomas deal with the two formulas of Roman law so often invoked in his day which seem to contradict flatly the two conditions above referred to? These two formulas are: first, "Whatever the prince wants [whatever his pleasure may be] has the vigor of law"; [35] and, secondly, "The prince is not bound by laws." (He is above the law.) [36]

[33] *S.* II-II, Q. 65, A. 2 *ad* 2.   [34] *Ibid.*, A. 1 and A. 2 *ad* 2.
[35] "Quod principi placuit legis habet vigorem" (*Digest* i.4.1).
[36] "Princeps legibus solutus" (*ibid.*, i.3.31).

These maxims could not be ignored or waved aside. They had intrigued political writers of all generations. They seemed to lead to an impasse; for, on the one hand, no Christian could deny that in some form or other positive law must derive from natural law and conform to divine law; and, on the other hand, it seemed difficult to repudiate norms which, though pagan in origin, had received the full sanction of Christian jurisprudence. The force of the autocratic formulas was further strengthened by imperial affirmations such as those of Justinian: "God subordinated all laws to the imperial sway (*fortuna imperialis*) in that He himself sent to mankind the Emperor as a living law." [37] And this animate law, he tells us, was providentially given because of the insufficiency of inanimate legislation. Since human nature constantly varies, he said, rigid legislation would soon become antiquated unless a man divinely prepared were on hand to adapt it to the new circumstances.[38]

Refusal to accept the doctrine that the ruler is above the law was felt to encounter this dilemma: either the ruler binds himself or he is bound by others. The first is not possible because a man may, indeed, bind himself by a vow or by a pledge, but cannot constrain himself legally. A law, it was pointed out, is the creation or rather the effect of a governing power and, as Aristotle teaches, such a power is the *principle of ruling* another *qua other*. A legal injunction presupposes a jurisdiction, and no man can have jurisdiction over himself except in a metaphorical sense. Coercion, implicit in the enforcement of law, demands two distinct parties: one which does the coercing, and one which suffers it; the *agent*, it was said, must be a different person from the *patient*. The ruler cannot appear in the double role of sovereign and subject.

The second alternative was not tenable, given the nature of supreme power, which admits of no control.

In facing this problem St. Thomas tried to reconcile the political with the moral side of the question. The supreme power of the ruler is indeed beyond the control of the subjects. They have no way of compelling him to respect the law. But supreme power is

[37] *Novella* 105.4.
[38] *Digest,* Preface ii.

not beyond the control of God, who brings the sovereign to a voluntary observance of this (the human) law.

The explanation which he gives [39] is the one that the Church has for a long time made its own. The law, he said, binds the sovereign by its *directive,* not by its *coercive* power. And by "coercive," he means a capacity of compelling obedience by punitive sanctions; and by "directive," a power which human law derives from eternal law and which makes it capable of creating obligations in the forum of conscience.

Coercion, he tells us, cannot be practiced at the level of sovereignty, because it would result in the last analysis in self-coercion, which, as it was said above, is not possible. From his wording, one gathers that he did not hold, as many did, that a ruler's exemption from law observance was simply a *de facto* matter, viz., that the reason why a ruler is not bound by law is merely the fact that there is no one to carry out a sentence delivered against him. On the contrary, for him the exemption is *de iure;* and the impossibility exists not in the executing of a sentence but in the making of it; for eventually the sovereign, being the supreme judge of the land, would have to judge his own case, and as all know, no man can be a judge in his own cause. Moreover, what could be the sense of a judgment that would forever remain inert?

Another force is therefore needed to make the ruler respect his laws (and those which he has inherited and accepted); a force that comes into existence when a properly formulated proposition of practical reason acquires that majesty that transforms it into a law. God, by whose authority this transformation is effected, has implanted in us the invincible conviction that the *power* to coerce, which He gives, implies an *obligation* on the part of the coercer to respect voluntarily that which he compels others to observe. Hence the power which law has to coerce subjects can never be dissociated from the power it has to make the ruler abide by it.[40] This latter power is exercised in our conscience by a voluntary submission to God, the author of this power, which, as we said, is called "directive"; and there is no difficulty here, for though a man cannot *coerce* himself, he is quite capable of *directing* himself.

[39] *S.* I-II, Q. 96, A. 5 *ad* 3, p. 74.   [40] *Ibid.*

The nature of this directive power requires a few words of explanation. The fact that a rational proposition can be made into an instrument whereby one or more individuals can dispose of the life, liberty, and property of their fellow men proves, people thought, that the power to do this—the public power that legislates —has its origin in God. Human law can do all it does because it is an emanation of eternal law. The condition which God imposes on society in bestowing upon it the benefit of law is that all, without distinction, accept the conditions that accompany it. The promulgation of a just law postulates the tacit acceptance of its provisions on the part of everybody. This, it was said, is a basic principle that all men discover in the depths of their conscience, and which lends to law its directive power.

For the greater protection of society, law is furnished with the other power, that of coercing, and this one, as was said, is applicable to all except the sovereign legislator.

It was stated above that this power of creating, in *everybody*, the directive obligation of law observance is communicated to positive law by eternal law. How is this done? The answer is: just as eternal law imprints itself on human law by the medium of natural law, so it is through natural law that the moral obligation which bids all men observe the human law comes before the tribunal of conscience. The question now is: which one of the precepts that natural reason dictates to man is at the basis of this universal validity?

Caietan, in his commentary to the text of St. Thomas above quoted, says that it is the command to *do to others what we would have others do to us*, and that therefore a ruler must not impose on others a law which he does not want applied to himself. Suarez thought this was not correct, and suggested the one which, coupled with its correlative, must be postulated for the existence of the political association. This inborn principle of the political animal says to the ruler: "Respect the law you make," and says to the subject: "The superior must be obeyed." [41] This is the natural law precept which St. Thomas adduces to show the validity of the

---

[41] *De legibus* iii. 35. 6. Of course, the *directive* power of law is entirely different from the *vis ostensiva,* such power as the *Laws* of both Plato and Cicero might have.

directive power of law. He finds confirmation of it in divine law (Matthew 23) and points to its embodiment in canon law. He also hints at the universality of it by quoting the maxim of an old Sage.[42] Of course this holds only when the matter and the *ratio* of a law are the same in the ruler and the ruled. Prohibition to carry weapons, therefore, cannot obligate the king. But the law of just price does.

The significance of the natural law precept above stated was shown thus: A law establishes a medium of some virtue as a step toward the common good. So, e.g., the law that regulates the price of goods fixes a means within the sphere of justice. The transgression of this medium is a repudiation of justice and therefore a sin. And sinning is not more tolerable in a ruler than it is in a subject.

The solution we find in St. Thomas was kept alive by subsequent jurists and theologians; Bossuet restates it in this form: "Kings are then, like everybody else, subject to the equity of the laws . . . but they are not subject to the penalties of the laws, or, to speak the language of theology, their submission is not to their *coercive* but to their *directive* power." [43]

The following objection might be raised: supposing the sovereign had not made a given law; he would then have been free to act without any consideration of the principle which eventually came to be incorporated in that law. This argument was met thus: eternal law, through its participant, natural law, is constantly acting on human reason so as to improve steadily the quality of legislation (St. Thomas accepts the doctrine of progress in lawmaking [44]). Eternal law is then one element; the other is the will of the legislator. The sovereign is not obliged to improve his code, but once he decides to do so and he issues a new law, then by virtue of the conditions above described and which attend to the formation of all laws, he binds himself to accept the directive power of the law he has made.

St. Thomas adds that the sovereign shows that he is above the

---

[42] Dionysius Cato.

[43] *Politique tirée des propres paroles de l' Écriture Sainte,* Book IV, art. 1, prop. 21.

[44] *S.* I-II, Q, 97, A. 1, pp. 78 ff.

law by the fact that he can change it. But again in its changed form he is obliged by its directive power to observe it.

The other statement, viz., that the will of the sovereign has the force of law, is explained by St. Thomas with the proviso that the will has this force when it is regulated by reason; which means that in the last resort the legislator, through a process of valid ratiocination based on the principles of natural law, must connect his enactments with eternal law. One must, of course, always recall that for St. Thomas the worst of all laws is preferable to anarchy.

2. Law

St. Thomas has left us a detailed treatise on law, embodied in those Questions of the First Part of the Second Part of the *Summa* which are here reprinted.[1] The problem comes up again in the Second Part of the Second Part, the relevant Questions of which are also included in this edition.[2] A comparison of the two is very illuminating, particularly in view of the disagreements to be found in them. In the first, St. Thomas is interested in deriving morality and legality from eternal law. In the latter, his intention is more juridical. He strives hard to present a theory that will embody Aristotle's teachings and, at the same time, reconcile some of the well-known contrasts in the field of law, especially natural law.

By demonstrating that a ruler must govern in accordance with laws and that the laws of a state must be derived from natural law, or at least must not go counter to them, St. Thomas proclaims that legality is conditioned by morality and that moral conduct is indeed action regulated by reason, but a reason that is aware that it must, if it will exist, proceed from principles which God has implanted in the soul of man—of every man—viz., the fundamental, inescapable principles of practical reason which constitute what is called natural law.

Natural law is the source of the norms of moral virtues,[3] but has

---

[1] Pp. 3 ff. [2] Pp. 92 ff.

[3] "Virtues perfect us as to the proper prosecution of the natural inclinations which pertain to natural law, and so for every natural inclination there is a properly ordered *special* virtue" (*S.* II-II, Q. 108, A. 2).

a distinct significance for a particular one of them, viz., justice, the social virtue par excellence, the precepts of which, properly formulated and promulgated, constitute the civil codes of the various states.

III. FORMS OF GOVERNMENT

Political differentiation in states is the outcome of different numerical relationships between ruler and ruled.[1] Of these only three are considered, viz., those relations or ratios of ruler to ruled in which the numerator is one, a few, or many.[2] The "many" may become "all." This classification is doubled by introducing a qualitative criterion: goodness—a government being good when it concerns itself with the *common* good and bad when it aims at *private* advantages.[3] The good government of a single man is called kingship, the bad one tyranny; the good government of the few, aristocracy, the bad, oligarchy; the good government of the many is timocracy or *politia*,[4] the bad, democracy (in the special Aristotelian sense).[5]

But the quantitative distinctions named above turn out to be accidental and derived—the outcome of something more funda-

---

[1] *In Pol.* iii. 6.　　[2] *Ibid.*, ii. 7; *In Eth.* viii. 10.　　[3] *In Pol.* iii. 6.

[4] St. Thomas, following Aristotle, uses this word in two principal senses. One, the generic, means "forms of government." Our word "regime," particularly in its broader sense, seems better suited than "constitution," which is often used as the English equivalent. The *"ordo* of the *civitas" (ibid.,* iv. 10) which is the relation between ruler and subjects, determines the form of government. So, therefore, *politia* is also defined as *"ordo* of the rulers" (*ibid.,* iv. 12) or again as *"ordinatio* of the *civitas* in relation to all ruling powers but especially to the principal one," i.e., the government (*ibid.,* iii. 5). The form of government determines the nature of the entire community: "it is the life of the state" (*ibid.,* iv. 3), so much so that "when the *politia* is changed, one cannot say that the *civitas* remains the same" (*ibid.,* iii. 2). The second meaning is that of a particular form of government: the good popular government in contrast with *democratia,* which is the bad. It was in this sense that, in the thirteenth century, the word "politicus" came to be used as the opposite of "despotic."

[5] *R.P.* I, § 11, p. 178.

mental.[6] What essentially differentiates one state from another is
the end or goal toward which a government strives. Of these ends
there are three: wealth, virtue, liberty. The wealthy, given the
nature of the economic urge, almost always concentrate in a small
group; they *happen* to form usually a numerically insignificant
minority. When this group succeeds in gaining power, they form
a government which, because of their very aspirations, must be
bad (self-seeking) and which, because of the paucity of numbers,
is called oligarchy, even though the characteristic feature is economic egoism rather than numbers. The virtuous too are few;
because of their very virtue, when they rise to power they concern
themselves with the common good as justice demands. If this small
minority dwindles down to unity, the regime that comes into existence is called *kingship*, provided that the ruler is a virtuous
man. Otherwise we have a tyranny.

A majority rule, therefore, cannot be the outcome of triumphant
zeal for virtue or greed for wealth, but comes into existence when
power falls into the hands of those who strive primarily for freedom.[7] Liberty in a state means self-government, which exists
when *all* subjects in turn may be rulers,[8] so that the basis of freedom is political equality, implying a control by the *poor*, who are
by far the most numerous. If this popular regime aims at the
public good (in which the interests of the wealthy must play a
part), then the form of government is *timocracy;* but if the regime
of liberty becomes domination by the populace, then we have what
has been called *democracy*.[9]

On the basis of these three fundamental aspirations, it is possible to establish a standard of value for each regime. As we saw
above, the dignity or excellence of a citizen in an aristocracy and
in a kingdom is measured by the practice of virtue, in an oligarchy
by financial success, in a democracy by devotion to freedom.[10]

These types are in no way fixed and immovable. Whatever the

---

[6] *In Pol.* iii. 6; iv. 2.

[7] The difficulty with the regime of freedom is that the citizens, having secured
political equality, tend to claim *absolute* equality. Cf. *In Eth.* v. 2.

[8] *In Pol.* i. 10.   [9] *R.P.* I, § 11, p. 178; *In Eth.* viii. 10.

[10] *S.* II-II, Q. 61, A. 2.

qualities of each may be, we find gradations that tend to destroy the rigidity of the type. Tyranny, for example, can be more or less severe; and because of these variations it is possible to say both that it is and that it is not the worst of all regimes.[11]

1. The Best Regime

A most important task of the political writers of antiquity and of their disciples in the Middle Ages was to determine the best form of government (the *optima civitas*). And naturally the question immediately arose: best for whom? St. Thomas was well aware of something that is still often forgotten, viz., that a political regime must be suitable to the cultural or moral level of the people concerned. In *S.* I-II, Q. 97, A. 1, he quotes approvingly this passage from St. Augustine:

If the people have a sense of moderation and responsibility and are most careful guardians of the common weal, it is right to enact a law allowing such a people to choose their own magistrates for the government of the commonwealth. But if, as time goes on, the same people become so corrupt as to sell their votes and entrust the government to scoundrels and criminals, then the right of appointing their public officials is rightly forfeit to such a people, and the choice devolves to a few good men.[1]

Circumstances, too, play an important role; a given regime which has been declared inferior to another from an *absolute* point of view becomes, under certain conditions, superior to it. So oligarchy, which is theoretically better than any kind of tyranny, becomes less desirable when the community is threatened by disruption, because, by its greater unity, the tyrannical rule, with all its vices, is better suited to stave off anarchy, which is the worst possible evil.[2]

Of this kind of relativism we find many evidences in St. Thomas, for he looks upon human conditions realistically and is convinced

---

[11] *R.P.* I §§ 21 ff. and 36 ff., pp. 181 ff., 186 ff

[1] P. 79 (*De lib. arb.* i. 6).

[2] Provided, of course, the tyrant does not completely crush his subjects (*ibid.*).

that the majority of men are not the material out of which the ideal state can be built. Not reason, but egoistic self-indulgence controls the actions of great numbers of citizens.[3]

In general, monarchy is the best form of government. The reason for this is stated repeatedly:

The best regime of a community is government by one person, which is made evident if we recall that the end for which a government exists is the maintenance of peace. Peace and unity of subjects is the goal of the ruler. But unity is more congruently the effect of one than of many.[4]

And again:

Now the welfare and safety of a multitude formed into a society lies in the preservation of its unity, which is called peace. If this is removed, the benefit of social life is lost and, moreover, the multitude in its disagreement becomes a burden to itself. The chief concern of the ruler of a multitude, therefore, is to procure the unity of peace. . . . Now it is manifest that what is itself one can more efficaciously bring about unity than a group of several. . . . Therefore the rule of one man is more useful than the rule of many.[5]

The state, too, must be one. But its unity is established by *order* which, because of social exigencies, demands diversities.[6] These diversities, of course, imply inequalities, as we saw above. In the monarchical rule an essential inequality is to be found in the very great superiority of the king: "A man cannot truly be

---

[3] "The majority of people follow the inclinations of sensuous nature rather than the order of reason" (*S.* I-II, Q. 71, A. 2 *ad* 3).
"The people for the most part fail to use reason" (*In Pol.* iv. 13).
"Now human law is framed for a number of human beings, the majority of whom are not perfect in virtue" (*S.* I-II, Q. 96, A. 2, p. 68).
[4] *C.G.* iv. 76.   [5] *R.P.* I, § 17, pp. 179-80.
[6] "Every perfect whole in natural things turns out to be constituted of specifically different parts. Since the state is a perfect whole, it must consist of parts which differ among themselves specifically" (*In Pol.* ii. 1). Therefore, complete unity destroys the state: "If the unity of a state progressed beyond a certain point, the state would become a household; and if the unity of the household proceeded too far, it would turn into one individual" (*ibid.*).

said to be king if he is not in himself equal to the task of ruling, which means that he must be super-excellent in all good endowments of mind and body and of external belongings." [7] Monarchy is a "regime in which one person excels and the others are by nature [8] constituted to obey." [9] This immense superiority is primarily a moral one. "It is necessary that the king differ *naturally* from his subjects through the possession of a certain greatness of goodness." [10] A kingly power would be unjustly exercised if the monarch were not "morally perfect" and if, in the exercise of his virtue, he differed from his subjects only quantitatively.[11] The specific kingly virtue is prudence, "which is found both in the ruler and in the subjects. But in the ruler as though in the architect; in the subjects as though in the hand-laborers." [12]

It is obvious that conditions are not always favorable to this state of affairs. There are, moreover, inherent disadvantages in a monarchical regime:

For it frequently happens that men living under a king strive more sluggishly for the common good, inasmuch as they consider that what they devote to the common good, they do not confer upon themselves but upon another, under whose power they see the common goods to be. But when they see that the common good is not under the power of one man, they do not attend to it as if it belonged to another, but each one attends to it as if it were his own.[13]

And this argument is strengthened by an example drawn from contemporary life:

Experience thus teaches that one city administered by rulers changing annually is sometimes able to do more than some kings having, perchance, two or three cities; and small services exacted

---

[7] *In Eth.* viii. 10.

[8] It must be recalled that nature sees to it that the needed farmers, philosophers, soldiers, etc., be always at hand: "The distribution of these functional aptitudes is done primarily by divine providence, but secondarily by natural causes, in virtue of which one man is better suited for one thing than for another" (*C.I.* ii. 31).

[9] *In Pol.* iii. 9.

[10] *Ibid.*, i. 10.   [11] *Ibid.*

[12] *S.* II-II, Q. 47, A. 12.   [13] *R.P.* I, § 31, p. 185.

by kings weigh more heavily than great burdens imposed by the community of citizens.[14]

A monarchical regime, moreover, fails to satisfy the natural ambition of people: "If a man of high value is the sole ruler, the many people who are deprived of the distinction of power resent it, and this resentment is the cause of dissension." [15] And dissension was for St. Thomas the worst political evil.

Both the monarchical and the aristocratic regime are defective in that they fail to take advantage of the fact that, good though an elite may be, it is never as good as the whole community which comprises, as one of its parts, the same elite. This fundamental consideration which St. Thomas encountered in commenting on the *Politics* of Aristotle [16] was to guide him in his choice of the best *practical* form of government.

2. The Mixed Government

The theoretically superior regime of monarchy can be maintained in practice provided certain conditions are met and certain difficulties obviated: first, the aspiration of all people to liberty and equality, which manifests itself in the claim to participate in public life. This is so strong that refusal to satisfy it may bring about dissension, which evil must be avoided at all costs:

In the earthly states . . . the variety and the abundance of public functions and roles helps to preserve the unity, because through them a great number of people are enabled to take part in public activities.[1]

A way must be found, therefore, to make the people feel that they have a stake in the public good. Secondly, the advantages of the kingly rule must not be impaired by the ever-suspended threat of relapse into tyrannical abuses. To avoid this the monarchy

---

[14] *Ibid.*, § 32; but cf. § 20, pp. 180-81: "This is also evident from experience. For provinces or cities which are not ruled by one person are torn with dissensions and tossed about without peace. . . . On the other hand, provinces and cities which are ruled under one king enjoy peace, flourish in justice, and delight in prosperity."   [15] *In Pol.* iii. 8, *et passim.*
[16] *Ibid.*, iii. 14.   [1] *S.* II-II, Q. 183, A. 2.

must be made "temperate" (*temperetur potestas*).[2] The solution was found by instituting a form of government in which the king's power would be limited and the people's desire satisfied. That form of government is what is called the "mixed regime."

The idea of fusing the main governmental forms goes back to classical days. Aristotle speaks of it and mentions the plan of some who deemed that all three forms should be compounded into one, and cited the example of Sparta.[3] Polybius further developed the idea,[4] but it was Cicero who gave it its widest scope. In the first book of *De republica,* he makes Scipio observe that the three above-named regimes tend regularly to degenerate [5] and to follow a cyclical course,[6] and that therefore, to avoid relapses and *recourses,* a fourth kind of governmental rule, composed of the said three, should be devised.[7] He makes Laelius say that the compound form is best, in that it embodies the *caritas* of the king, the *consilium* of the aristocracy, and the *libertas* of the popular regime.[8] Rome, of course, exemplified this threefold *conflatum* regime by its consuls, its senate, and its *comitia* of the people.[9]

It is difficult to say where St. Thomas got the idea of the mixed regime. In substance it is very close to Cicero's. He claims, however, that it is a generalization of what was formerly put into practice by the Hebrews:

For Moses and his successors governed the people in such a way that each of them was ruler over all, so that there was a kind of kingdom. Moreover, seventy-two men were chosen, who were elders

2 *R.P.* I, Ch. VI, pp. 188 ff. The word "moderatum" is also used. Cf. *R.P.* II, Ch. VIII, and Cicero, *De repub.* i. 29 (45): "moderatum et permixtum." The two attributes, "moderate" and "temperate," had already been joined by classical authors.

3 *Pol.* ii. 6.   4 *Hist.* vi.1.3.3.8.9.

5 "iter ad finitimum quoddam malum praeceps ac lubricum" (*De repub.* i. 29).

6 "orbes et quasi circuitus in rebus publicis commutationum et vicissitudinum" (*ibid.*).   7 "moderatum et permixtum tribus" (*ibid.*).

8 *Ibid.,* i. 35 (55). How this regime was to be organized we are told in *S.* I-II, Q. 105, A. 1, pp. 86 ff.

9 *Ibid.,* i. 32 (56). Venice, too, claimed that its government was a fusion of the three basic forms, with the regal power in the Doge, the aristocratic in the Senate, and the democratic in the greater Council.

in virtue . . . so that there was an element of aristocracy. But it was a democratical government in so far as the rulers were chosen from all the people.[10]

3. Tyranny

In treating of tyranny and of the justification of tyrannicide, a question often discussed in antiquity and brought to the fore again by John of Salisbury, St. Thomas moves very cautiously and, as usual, is more concerned with the stability of the state than with the upholding of individual *political* rights.

In the *Commentary to the Sentences* he seems to countenance tyrannicide by what might be looked upon as a partial approval of a statement of Cicero. He says:

Cicero here considers the case in which power was seized by an act of violence either against the will of the subjects or with a consent which was wrested by coercion, and in conditions such that no recourse could be had to a higher authority capable of passing judgment on the usurper. In these circumstances he who kills the tyrant in order to free his country is praised and rewarded.[1]

But such extreme measures proved to be not to his liking. He could not of course accept the doctrine that rulers are always right, that the king can do no wrong. So when he came to face the problem raised by St. .Paul in his *Epistle to the Romans:* "Princes are not a terror to good works but to the evil," [2] he hesitates between two interpretations: one, aiming at a doctrine that did not acquiesce in extreme resignation, is, from the point of view of the exegesis, somewhat daring. "Princes," he says, "*are not instituted* to be a terror, etc."; and later, "to be a terror to the good is not part of a Prince's function." [3] Realizing perhaps that this interpretation, though very acceptable from one point of view, was doing violence to the text and was departing from the old tradition, he fell back on the accepted explanation. Bad rulers, for such no doubt exist, cannot terrorize the good, for,

although they at times unjustly persecute the well-doers, yet the latter have no cause to fear, because the harm they suffer, if they

[10] *S.* I-II, Q. 105, A. 1, p. 88.   [1] II *Sent.* 2.2.2.5.
[2] Rom. xiii. 3.   [3] *In Ep. ad Rom.* xiii. 1.

will but patiently bear it, will turn out to their advantage, in accordance with the First Epistle of St. Peter: "But if also you suffer anything for justice's sake, blessed are ye." [4] Thus it may be seen why those who resist power bring upon themselves condemnation, whether it is that which is inflicted by rulers upon rebels or that by which God punishes men.[5]

Bad kings, he concludes, come into the world with God's consent, to punish the wicked and test the good.

When, however, St. Thomas came to discuss the situation from a more political point of view, he suggested measures which are in line with his constant practice of stressing above all the conservation of the state and of discouraging any acts that might result in a revolution. He feared that removal of a tyrant might bring about fatal dissensions among the people and possibly give rise to some worse kind of tyrannical rule. His practical suggestions as to how to deal with the matter are the following:

If tyranny is not too oppressive, the subjects should put up with it for the reasons above stated. For extreme cases some, he tells us, have suggested tyrannicide, that is, execution by private persons. The individual act of one who exposes himself to rid the state of a tyrant has often been admired and was approved by the Old Testament. However, says the Angelic Doctor, the New Testament does not countenance this practice—witness St. Peter, who says: "Be subjects to your masters, not only to the good and gentle but also to the forward." [6] And he goes on to say that the attitude of the martyrs, who died but did not rebel, confirmed this doctrine. Sound political prudence likewise condemns tyrannicide, for it would be a great hazard for the people and for the government if individuals, by private presumption, were to attempt to take the life of rulers, tyrannical though they may be; and he warns us that frequently those who are quick to have recourse to violence are inferior elements of society.[7]

Not individual violence, then, but lawful opposition should be resorted to against tyranny: "We must proceed not by private presumption, but by public authority." And defense against tyr-

---

[4] I Pet. iii. 14.   [5] *In Ep. ad Rom.* xiii. 1.
[6] I Pet. ii. 18.   [7] *R.P.* I, § 47, p. 190.

anny may take several forms. If the ruler has been elected by the people, he may justly be checked or even deposed for abuse of power. Nor do the people break their contract if they depose a sovereign whom they had elected for life, inasmuch as they are not held to abide by the terms of an agreement which the ruler himself has already voided by his actions.[8]

But if the tyrant wields power by delegation from a higher authority, it is the duty of this superior power to remove him. Finally, if no remedy can be found in human procedures, we must turn to God, the Universal Ruler. He may, if he wishes, change the heart of the tyrant; and those whom he deems unworthy of conversion he removes or degrades. We should have recourse to prayer; but before we request divine intervention against a tyrannical ruler, we must be sure that we deserve to be helped. For frequently God permits tyrants to rule, so that they may chastise the subjects for their sinful conduct.

IV. PLENITUDO POTESTATIS

We can gather from what has already been said that no state can possess absolute power, and we can infer that there is no room in St. Thomas' theory of government for a lay world-emperor. The Angelic Doctor says explicitly that the ultimate goal of an assembled multitude is not to live in accordance with virtue, but, by means of a virtuous life, to attain divine fruition. If indeed this end could be reached by the virtue of human nature, it would of necessity be in the power of the lay ruler to direct men to this goal. However, since man rises to the possession of God not by human but by divine power, the guidance to that goal must be the task not of a human but of a divine government.[1]

In St. Thomas' own words:

In order that spiritual matters might be kept separate from temporal ones, the ministry of this kingdom was entrusted not to earthly kings, but to priests and especially to the highest of them, the suc-

[8] *Ibid.*   [1] *R.P.* II, §§ 107-108.

cessor of St. Peter, vicar of Christ, the Roman Pontiff, to whom all
kings must be subject just as they are subject to Our Lord Jesus.
For, those to whom the care of an intermediate end pertains should
be subject to him to whom the care of the ultimate end belongs and
be directed by his rule.[2]

More uncompromising still, even if stated in feudal parlance,
is the pronouncement of *Quaestiones Quodlibetales* xii. 19:

In old Roman days, monarchs opposed Christ. But now kings
comprehend, and because of what they have learned, they serve
Our Lord Jesus Christ in fear; and, therefore, today kings are
vassals of the Church.

Nor is the Pope's power that of a supreme potentate removed
from the actual administration of things and therefore in need of
a vicar or an associate to assume his political functions and to
act as a universal emperor over all earthly kings and rulers. There
can be no lay King of Kings; it is the Pope who is the sovereign
of all rulers: "In the Pope the secular power is joined to the spiritual. He holds the apex of both powers, spiritual and secular, by
the will of Him who is Priest and King unto eternity, King of
Kings and Dominus Dominantium." [3]

An indirect power (*ratione peccati*) over the worldly rulers is
exercised by the other princes of the Church:

Secular power is subject to the spiritual power as the body is subject to the soul, and therefore it is not a usurpation of authority
if the spiritual prelate interferes in temporal things concerning
those matters in which the secular power is subject to him, or concerning those matters the care of which has been entrusted to him
by the secular power.[4]

But the authority of the Pope is quite other. For though there is a
sphere of authority reserved for political power, the Pope is not ex-
cluded from it:

---

[2] *Ibid.;* § 110.
[3] II *Sent.* 44 expositio textus.
[4] *S.* II-II, Q. 60, A. 6. This analogical argumentation is constantly resorted
to: "In the Church the Pope holds the place of the head and the major
prelates hold the place of the principal limbs" (*In Ep. ad Rom.* xii. 2).

In matters pertaining to salvation of the soul we should obey spiritual rather than temporal authority, but in those which pertain to the political good we should obey the temporal rather than the spiritual, for, as Matthew says, "Give unto Caesar, etc.," unless when it happens that *the spiritual and the civil power are joined in one person as in the case of the Pope,* who holds the summit of power both spiritual and secular, because of the will of Him who is both King and Priest, Priest unto Eternity according to the order of Melchisedech.[5]

The uniqueness of the Pope's authority is explained in the passage that follows:

Sometimes the inferior power emanates in its totality from the superior, in which case the entire potence of the former is founded upon the potence of the latter, so that obedience is due to the higher at all times and without exceptions. Such is the superiority of the Emperor's power over that of the Proconsul [quoted from St. Augustine]; such that of the Pope over all spiritual powers in the Church, since the ecclesiastical hierarchies are ordained and disposed by him, and his power is in some manner the foundation of the Church as it appears from Matthew 16. Hence we are required in all these things to obey him rather than the bishop or archbishop and to him the monk owes obedience in preference to his abbot. But two powers may be such that both arise from a third and supreme authority, and their relative rank then depends upon the will of this uppermost power. When this is the case, either one of the two subordinate authorities controls the other only in those matters in which its superiority has been recognized by the uppermost power. Of such nature is the authority exercised by *rulers,* by bishops, archbishops, etc., over their subjects, for all of them have received it from the Pope and with it the conditions and limitations of its use.[6]

St. Thomas could tolerate no other adjustment: "Mankind," he says, "is considered like one body, which is called the mystic body, whose head is Christ *both as to soul and as to body*." [7] Christ has one vicar, the Pope,[8] and the Pope is the "head of the republic of Christ." [9] The *ecclesia* includes the *res publica.*

[5] II *Sent.* 44 explicatio textus. Some apply this solely to the Pontifical State. But such an interpretation does not seem to be tenable.
[6] *Ibid.* [7] *S.* III, Q. 8, A. 1.
[8] *C.G.* iv. 76. [9] *Contra errores Graecorum* ii. 32.

The law by which the Pope governs is the divine law, which, as we saw above, includes all that natural law teaches and something else besides. Divine law includes natural law but does not abolish it. In other words, if the state remains within the limits set to it by natural law, no interference is justified. No one is allowed to appeal to divine law against the just obligations imposed by the state. According to St. Thomas, the faith of Christ is the principle and cause of justice. Hence the order of justice is not destroyed but rather enhanced by this faith. But the order of justice demands that inferiors obey superiors, for otherwise human society could not exist. Hence men may not invoke their faith in Christ as an excuse for disobeying secular rulers.[10]

St. Thomas recognizes the autonomy of the state, and this recognition is utilized in settling important questions such as that of the right of infidel rulers to demand obedience of their Christian subjects: "Infidelity in itself does not destroy the justness of power, because power was instituted by *ius gentium*, a human law, and the distinction between believers and infidels exists by virtue of divine law, which does not destroy human law." [11] An infidel, like any other ruler, may, of course, lose his power because of sins he commits; and it may well be that such sins, in that case, have some connection with his religion. "It does not pertain to the Church," he adds, "to punish the infidelity of those who never took up the faith, according to St. Paul's I Corinthians (v. 12)." [12] However, the situation of heretics is different: The Church "can sententially punish the infidelity of those who had previously accepted the faith [13] . . . and, therefore, as soon as a sentence of excommunication has been delivered against a ruler on account of apostasy from the faith, *ipso facto* his subjects are released from his control and from their oath of fidelity." [14]

Existing infidel rulers are therefore authorized to continue in existence, but no new infidel formations are to be permitted:

The Church cannot allow that infidels proceed to gain control over believers or that they be in any way placed in a commanding

---

[10] S. II-II, Q. 104, A. 6, pp. 171-2.   [11] *Ibid.*, Q. 12, A. 2.   [12] *Ibid.*
[13] Here follows the reason why heresy and not infidelity is punishable.
[14] S. II-II, Q. 12, A. 2.

position over them. But we can speak differently about powers or authorities already existing. For, as we have seen, power and authority have been instituted by human law, whereas the distinction between infidels and believers exists in virtue of divine law. But divine law, which comes from Grace, does not destroy human law, which comes from nature.[15]

This apparently was a strong statement, for St. Thomas immediately introduced a clause that justified exceptional procedures on the part of the Church, on the basis of its possessing the "authority of God." It is important, however, to notice that here, as everywhere else, the point that St. Thomas stresses is the stability of the political order. For its sake the Church refrains from going the whole length in imposing this God-given authority. It is because of this fear of political disturbances that St. Thomas decides against the manumission of Christian slaves owned by Jews.

Over the natural state so organized the Pope ordinarily exercises no immediate jurisdiction. He does not wield the two swords. One of them, that of earthly justice, he hands over to the secular ruler, who is to unsheathe it, however, at his beck (*ad nutum*).[16] It is interesting, nevertheless, to see that in one sphere the Pope exercises direct political authority: The *civil* authorities, St. Thomas says, have, according to Aristotle, the power to regulate the instruction of the citizens, to decide to what pursuits individual men should dedicate themselves, and how far these should be carried. "And so it is clear that the ordaining of a university pertains to him who is at the head of the state, and especially to the authority of the Apostolic See by which the Universal Church is ruled, the intellectual interests of which are taken care of in the higher institution of learning." [17]

DINO BIGONGIARI

COLUMBIA UNIVERSITY
April, 1952

---

[15] *Ibid.*, Q. 10, A. 10.
[16] IV *Sent.* 37 expositio textus; cf. *S.* II-II, Q. 64, A. 4. *ad* 3. Cf. St. Bernard, *De consideratione* iv. 3. 7, and Epist. 256.
[17] *C.I.* i. 8.

NOTE ON THE TEXT

This edition presents the ideas of St. Thomas Aquinas on politics, justice, and social problems as set forth in *The Summa Theologica*, and on forms of government as set forth in *De Regimine Principum*.

Selections from *The Summa Theologica* have been taken from the translation of the Fathers of the English Dominican Province, published by Burns, Oates and Washbourne, Ltd., London, Publishers to the Holy See. Where a passage has been newly translated by the editor, it appears in brackets, and the version of the Dominican Fathers is given below in a footnote. In instances where the Douay and Vulgate versions of a biblical passage differ, as indicated by the Dominican Fathers, this distinction has been preserved. Explanatory notes on the text, contributed by the editor, appear both in bracketed footnotes and in the Appendix. The editor has also supplied a glossary of unusual terms and familiar words used in a limited sense.

Selections from *De Regimine Principum*, with accompanying notes, have been taken from the Phelan-Eschmann translation, published under the title *On Kingship, To the King of Cyprus*, and are here reprinted by permission of the publisher, the Pontifical Institute of Mediaeval Studies, Toronto, Canada.

For the reader's convenience, the editors of the "Hafner Library of Classics" have removed references to source material other than passages included in this volume from the text to the Appendix and have supplied a list of abbreviated titles of works cited. Punctuation and spelling have been revised in accordance with present-day American usage.

O. P.

THE SUMMA THEOLOGICA

[Selections from I-II and II-II]

THE SUMMA THEOLOGICA

[First Part of the Second Part]

QUESTION 90

OF THE ESSENCE OF LAW

(*In Four Articles*)

WE have now to consider the extrinsic principles of acts. Now the extrinsic principle inclining to evil is the devil, of whose temptations we have spoken in the First Part (Q. 114). But the extrinsic principle moving to good is God, Who both instructs us by means of His law and assists us by His grace; wherefore in the first place we must speak of law; in the second place, of grace.

Concerning law, we must consider (1) law itself in general, (2) its parts. Concerning law in general three points offer themselves for our consideration: (1) its essence; (2) the different kinds of law; (3) the effects of law.

Under the first head there are four points of inquiry: (1) whether law is something pertaining to reason? (2) concerning the end of law; (3) its cause; (4) the promulgation of law.

FIRST ARTICLE

WHETHER LAW IS SOMETHING PERTAINING TO REASON?

We proceed thus to the First Article:

Objection 1. It would seem that law is not something pertaining to reason. For the Apostle says: "I see another law in my members," etc.[1] But nothing pertaining to reason is in the members, since the reason does not make use of a bodily organ. Therefore law is not something pertaining to reason.

Obj. 2. Further, in the reason there is nothing else but power, habit, and act. But law is not the power itself of reason. In like manner, neither is it a habit of reason, because the habits of reason are the intellectual virtues of which we have spoken above.[2] Nor again is it an act of reason, because then law would cease when the act of reason ceases, for instance, while we are asleep. Therefore law is nothing pertaining to reason.

Obj. 3. Further, the law moves those who are subject to it to act aright. But it belongs properly to the will to move to act, as is evident from what has been said above.[3] Therefore law pertains not to the reason, but to the will, according to the words of the Jurist:[a] "Whatever pleases the sovereign, has the force of law." [4]

On the contrary, It belongs to the law to command and to forbid. But it belongs to reason to command, as stated above.[5] Therefore law is something pertaining to reason.

I answer that, Law is a rule and measure of acts whereby man is induced to act or is restrained from acting; for *lex* (law) is derived from *ligare* (to bind), because it binds one to act. Now the rule and measure of human acts is the reason, which is the first principle of human acts, as is evident from what has been stated above,[6] since it belongs to the reason to direct to the end, which is the first principle in all matters of action,[7] according to the Philosopher.[b] Now that which is the principle in any genus is the rule and measure of that genus: for instance, unity in the genus of numbers, and the first movement in the genus of movements. Consequently it follows that law is something pertaining to reason.

Reply Obj. 1. Since law is a kind of rule and measure, it may be in something in two ways. First, as in that which measures and rules; and since this is proper to reason, it follows that, in this way, law is in the reason alone.—Secondly, as in that which is measured and ruled. In this way law is in all those things that are inclined to something by reason of some law, so that any inclination arising from a law may be called a law, not essentially but by participation as it were. And thus the inclination of the members to concupiscence is called "the law of the members."

a [Ulpian (170?-228 A.D.).]
b [Aristotle.]

Reply Obj. 2. Just as, in external action, we may consider the work and the work done—for instance, the work of building and the house built, so in the acts of reason we may consider the act itself of reason, i.e., to understand and to reason, and something produced by this act. With regard to the speculative reason, this is first of all the definition; secondly, the proposition; thirdly, the syllogism or argument. And since also the practical reason makes use of a syllogism in respect of the work to be done,[c] as stated above [8] and as the Philosopher teaches,[9] hence we find in the practical reason something that holds the same position in regard to operations as, in the speculative intellect, the proposition holds in regard to conclusions. Suchlike universal propositions of the practical intellect that are directed to actions have the nature of law. And these propositions are sometimes under our actual consideration, while sometimes they are retained in the reason by means of a habit.

Reply Obj. 3. Reason has its power of moving from the will, as stated above,[10] for it is due to the fact that one wills the end that the reason issues its commands as regards things ordained to the end. But in order that the volition of what is commanded may have the nature of law, it needs to be in accord with some rule of reason. And in this sense is to be understood the saying that the will of the sovereign has the force of law; otherwise the sovereign's will would savor of lawlessness rather than of law.

SECOND ARTICLE

WHETHER THE LAW IS ALWAYS DIRECTED TO THE COMMON GOOD?

We proceed thus to the Second Article:

Objection 1. It would seem that the law is not always directed to the common good as to its end. For it belongs to law to command and to forbid. But commands are directed to certain individual goods. Therefore the end of the law is not always the common good.

[c] [I.e., makes use of a syllogism of a sort in its (practical) activities.]

Obj. 2. Further, the law directs man in his actions. But human actions are concerned with particular matters. Therefore the law is directed to some particular good.

Obj. 3. Further, Isidore says: "If the law is based on reason, whatever is based on reason will be a law." [11] But reason is the foundation not only of what is ordained to the common good, but also of that which is directed to private good. Therefore the law is not only directed to the good of all, but also to the private good of an individual.

On the contrary, Isidore says that "laws are enacted for no private profit, but for the common benefit of the citizens." [12]

I answer that, As stated above (A. 1), the law belongs to that which is a principle of human acts, because it is their rule and measure. Now as reason is a principle of human acts, so in reason itself there is something which is the principle in respect of all the rest; wherefore to this principle chiefly and mainly law must needs be referred.—Now the first principle in practical matters, which are the object of the practical reason, is the last end; and the last end of human life is bliss or happiness, as stated above.[13] Consequently the law must needs regard principally the relationship to happiness. Moreover, since every part is ordained to the whole, as imperfect to perfect; and since one man is a part of the perfect community, the law must needs regard properly the relationship to universal happiness. Wherefore the Philosopher, in the above definition of legal matters, mentions both happiness and the body politic, for he says that we call those legal matters *just,* "which are adapted to produce and preserve happiness and its parts for the body politic," [14] since the state is a perfect community, as he says in *Politics* i. 1.

[Now, in every genus that thing which reaches the highest degree is the principle (cause) of the rest (in that genus), and these others are graded with respect to it. So fire, which possesses heat in the highest degree, is the cause of heat in mixed bodies],[d] and

---

[d] D.F. Tr.: Now in every genus, that which belongs to it chiefly is the principle of the others, and the others belong to that genus in subordination to that thing: thus fire, which is chief among hot things, is the cause of heat in mixed bodies.

these are said to be hot in so far as they have a share of fire. Consequently, since the law is chiefly ordained to the common good, any other precept in regard to some individual work must needs be devoid of the nature of a law, save in so far as it regards the common good. Therefore every law is ordained to the common good.

Reply Obj. 1. A command denotes an application of a law to matters regulated by the law. Now the order to the common good, at which the law aims, is applicable to particular ends. And in this way commands are given even concerning particular matters.

Reply Obj. 2. Actions are indeed concerned with particular matters, but those particular matters are referable to the common good, not as to a common genus or species, but as to a common final cause, according as the common good is said to be the common end.

Reply Obj. 3. Just as nothing stands firm with regard to the speculative reason except that which is traced back to the first indemonstrable principles, so nothing stands firm with regard to the practical reason unless it be directed to the last end which is the common good; and whatever stands to reason in this sense has the nature of a law.

THIRD ARTICLE

WHETHER THE REASON OF ANY MAN IS COMPETENT TO MAKE LAWS?

We proceed thus to the Third Article:

Objection 1. It would seem that the reason of any man is competent to make laws. For the Apostle says that "when the Gentiles, who have not the law, do by nature those things that are of the law . . . they are a law to themselves." [15] Now he says this of all in general. Therefore anyone can make a law for himself.

Obj. 2. Further, as the Philosopher says, "The intention of the lawgiver is to lead men to virtue." [16] But every man can lead another to virtue. Therefore the reason of any man is competent to make laws.

Obj. 3. Further, just as the sovereign of a state governs the state, so every father of a family governs his household. But the sovereign of a state can make laws for the state. Therefore every father of a family can make laws for his household.

On the contrary, Isidore says: "A law is an ordinance of the people, whereby something is sanctioned by the Elders together with the Commonalty." [17]

I answer that, A law, properly speaking, regards first and foremost the order to the common good. Now to order anything to the common good belongs either to the whole people or to someone who is the vicegerent of the whole people. And therefore the making of a law belongs either to the whole people or to a public personage who has care of the whole people, since in all other matters the directing of anything to the end concerns him to whom the end belongs.

Reply Obj. 1. As stated above (A. 1 *ad* 1), a law is in a person not only as in one that rules, but also by participation as in one that is ruled. In the latter way each one is a law to himself, in so far as he shares the direction that he receives from one who rules him. Hence the same text goes on, "who show the work of the law written in their hearts."

Reply Obj. 2. A private person cannot lead another to virtue efficaciously, for he can only advise, and if his advice be not taken, it has no coercive power, such as the law should have in order to prove an efficacious inducement to virtue, as the Philosopher says.[18] But this coercive power is vested in the whole people or in some public personage to whom it belongs to inflict penalties, as we shall state further on (Q. 92, A. 2 *ad* 3; II-II, Q. 64, A. 3). Wherefore the framing of laws belongs to him alone.

Reply Obj. 3. As one man is a part of the household, so a household is a part of the state; and the state is a perfect community, according to *Politics* i. 1. And therefore, as the good of one man is not the last end, but is ordained to the common good, so, too, the good of one household is ordained to the good of a single state, which is a perfect community. Consequently he that governs a family can indeed make certain commands or ordinances, but not such as to have properly the force of law.

FOURTH ARTICLE

WHETHER PROMULGATION IS ESSENTIAL TO A LAW?

We proceed thus to the Fourth Article:

Objection 1. It would seem that promulgation is not essential to a law. For the natural law above all has the character of law. But the natural law needs no promulgation. Therefore it is not essential to a law that it be promulgated.

Obj. 2. Further, it belongs properly to a law to bind one to do or not to do something. But the obligation of fulfilling a law touches not only those in whose presence it is promulgated, but also others. Therefore promulgation is not essential to a law.

Obj. 3. Further, the binding force of a law extends even to the future, since "laws are binding in matters of the future," as the jurists say.[19] But promulgation concerns those who are present. Therefore it is not essential to a law.

On the contrary, It is laid down in the *Decretals,* dist. 4, that "laws are established when they are promulgated."

I answer that, As stated above (A. 1), a law is imposed on others by way of a rule and measure. Now a rule or measure is imposed by being applied to those who are to be ruled and measured by it. Wherefore, in order that a law obtain the binding force which is proper to a law, it must needs be applied to the men who have to be ruled by it. Such application is made by its being notified to them by promulgation. Wherefore promulgation is necessary for the law to obtain its force.

Thus from the four preceding articles the definition of law may be gathered; and it is nothing else than an ordinance of reason for the common good, made by him who has care of the community, and promulgated.

Reply Obj. 1. The natural law is promulgated by the very fact that God instilled it into man's mind so as to be known by him naturally.

Reply Obj. 2. Those who are not present when a law is promulgated are bound to observe the law, in so far as it is notified or can be notified to them by others, after it has been promulgated.

Reply Obj. 3. The promulgation that takes place now extends to future time by reason of the durability of written characters, by which means it is continually promulgated. Hence Isidore says that *"lex* (law) is derived from *legere* (to read) because it is written." [20]

QUESTION 91

OF THE VARIOUS KINDS OF LAW

(*In Six Articles*)

WE must now consider the various kinds of law, under which head there are six points of inquiry: (1) Whether there is an eternal law? (2) Whether there is a natural law? (3) Whether there is a human law? (4) Whether there is a divine law? (5) Whether there is one divine law or several? (6) Whether there is a law of sin?

FIRST ARTICLE

WHETHER THERE IS AN ETERNAL LAW?

We proceed thus to the First Article:

Objection 1. It would seem that there is no eternal law. Because every law is imposed on someone. But there was not someone from eternity on whom a law could be imposed, since God alone was from eternity. Therefore no law is eternal.

Obj. 2. Further, promulgation is essential to law. But promulgation could not be from eternity, because there was no one to whom it could be promulgated from eternity. Therefore no law can be eternal.

Obj. 3. Further, a law implies order to an end. But nothing ordained to an end is eternal, for the last end alone is eternal. Therefore no law is eternal.

On the contrary, Augustine says: "That Law which is the Supreme Reason cannot be understood to be otherwise than unchangeable and eternal." [1]

I answer that, As stated above (Q. 90, A. 1 *ad* 2; AA. 3, 4), a law is nothing else but a dictate of practical reason emanating from the ruler who governs a perfect community. Now it is evident, granted that the world is ruled by divine providence, as was stated in the First Part,[2] that the whole community of the universe is governed by divine reason. Wherefore the very Idea of the government of things in God the Ruler of the universe has the nature of a law. And since the divine reason's conception of things is not subject to time but is eternal, according to Proverbs viii. 23, therefore it is that this kind of law must be called eternal.

Reply Obj. 1. Those things that are not in themselves exist with God, inasmuch as they are foreknown and preordained by Him, according to Romans iv. 17, "Who calls those things that are not, as those that are." Accordingly the eternal concept of the divine law bears the character of an eternal law in so far as it is ordained by God to the government of things foreknown by Him.

Reply Obj. 2. Promulgation is made by word of mouth or in writing; and in both ways the eternal·law is promulgated, because both the divine word and the writing of the Book of Life are eternal. But the promulgation cannot be from eternity on the part of the creature that hears or reads.

Reply Obj. 3. The law implies order to the end actively, in so far as it directs certain things to the end, but not passively—that is to say, the law itself is not ordained to the end—except accidentally, in a governor whose end is extrinsic to him, and to which end his law must needs be ordained. But the end of the divine government is God Himself, and His law is not distinct from Himself. Wherefore the eternal law is not ordained to another end.

SECOND ARTICLE

WHETHER THERE IS IN US A NATURAL LAW?

We proceed thus to the Second Article:

Objection 1. It would seem that there is no natural law in us. Because man is governed sufficiently by the eternal law; for Augustine says that "the eternal law is that by which it is right that all things should be most orderly."[3] But nature does not abound in superfluities, as neither does she fail in necessaries. Therefore no law is natural to man.

Obj. 2. Further, by the law man is directed in his acts to the end, as stated above (Q. 90, A. 2). But the directing of human acts to their end is not a function of nature, as is the case in irrational creatures, which act for an end solely by their natural appetite; whereas man acts for an end by his reason and will. Therefore no law is natural to man.

Obj. 3. Further, the more a man is free, the less is he under the law. But man is freer than all the animals, on account of his free will, with which he is endowed above all other animals. Since therefore other animals are not subject to a natural law, neither is man subject to a natural law.

On the contrary, A gloss on Romans ii. 14: "When the Gentiles, who have not the law, do by nature those things that are of the law," comments as follows: "Although they have no written law, yet they have the natural law, whereby each one knows, and is conscious of, what is good and what is evil."

I answer that, As stated above (Q. 90, A. 1 *ad* 1), law, being a rule and measure, can be in a person in two ways: in one way, as in him that rules and measures; in another way, as in that which is ruled and measured, since a thing is ruled and measured in so far as it partakes of the rule or measure. Wherefore, since all things subject to divine providence are ruled and measured by the eternal law, as was stated above (A. 1), it is evident that all things partake somewhat of the eternal law, in so far as, namely, from its being imprinted on them, they derive their respective inclinations to their proper acts and ends. Now among all others the rational creature is subject to divine providence in the most excellent way, in so far as it partakes of a share of providence, by being provident both for itself and for others. Wherefore it has a share of the eternal reason, whereby it has a natural inclination to its proper act and end: and this participation of the eternal law in the rational creature is called the natural law. Hence the Psalmist after saying: "Offer up the sacrifice of justice," as though someone asked what the works of justice are, adds: "Many say, Who showeth us good things?" in answer to which question he says: "The light of Thy countenance, O Lord, is signed upon us"; [4] thus implying that the light of natural reason, whereby we discern what is good and what is evil, which is the function of the natural law, is nothing else than an imprint on us of the divine light. It is therefore evident that the natural law is nothing else than the rational creature's participation of the eternal law.

Reply Obj. 1. This argument would hold if the natural law were something different from the eternal law, whereas it is nothing but a participation thereof, as stated above.

Reply Obj. 2. Every act of reason and will in us is based on that which is according to nature, as stated above; [5] for every act of reasoning is based on principles that are known naturally, and every act of appetite in respect of the means is derived from the natural appetite in respect of the last end. Accordingly the first direction of our acts to their end must needs be in virtue of the natural law.

Reply Obj. 3. Even irrational animals partake in their own way of the eternal reason, just as the rational creature does. But because the rational creature partakes thereof in an intellectual and rational manner, therefore the participation of the eternal law in the rational creature is properly called a law, since a law is something pertaining to reason, as stated above (Q. 90, A. 1). Irrational creatures, however, do not partake thereof in a rational manner, wherefore there is no participation of the eternal law in them, except by way of similitude.

Third Article

WHETHER THERE IS A HUMAN LAW?

We proceed thus to the Third Article:

Objection 1. It would seem that there is not a human law. For the natural law is a participation of the eternal law, as stated above (A. 2). Now through the eternal law "all things are most orderly," as Augustine states.[6] Therefore the natural law suffices for the ordering of all human affairs. Consequently there is no need for a human law.

Obj. 2. Further, a law bears the character of a measure, as stated above (Q. 90, A. 1). But human reason is not a measure of things, but vice versa, as stated in *Metaphysics* x. text. 5. Therefore no law can emanate from human reason.

Obj. 3. Further, a measure should be most certain, as stated in *Metaphysics* x. text. 3. But the dictates of human reason in matters of conduct are uncertain, according to Wisdom ix. 14: "The thoughts of mortal men are fearful, and our counsels uncertain." Therefore no law can emanate from human reason.

On the contrary, Augustine distinguishes two kinds of law—the one eternal; the other temporal, which he calls human.[7]

I answer that, As stated above (Q. 90, A. 1, *ad* 2), a law is a dictate of the practical reason. Now it is to be observed that the same procedure takes place in the practical and in the speculative reason, for each proceeds from principles to conclusions, as stated above (*ibid.*). Accordingly we conclude that just as, in the speculative reason, from naturally known indemonstrable principles we draw the conclusions of the various sciences, the knowledge of which is not imparted to us by nature, but acquired by the efforts of reason; so, too, it is from the precepts of the natural law, as from general and indemonstrable principles, that the human reason needs to proceed to the more particular determination of certain matters. These particular determinations, devised by human reason, are called human laws, provided the other essential conditions of law be observed, as stated above (Q. 90, AA. 2, 3, 4). Wherefore Cicero says in his *Rhetoric* that "justice has its source in nature; thence certain things came into custom by reason of their utility; afterward these things which emanated from nature and were approved by custom were sanctioned by fear and reverence for the law."[8]

Reply Obj. 1. The human reason cannot have a full participation of the dictate of the divine reason but according to its own mode, and imperfectly. Consequently, as on the part of the speculative reason, by a natural participation of divine wisdom, there is in us the knowledge of certain general principles, but not proper knowledge of each single truth, such as that contained in the divine wisdom; so, too, on the part of the practical reason man has a natural participation of the eternal law, according to certain general principles, but not as regards the particular determinations of individual cases, which are, however, contained in the eternal law. [Hence the necessity that human reason proceed to certain particular sanctions of law.] ᵃ

Reply Obj. 2. Human reason is not of itself the rule of things, but the principles impressed on it by nature are general rules and measures of all things relating to human conduct, whereof the natural reason is the rule and measure, although it is not the measure of things that are from nature.

Reply Obj. 3. The practical reason is concerned with practical matters, which are singular and contingent, but not with necessary things, with which the speculative reason is concerned. Wherefore human laws cannot have that inerrancy that belongs to the demonstrated conclusions of sciences. Nor is it necessary for every measure to be altogether unerring and certain, but according as it is possible in its own particular genus.

FOURTH ARTICLE

WHETHER THERE WAS ANY NEED FOR A DIVINE LAW?

We proceed thus to the Fourth Article:

Objection 1. It would seem that there was no need for a divine law. Because, as stated above (A. 2), the natural law is a participation in us of the eternal law. But the eternal law is a divine law, as stated above (A. 1). Therefore there is no need for a divine law in addition to the natural law and human laws derived therefrom.

Obj. 2. Further, it is written that "God left man in the hand of his own counsel." [9] Now counsel is an act of reason, as stated above.[10] Therefore man was left to the direction of his reason. But a dictate of human reason is a human law, as stated above (A. 3). Therefore there is no need for man to be governed also by a divine law.

Obj. 3. Further, human nature is more self-sufficing than irrational creatures. But irrational creatures have no divine law be-

ᵃ D.F. Tr.: Hence the need for human reason to proceed further to sanction them by law.

sides the natural inclination impressed on them. Much less, therefore, should the rational creature have a divine law in addition to
the natural law.

On the contrary, David prayed God to set His law before him,
saying: "Set before me for a law the way of Thy justifications, O
Lord." [11]

I answer that, Besides the natural and the human law it was
necessary for the directing of human conduct to have a divine law.
And this for four reasons. First, because it is by law that man is
directed how to perform his proper acts in view of his last end. And
indeed, if man were ordained to no other end than that which is
proportionate to his natural faculty, there would be no need for
man to have any further direction on the part of his reason besides
the natural law and human law which is derived from it. But since
man is ordained to an end of eternal happiness which is inpro-
portionate to man's natural faculty, as stated above,[12] therefore it
was necessary that, besides the natural and the human law, man
should be directed to his end by a law given by God.

Secondly, because, on account of the uncertainty of human
judgment, especially on contingent and particular matters, different people form different judgments on human acts; whence also
different and contrary laws result. In order, therefore, that man
may know without any doubt what he ought to do and what he
ought to avoid, it was necessary for man to be directed in his
proper acts by a law given by God, for it is certain that such a law
cannot err.

Thirdly, because man can make laws in those matters of which
he is competent to judge. But man is not competent to judge of
interior movements that are hidden, but only of exterior acts which
appear; and yet for the perfection of virtue it is necessary for man
to conduct himself aright in both kinds of acts. Consequently human law could not sufficiently curb and direct interior acts, and it
was necessary for this purpose that a divine law should supervene.

Fourthly, because, as Augustine says, human law cannot punish
or forbid all evil deeds; since while aiming at doing away with all
evils, it would do away with many good things, and would hinder
the advance of the common good, which is necessary for human

intercourse.[13] In order, therefore, that no evil might remain unforbidden and unpunished, it was necessary for the divine law to supervene, whereby all sins are forbidden.

And these four causes are touched upon in Psalm cxviii. 8, where it is said: "The law of the Lord is unspotted," i.e., allowing no foulness of sin; "converting souls," because it directs not only exterior but also interior acts; "the testimony of the Lord is faithful," because of the certainty of what is true and right; "giving wisdom to little ones," by directing man to an end supernatural and divine.

Reply Obj. 1. By natural law the eternal law is participated in proportionately to the capacity of human nature. But to his supernatural end man needs to be directed in a yet higher way. Hence the additional law given by God, whereby man shares more perfectly in the eternal law.

Reply Obj. 2. Counsel is a kind of inquiry; hence it must proceed from some principles. Nor is it enough for it to proceed from principles imparted by nature, which are the precepts of the natural law, for the reasons given above; but there is need for certain additional principles, namely, the precepts of the divine law.

Reply Obj. 3. Irrational creatures are not ordained to an end higher than that which is proportionate to their natural powers; consequently the comparison fails.

FIFTH ARTICLE

WHETHER THERE IS BUT ONE DIVINE LAW?

We proceed thus to the Fifth Article:

Objection 1. It would seem that there is but one divine law. Because where there is one king in one kingdom there is but one law. Now the whole of mankind is compared to God as to one king, according to Psalm xlvi. 8: "God is the King of all the earth." Therefore there is but one divine law.

Obj. 2. Further, every law is directed to the end which the lawgiver intends for those for whom he makes the law. But God intends one and the same thing for all men; since, according to

I Timothy ii. 4, "He will have all men to be saved, and to come to the knowledge of the truth." Therefore there is but one divine law.

Obj. 3. Further, the divine law seems to be more akin to the eternal law, which is one, than the natural law, according as the revelation of grace is of a higher order than natural knowledge. Therefore much more is the divine law but one.

On the contrary, The Apostle says: "The priesthood being translated, it is necessary that a translation also be made of the law." [14] But the priesthood is twofold, as stated in the same passage, viz., the levitical priesthood and the priesthood of Christ. Therefore the divine law is twofold, namely, the Old Law and the New Law.

I answer that, As stated in the First Part,[15] distinction is the cause of number. Now things may be distinguished in two ways. First, as those things that are altogether specifically different, e.g., a horse and an ox. Secondly, as perfect and imperfect in the same species, e.g., a boy and a man; and in this way the divine law is divided into Old and New. Hence the Apostle compares the state of man under the Old Law to that of a child "under a pedagogue"; but the state under the New Law to that of a full-grown man who is "no longer under a pedagogue." [16]

Now the perfection and imperfection of these two laws is to be taken in connection with the three conditions pertaining to law, as stated above. For, in the first place, it belongs to law to be directed to the common good as to its end, as stated above (Q. 90, A. 2). This good may be twofold. It may be a sensible and earthly good; and to this, man was directly ordained by the Old Law; wherefore, at the very outset of the law, the people were invited to the earthly kingdom of the Chananaeans.[17] Again it may be an intelligible and heavenly good; and to this, man is ordained by the New Law. Wherefore, at the very beginning of His preaching, Christ invited men to the kingdom of heaven, saying: "Do penance, for the kingdom of heaven is at hand." [18] Hence Augustine says that "promises of temporal goods are contained in the Old Testament, for which reason it is called old; but the promise of eternal life belongs to the New Testament." [19]

Secondly, it belongs to the law to direct human acts according to the order of righteousness (A. 4), wherein also the New Law surpasses the Old Law, since it directs our internal acts, according to Matthew v. 20: "Unless your justice abound more than that of the Scribes and Pharisees, you shall not enter into the kingdom of heaven." Hence the saying that "the Old Law restrains the hand, but the New Law controls the mind." [b]

Thirdly, it belongs to the law to induce men to observe its commandments. This the Old Law did by the fear of punishment; but the New Law, by love, which is poured into our hearts by the grace of Christ, bestowed in the New Law, but foreshadowed in the Old. Hence Augustine says that "there is little difference [c] between the Law and the Gospel—fear and love." [20]

Reply Obj. 1. As the father of a family issues different commands to the children and to the adults, so also the one King, God, in His one kingdom, gave one law to men while they were yet imperfect, and another more perfect law when, by the preceding law, they had been led to a greater capacity for divine things.

Reply Obj. 2. The salvation of man could not be achieved otherwise than through Christ, according to Acts iv. 12: "There is no other name . . . given to men, whereby we must be saved." Consequently the law that brings all to salvation could not be given until after the coming of Christ. But before His coming it was necessary to give to the people of whom Christ was to be born a law containing certain rudiments of righteousness unto salvation in order to prepare them to receive Him.

Reply Obj. 3. The natural law directs man by way of certain general precepts, common to both the perfect and the imperfect; wherefore it is one and the same for all. But the divine law directs man also in certain particular matters to which the perfect and imperfect do not stand in the same relation. Hence the necessity for the divine law to be twofold, as already explained.

[b] [Isidore, *Libri tres Sententiarum* D. xl.]
[c] The "little difference" refers to the Latin words *timor* and *amor*—"fear" and "love."

SIXTH ARTICLE

WHETHER THERE IS A LAW IN THE FOMES OF SIN?

We proceed thus to the Sixth Article:

Objection 1. It would seem that there is no law of the "fomes" of sin. For Isidore says that the "law is based on reason." [21] But the "fomes" of sin is not based on reason, but deviates from it. Therefore the "fomes" has not the nature of a law.

Obj. 2. Further, every law is binding, so that those who do not obey it are called transgressors. But man is not called a transgressor from not following the instigations of the "fomes," but rather from his following them. Therefore the "fomes" has not the nature of a law.

Obj. 3. Further, the law is ordained to the common good, as stated above (Q. 90, A. 2). But the "fomes" inclines us, not to the common, but to our own private good. [Therefore the "fomes" does not have the nature of a law.] [d]

On the contrary, The Apostle says: "I see another law in my members, fighting against the law of my mind." [22]

I answer that, As stated above (A. 2; Q. 90, A. 1 *ad* 1), the law, as to its essence, resides in him that rules and measures; but, by way of participation, in that which is ruled and measured, so that every inclination or ordination which may be found in things subject to the law is called a law by participation, as stated above (*ibid.*). Now those who are subject to a law may receive a twofold inclination from the lawgiver. First, in so far as he directly inclines his subjects to something, sometimes indeed different subjects to different acts; in this way we may say that there is a military law and a mercantile law. Secondly, indirectly; thus by the very fact that a lawgiver deprives a subject of some dignity, the latter passes into another order, so as to be under another law, as it were: thus if a knight is dropped from chivalry,[e] he becomes a subject of rural or mercantile legislation.

Accordingly under the divine lawgiver various creatures have vari-

[d] D.F. Tr.: Therefore the "fomes" has not the nature of sin.
[e] D.F. Tr.: if a soldier be turned out of the army.

ous natural inclinations, so that what is, as it were, a law for one is against the law for another: thus I might say that fierceness is, in a way, the law of a dog, but against the law of a sheep or another meek animal. And so the law of man, which, by the divine ordinance, is allotted to him according to his proper natural condition, is that he should act in accordance with reason; and this law was so effective in the primitive state that nothing either beside or against reason could take man unawares. But when man turned his back on God, he fell under the influence of his sensual impulses—in fact this happens to each one individually the more he deviates from the path of reason—so that, after a fashion, he is likened to the beasts that are led by the impulse of sensuality, according to Psalm xlviii. 21: "Man, when he was in honour, did not understand: he hath been compared to senseless beasts, and made like to them."

So, then, this very inclination of sensuality which is called the "fomes," in other animals has simply the nature of a law (yet only in so far as a law may be said to be in such things), by reason of a direct inclination. But in man, it has not the nature of law in this way, rather is it a deviation from the law of reason. But since, by the just sentence of God, man is destitute of original justice and his reason bereft of its vigor, this impulse of sensuality whereby he is led, in so far as it is a penalty following from the divine law depriving man of his proper dignity, has the nature of a law.

Reply Obj. 1. This argument considers the "fomes" in itself, as an incentive to evil. It is not thus that it has the nature of a law, as stated above, but according as it results from the justice of the divine law: [it is as though one were to say that it is legal to authorize that a nobleman, because of his transgressions, be made to perform the tasks of a slave].*

Reply Obj. 2. This argument considers law in the light of a rule or measure, for it is in this sense that those who deviate from the law become transgressors. But the "fomes" is not a law in this respect, but by a kind of participation, as stated above.

---

* D.F. Tr.: it is as though we were to say that the law allows a nobleman to be condemned to hard labor for some misdeed.

Reply Obj. 3. This argument considers the "fomes" as to its proper inclination, and not as to its origin. And yet if the inclination of sensuality be considered as it is in other animals, thus it is ordained to the common good, namely, to the preservation of nature in the species or in the individual. And this is in man also, in so far as sensuality is subject to reason. But it is called the "fomes" in so far as it strays from the order of reason.

QUESTION 92

OF THE EFFECTS OF LAW

(*In Two Articles*)

We must now consider the effects of law; under which head there are two points of inquiry: (1) Whether an effect of law is to make men good? (2) Whether the effects of law are to command, to forbid, to permit, and to punish, as the Jurist states?

FIRST ARTICLE

WHETHER AN EFFECT OF LAW IS TO MAKE MEN GOOD?

We proceed thus to the First Article:

Objection 1. It seems that it is not an effect of law to make men good. For men are good through virtue, since virtue, as stated in *Ethics* ii. 6, is "that which makes its subject good." But virtue is in man from God alone, because He it is Who "works it in us without us," as we stated above [1] in giving the definition of virtue. Therefore the law does not make men good.

Obj. 2. Further, law does not profit a man unless he obeys it. But the very fact that a man obeys a law is due to his being good. Therefore in man goodness is presupposed to the law. Therefore the law does not make men good.

Obj. 3. Further, law is ordained to the common good, as stated above (Q. 90, A. 2). But some behave well in things regarding the community, who behave ill in things regarding themselves. Therefore it is not the business of the law to make men good.

Obj. 4. Further, some laws are tyrannical, as the Philosopher says.[2] But a tyrant does not intend the good of his subjects, but considers only his own profit. Therefore law does not make men good.

On the contrary, The Philosopher says that the "intention of every lawgiver is to make good citizens." [3]

I answer that, As stated above (Q. 90, A. 1 *ad* 2; AA. 3, 4), a law is nothing else than a dictate of reason in the ruler by [which][a] his subjects are governed. Now the virtue of any subordinate thing consists in its being well subordinated to that by which it is regulated; thus we see that the virtue of the irascible and concupiscible faculties consists in their being obedient to reason; and accordingly "the virtue of every subject consists in his being well subjected to his ruler," as the Philosopher says.[4] But every law aims at being obeyed by those who are subject to it. Consequently it is evident that the proper effect of law is to lead its subjects to their proper virtue; and since virtue is "that which makes its subject good," it follows that the proper effect of law is to make those to whom it is given good, either simply or in some particular respect. For if the intention of the lawgiver is fixed on true good, which is the common good regulated according to divine justice, it follows that the effect of the law is to make men good simply. If, however, the intention of the lawgiver is fixed on that which is not simply good, but useful or pleasurable to himself, or in opposition to divine justice, then the law does not make men good simply, but in respect to that particular government. In this way good is found even in things that are bad of themselves: thus a man is called a good robber because he works in a way that is adapted to his end.

Reply Obj. 1. Virtue is twofold, as explained above,[5] viz., acquired and infused. Now the fact of being accustomed to an action contributes to both, but in different ways; for it causes the acquired virtue, while it disposes to infused virtue, and preserves and fosters it when it already exists. And since law is given for the purpose of directing human acts as far as human acts conduce to virtue, so far does law make men good. Wherefore the Philosopher says in the second book of the *Politics* [*Ethics* ii] that "lawgivers make men good by habituating them to good works."

Reply Obj. 2. It is not always through perfect goodness of virtue that one obeys the law, but sometimes it is through fear of punishment, and sometimes from the mere dictate of reason, which is a beginning of virtue, as stated above.[6]

Reply Obj. 3. The goodness of any part is considered in com-

[a] D.F. Tr.: whom.

parison with the whole; hence Augustine says that "unseemly is the part that harmonizes not with the whole." [7] Since then every man is a part of the state, it is impossible that a man be good unless he be well proportionate to the common good; nor can the whole be well consistent unless its parts be proportionate to it. Consequently the common good of the state cannot flourish unless the citizens be virtuous, at least those whose business it is to govern. But it is enough for the good of the community that the other citizens be so far virtuous that they obey the commands of their rulers. Hence the Philosopher says that "the virtue of a sovereign is the same as that of a good man, but the virtue of any common citizen is not the same as that of a good man." [8]

Reply Obj. 4. A tyrannical law, through not being according to reason, is not a law, absolutely speaking, but rather a perversion of law; and yet in so far as it is something in the nature of a law, it aims at the citizens being good. For all it has in the nature of a law consists in its being an ordinance made by a superior to his subjects, and aims at being obeyed by them, which is to make them good, not simply, but with respect to that particular government.

SECOND ARTICLE

WHETHER THE ACTS OF LAW ARE SUITABLY ASSIGNED?

We proceed thus to the Second Article:

Objection 1. It would seem that the acts of law are not suitably assigned as consisting in "command," "prohibition," "permission," and "punishment." For "every law is a general precept," as the Jurist states.[9] But command and precept are the same. Therefore the other three are superfluous.

Obj. 2. Further, the effect of a law is to induce its subjects to be good, as stated above (A. 1). But counsel aims at a higher good than a command does. Therefore it belongs to law to counsel rather than to command.

Obj. 3. Further, just as punishment stirs a man to good deeds, so does reward. Therefore, if to punish is reckoned an effect of law, so also is to reward.

Obj. 4. Further, the intention of a lawgiver is to make men good, as stated above (A. 1). But he that obeys the law merely through fear of being punished is not good, because "although a good deed may be done through servile fear, i.e., fear of punishment, it is not done well," as Augustine says.[10] Therefore punishment is not a proper effect of law.

On the contrary, Isidore says: "Every law either permits something, as: 'A brave man may demand his reward'; or forbids something, as: 'No man may ask a consecrated virgin in marriage'; or punishes, as: 'Let him that commits a murder be put to death.' "[11]

I answer that, Just as an assertion is a dictate of reason asserting something, so is a law a dictate of reason commanding something. Now it is proper to reason to lead from one thing to another. Wherefore just as, in demonstrative sciences, the reason leads us from certain principles to assent to the conclusion, so it induces us by some means to assent to the precept of the law.

Now the precepts of law are concerned with human acts, in which the law directs, as stated above (Q. 90, AA. 1, 2; Q. 91, A. 4). Again, there are three kinds of human acts; for, as stated above,[12] some acts are good generically, viz., acts of virtue; and in respect of these the act of the law is a precept or command, for "the law commands all acts of virtue" (*Ethics* v. 1). Some acts are evil generically, viz., acts of vice, and in respect of these the law forbids. Some acts are generically indifferent, and in respect of these the law permits; and all acts that are either not distinctly good or not distinctly bad may be called indifferent.—And it is the fear of punishment that law makes use of in order to ensure obedience, in which respect punishment is an effect of law.

Reply Obj. 1. Just as to cease from evil is a kind of good, so a prohibition is a kind of precept; and accordingly, taking precept in a wide sense, every law is a kind of precept.

Reply Obj. 2. To advise is not a proper act of law, but may be within the competency even of a private person, who cannot make a law. Wherefore, too, the Apostle, after giving a certain counsel says: "I speak, not the Lord." [13] Consequently it is not reckoned as an effect of law.

Reply Obj. 3. To reward may also pertain to anyone; but to punish pertains to none but the framer of the law, by whose authority the pain is inflicted. Wherefore to reward is not reckoned an effect of law, but only to punish.

Reply Obj. 4. From becoming accustomed to avoid evil and fulfill what is good, through fear of punishment, one is sometimes led on to do so likewise, with delight and of one's own accord. Accordingly, law, even by punishing, leads men on to being good.

QUESTION 93

OF THE ETERNAL LAW

(*In Six Articles*)

WE must now consider each law by itself; and (1) the eternal law, (2) the natural law, (3) the human law, (4) the Old Law, (5) the New Law, which is the law of the Gospel. Of the sixth law, which is the law of the "fomes," suffice what we have said when treating of original sin.

Concerning the first there are six points of inquiry: (1) What is the eternal law? (2) Whether it is known to all? (3) Whether every law is derived from it? (4) Whether necessary things are subject to the eternal law? (5) Whether natural contingencies are subject to the eternal law? (6) Whether all human things are subject to it?

FIRST ARTICLE

WHETHER THE ETERNAL LAW IS A SOVEREIGN TYPE [a] EXISTING IN GOD?

We proceed thus to the First Article:

Objection 1. It would seem that the eternal law is not a sovereign type existing in God. For there is only one eternal law. But there are many types of things in the divine mind; for Augustine says that God "made each thing according to its type." [1] Therefore the eternal law does not seem to be a type existing in the divine mind.

Obj. 2. Further, it is essential to a law that it be promulgated by word, as stated above (Q. 90, A. 4). But Word is a *personal* name in God, as stated in the First Part; [2] whereas type refers to the *essence*. Therefore the eternal law is not the same as a divine type.

[a] Ratio.

Obj. 3. Further, Augustine says: "We see a law above our minds, which is called truth." [3] But the law which is above our minds is the eternal law. Therefore truth is the eternal law. But the idea of truth is not the same as the idea of a type. Therefore the eternal law is not the same as the sovereign type.

On the contrary, Augustine says that "the eternal law is the sovereign type, to which we must always conform." [4]

I answer that, Just as in every artificer there pre-exists a type of the things that are made by his art, so too in every governor there must pre-exist the type of the order of those things that are to be done by those who are subject to his government. And just as the type of the things yet to be made by an art is called the art or exemplar of the products of that art, so too the type in him who governs the acts of his subjects bears the character of a law, provided the other conditions be present which we have mentioned above (Q. 90). Now God, by His wisdom, is the creator of all things, in relation to which He stands as the artificer to the products of his art, as stated in the First Part. [5] Moreover, He governs all the acts and movements that are to be found in each single creature, as was also stated in the First Part. [6] Wherefore as the type of the divine wisdom, inasmuch as by it all things are created, has the character of art, exemplar or idea, so the type of divine wisdom, as moving all things to their due end, bears the character of law. Accordingly, the eternal law is nothing else than the type of divine wisdom, as directing all actions and movements.

Reply Obj. 1. Augustine is speaking in that passage of the ideal types which regard the proper nature of each single thing; and consequently in them there is a certain distinction and plurality, according to their different relations to things, as stated in the First Part. [7] But law is said to direct human acts by ordaining them to the common good, as stated above (Q. 90, A. 2). And things, which are in themselves different, may be considered as one, according as they are ordained to one common thing. Wherefore the eternal law is one, since it is the type of this order.

Reply Obj. 2. With regard to any sort of word, two points may be considered: viz., the word itself and that which is expressed by the word. For the spoken word is something uttered by the mouth of man and expresses that which is signified by the human word. The same applies to the human mental word, which is nothing else than something conceived by the mind, by which man expresses his thoughts mentally. So then in God the Word conceived by the intellect of the Father is the name of a person, but all things that are in the Father's knowledge, whether they refer to the essence or to the persons, or to the works of God, are expressed by this Word, as Augustine declares.[8] And, among other things expressed by this Word, the eternal law itself is expressed thereby. Nor does it follow that the eternal law is a personal name in God, yet it is appropriated to the Son, on account of the kinship between type and word.

Reply Obj. 3. The types of the divine intellect do not stand in the same relation to things, as the types of the human intellect. For the human intellect is measured by things, so that a human concept is not true by reason of itself, but by reason of its being consonant with things, since [the fact that a thing is or is not determines whether the opinion is true or false].[b] But the divine intellect is the measure of things, since each thing has so far truth in it as it represents the divine intellect, as was stated in the First Part.[9] Consequently the divine intellect is true in itself, and its type is truth itself.

SECOND ARTICLE

WHETHER THE ETERNAL LAW IS KNOWN TO ALL?

We proceed thus to the Second Article:

Objection 1. It would seem that the eternal law is not known to all. Because, as the Apostle says, "the things that are of God no man knoweth, but the Spirit of God." [10] But the eternal law is a type existing in the divine mind. Therefore it is unknown to all save God alone.

Obj. 2. Further, as Augustine says, "the eternal law is that by which it is right that all things should be most orderly." [11]

[b] D.F. Tr.: an opinion is true or false according as it answers to the reality.

But all do not know how all things are most orderly. Therefore all do not know the eternal law.

Obj. 3. Further, Augustine says that "the eternal law is not subject to the judgment of man." [12] But according to *Ethics* i, "Any man can judge well of what he knows." Therefore the eternal law is not known to us.

On the contrary, Augustine says that "knowledge of the eternal law is imprinted on us." [13]

I answer that, A thing may be known in two ways: first, in itself; secondly, in its effect, wherein some likeness of that thing is found; thus someone not seeing the sun in its substance may know it by its rays. So then no one can know the eternal law as it is in itself, except the blessed who see God in His essence. But every rational creature knows it in its reflection, greater or less. For every knowledge of truth is a kind of reflection and participation of the eternal law, which is the unchangeable truth, as Augustine says.[14] Now all men know the truth to a certain extent, at least as to the common principles of the natural law; and as to the others, they partake of the knowledge of truth, some more, some less; and in this respect are more or less cognizant of the eternal law.

Reply Obj. 1. We cannot know the things that are of God as they are in themselves; but they are made known to us in their effects, according to Romans i. 20: "The invisible things of God . . . are clearly seen, being understood by the things that are made."

Reply Obj. 2. Although each one knows the eternal law according to his own capacity, in the way explained above, yet none can comprehend it, for it cannot be made perfectly known by its effects. Therefore it does not follow that anyone who knows the eternal law in the way aforesaid knows also the whole order of things, whereby they are most orderly.

Reply Obj. 3. To judge of a thing may be understood in two ways. First, as when a cognitive power judges of its proper object, according to Job xii. 11: "Doth not the ear discern words, and the palate of him that eateth, the taste?" It is to this kind of judgment that the Philosopher alludes when he says that "anyone can judge well of what he knows," by judging, namely, whether what is put forward is true. In another way we speak of a superior judging of a subordinate by a kind of practical judgment, as to whether he should be such and such or not. And thus none can judge of the eternal law.

THIRD ARTICLE

WHETHER EVERY LAW IS DERIVED FROM THE ETERNAL LAW?

We proceed thus to the Third Article:

Objection 1. It would seem that not every law is derived from the eternal law. For there is a law of the "fomes," as stated above (Q. 91, A. 6), which is not derived from that divine law which is the eternal law, since thereunto pertains the "prudence of the flesh," of which the Apostle says that "it cannot be subject to the law of God." [15] Therefore not every law is derived from the eternal law.

Obj. 2. Further, nothing unjust can be derived from the eternal law, because, as stated above (A. 2, *Obj.* 2), "the eternal law is that according to which it is right that all things should be most orderly." But some laws are unjust, according to Isaias x. 1: "Woe to them that make wicked laws." Therefore not every law is derived from the eternal law.

Obj. 3. Further, Augustine says that "the law which is framed for ruling the people rightly permits many things which are punished by divine providence." [16] But the type of divine providence is the eternal law, as stated above (A. 1). Therefore not even every good law is derived from the eternal law.

On the contrary, divine wisdom says: "By Me kings reign, and lawgivers decree just things." [17] But the type of divine wisdom is the eternal law, as stated above (A. 1). Therefore all laws proceed from the eternal law.

I answer that, As stated above (Q. 90, AA. 1, 2), law denotes a kind of plan directing acts toward an end. Now wherever there are movers ordained to one another, the power of the second mover must needs be derived from the power of the first mover, since the second mover does not move except in so far as it is moved by the first. Wherefore we observe the same in all those who govern, so that the plan of government is derived by secondary governors from the governor-in-chief: thus the plan of what is to be done in a state flows from the king's command to his inferior administrators; and again in things of art the plan of whatever is to be done by art flows from the chief craftsman to the under-craftsmen who work with their hands. Since then the eternal law is the plan of government in the Chief Governor, all the plans of government in the inferior governors must be derived from the eternal law. But these plans of inferior governors are all other laws besides the eternal law. Therefore all laws, in so far as they partake of right reason, are derived from the eternal law. Hence Augustine says that "in temporal law there is nothing just and lawful but what man has drawn from the eternal law." [18]

Reply Obj. 1. The "fomes" has the nature of law in man in so far as it is a punishment resulting from divine justice; and in this respect it is evident that it is derived from the eternal law. But in so far as it denotes a proneness to sin, it is contrary to the divine law and has not the nature of law, as stated above (Q. 91, A. 6).

Reply Obj. 2. Human law has the nature of law in so far as it partakes of right reason; and it is clear that, in this respect, it is derived from the eternal law. But in so far as it deviates from reason, it is called an unjust law and has the nature, not of law, but of violence. Nevertheless even an unjust law, in so far as it retains some appearance of law, through being framed by one who is in power, is derived from the eternal law, since all power is from the Lord God, according to Romans xiii. 1.

Reply Obj. 3. Human law is said to permit certain things, not as approving of them, but as being unable to direct them. And many things are directed by the divine law which human law is unable to direct, because more things are subject to a higher than to a lower cause. Hence the very fact that human law does not meddle with matters it cannot direct comes under the ordination of the eternal law. It would be different were human law to sanction what the eternal law condemns. Consequently it does not follow that human law is not derived from the eternal law, but that it is not on a perfect equality with it.

WHETHER NECESSARY AND ETERNAL THINGS ARE SUBJECT TO THE ETERNAL LAW?

We proceed thus to the Fourth Article:

Objection 1. It would seem that necessary and eternal things are subject to the eternal law. For whatever is reasonable is subject to reason. But the divine will is reasonable, for it is just. Therefore it is subject to (the divine) reason. But the eternal law is the divine reason. Therefore God's will is subject to the eternal law. But God's will is eternal. Therefore eternal and necessary things are subject to the eternal law.

Obj. 2. Further, whatever is subject to the King is subject to the King's law. Now the Son, according to 1 Corinthians xv. 28, 24, "shall be subject . . . to God and the Father . . . when He shall have delivered up the Kingdom to Him." Therefore the Son, Who is eternal, is subject to the eternal law.

Obj. 3. Further, the eternal law is divine providence as a type. But many necessary things are subject to divine providence: for instance, the stability of incorporal substances and of the heavenly bodies. Therefore even necessary things are subject to the eternal law.

On the contrary, Things that are necessary cannot be otherwise, and consequently need no restraining. But laws are imposed on men in order to restrain them from evil, as explained above (Q. 92, A. 2). Therefore necessary things are not subject to the law.[c]

I answer that, As stated above (A. 1), the eternal law is the type of the divine government. Consequently whatever is subject to the divine government is subject to the eternal law, while if any-

[c] D.F. Tr.: eternal law.

thing is not subject to the divine government, neither is it subject to the eternal law. The application of this distinction may be gathered by looking around us. For those things are subject to human government which can be done by man; but what pertains to the nature of man is not subject to human government; for instance, that he should have a soul, hands, or feet. Accordingly all that is in things created by God, whether it be contingent or necessary, is subject to the eternal law, while things pertaining to the divine nature or essence are not subject to the eternal law, but are the eternal law itself.

Reply Obj. 1. We may speak of God's will in two ways. First, as to the will itself; and thus, since God's will is His very essence, it is subject neither to the divine government, nor to the eternal law, but is the same thing as the eternal law. Secondly, we may speak of God's will as to the things themselves that God wills about creatures; which things are subject to the eternal law in so far as they are planned by divine wisdom. In reference to these things God's will is said to be reasonable (*rationalis*), though regarded in itself it should rather be called their type (*ratio*).

Reply Obj. 2. God the Son was not made by God, but was naturally born of God. Consequently He is not subject to divine providence or to the eternal law, but rather is Himself the eternal law by a kind of appropriation, as Augustine explains.[19] But He is said to be subject to the Father by reason of His human nature, in respect of which also the Father is said to be greater than He.

The third objection we grant, because it deals with those necessary things that are created.

Reply Obj. 4.[d] As the Philosopher says, some necessary things have a cause of their necessity, and thus they derive from something else the fact that they cannot be otherwise.[20] And this is in itself a most effective restraint, for whatever is restrained is said to be restrained in so far as it cannot do otherwise than it is allowed to.

[d] [This deals with *On the contrary*.]

FIFTH ARTICLE

WHETHER NATURAL CONTINGENTS ARE SUBJECT TO THE ETERNAL LAW?

We proceed thus to the Fifth Article:

Objection 1. It would seem that natural contingents are not subject to the eternal law, because promulgation is essential to law, as stated above (Q. 90, A. 4). But a law cannot be promulgated except to rational creatures to whom it is possible to make an announcement. Therefore none but rational creatures are subject to the eternal law; and consequently natural contingents are not.

Obj. 2. Further, "Whatever obeys reason partakes somewhat of reason," as stated in *Ethics* i. But the eternal law is the supreme type, as stated above (A. 1). Since, then, natural contingents do not partake of reason in any way, but are altogether void of reason, it seems that they are not subject to the eternal law.

Obj. 3. Further, the eternal law is most efficient. But in natural contingents defects occur. Therefore they are not subject to the eternal law.

On the contrary, It is written: "When He compassed the sea with its bounds, and set a law to the waters, that they should not pass their limits." [21]

I answer that, We must speak otherwise of the law of man than of the eternal law, which is the law of God. For the law of man extends only to rational creatures subject to man. The reason of this is because law directs the actions of those that are subject to the government of someone; wherefore, properly speaking, none imposes a law on his own actions. Now whatever is done regarding the use of irrational things subject to man is done by the act of man himself moving those things, for these irrational creatures do not move themselves, but are moved by others, as stated above.[22] Consequently man cannot impose laws on irrational beings, however much they may be subject to him. But he can impose laws on rational beings subject to him, in so far as by his command or pronouncement of any kind he imprints on their minds a rule which is a principle of action.

Now just as man, by such pronouncement, impresses a kind of inward principle of action on the man that is subject to him, so God imprints on the whole of nature the principles of its proper actions. And so, in this way, God is said to command the whole of nature, according to Psalm cxlviii. 6: "He hath made a decree, and it shall not pass away." And thus all actions and movements of the whole of nature are subject to the eternal law. Consequently irrational creatures are subject to the eternal law through being moved by divine providence, but not, as rational creatures are, through understanding the divine commandment.

Reply Obj. 1. The impression of an inward active principle is to natural things what the promulgation of law is to men, because law, by being promulgated, imprints on man a directive principle of human actions, as stated above.

Reply Obj. 2. Irrational creatures neither partake of, nor are obedient to, human reason, whereas they do partake of the divine reason by obeying it, because the power of divine reason extends over more things than human reason does. And as the members of the human body are moved at the command of reason, and yet do not partake of reason, since they have no apprehension subordinate to reason, so, too, irrational creatures are moved by God, without, on that account, being rational.

Reply Obj. 3. Although the defects which occur in natural things are outside the order of particular causes, they are not outside the order of universal causes, especially of the First Cause, i.e., God, from Whose providence nothing can escape, as stated in the First Part. [23] And since the eternal law is the type of divine providence, as stated above (A. 1), hence the defects of natural things are subject to the eternal law.

SIXTH ARTICLE

WHETHER ALL HUMAN AFFAIRS ARE SUBJECT TO THE ETERNAL LAW?

We proceed thus to the Sixth Article:

Objection 1. It would seem that not all human affairs are subject to the eternal law. For the Apostle says: "If you are led by the spirit you are not under the law." [24] But the righteous, who are the sons of God by adoption, are led by the spirit of God, according to Romans viii. 14: "Whosoever are led by the Spirit of God, they are the sons of God." Therefore not all men are under the eternal law.

Obj. 2. Further, the Apostle says: "The prudence [e] of the flesh is an enemy to God, for it is not subject to the law of God." [25] But many are those in whom the prudence of the flesh dominates. Therefore all men are not subject to the eternal law, which is the law of God.

Obj. 3. Further, Augustine says that "the eternal law is that by which the wicked deserve misery, the good, a life of blessedness." [26] But those who are already blessed, and those who are already lost, are not in the state of merit. Therefore they are not under the eternal law.

On the contrary, Augustine says: "Nothing evades the laws of the most high Creator and Governor, for by Him the peace of the universe is administered." [27]

I answer that, There are two ways in which a thing is subject to the eternal law, as explained above (A. 5): first, by partaking of the eternal law by way of knowledge; secondly, by way of action and passion, i.e., by partaking of the eternal law by way of an inward motive principle; and in this second way, irrational creatures are subject to the eternal law, as stated above (*ibid.*). But since the rational nature, together with that which it has in common with all creatures, has something proper to itself inasmuch as it is rational, consequently it is subject to the eternal law in both ways; because while each rational creature has some

e Vulg.: wisdom.

knowledge of the eternal law, as stated above (A. 2), it also has a natural inclination to that which is in harmony with the eternal law, for "we are naturally adapted to be the recipients of virtue" (*Ethics* ii. 1).

Both ways, however, are imperfect and to a certain extent destroyed in the wicked, because in them the natural inclination to virtue is corrupted by vicious habits, and, moreover, the natural knowledge of good is darkened by passions and habits of sin. But in the good both ways are found more perfect, because in them, besides the natural knowledge of good, there is the added knowledge of faith and wisdom; and again, besides the natural inclination to good, there is the added interior motive of grace and virtue.

Accordingly the good are perfectly subject to the eternal law, as always acting according to it, whereas the wicked are subject to the eternal law, imperfectly as to their actions, indeed, since both their knowledge of good and their inclination thereto are imperfect; but this imperfection on the part of action is supplied on the part of passion in so far as they suffer what the eternal law decrees concerning them, according as they fail to act in harmony with that law. Hence Augustine says: "I esteem that the righteous act according to the eternal law"; [28] and: "Out of the just misery of the souls which deserted Him, God knew how to furnish the inferior parts of His creation with most suitable laws." [29]

Reply Obj. 1. This saying of the Apostle may be understood in two ways. First, so that a man is said to be under the law through being pinned down thereby, against his will, as by a load. Hence, on the same passage, a gloss says that "he is under the law who refrains from evil deeds through fear of the punishment threatened by the law, and not from love of virtue." In this way the spiritual man is not under the law, because he fulfills the law willingly, through charity which is poured into his heart by the Holy Ghost. Secondly, it can be understood as meaning that the works of a man who is led by the Holy Ghost are works of the Holy Ghost rather than his own. Therefore, since the Holy Ghost is not under the law, as neither is the Son, as stated above (A. 4 *ad* 2), it follows that such works, in so far as they are of the Holy Ghost, are not under the law. The Apostle witnesses to this when he says: "Where the Spirit of the Lord is, there is liberty." [30]

Reply Obj. 2. The prudence of the flesh cannot be subject to the law of God as regards action, since it inclines to actions contrary to the ... yet it is subject to the law of God as regards passi... to suffer punishment according to the law of ... in no man does the prudence of ... ...troy the whole good of his n... ...s in man the inclination to ... ...aw. For we have seen above ... ...the good of nature.

R... ... the end and moved toward the e... ...use: thus gravity which makes a heavy bo... ...place is also the cause of its being moved thither. W... ...reply that as it is according to the eternal law that some des... ...e happiness, others unhappiness, so is it by the eternal law that some are maintained in a happy state, others in an unhappy state. Accordingly both the blessed and the damned are under the eternal law.

QUESTION 94

OF THE NATURAL LAW

(*In Six Articles*)

WE must now consider the natural law, concerning which there are six points of inquiry: (1) What is the natural law? (2) What are the precepts of the natural law? (3) Whether all acts of virtue are prescribed by the natural law? (4) Whether the natural law is the same in all? (5) Whether it is changeable? (6) Whether it can be abolished from the heart of man?

FIRST ARTICLE

WHETHER THE NATURAL LAW IS A HABIT?

We proceed thus to the First Article:

Objection 1. It would seem that the natural law is a habit. Because, as the Philosopher says, "there are three things in the soul: power, habit, and passion." [1] But the natural law is not one of the soul's powers, nor is it one of the passions, as we may see by going through them one by one. Therefore the natural law is a habit.

Obj. 2. Further, Basil says that the conscience or "*synderesis* is the law of our mind," [2] which can only apply to the natural law. But the *synderesis* is a habit, as was shown in the First Part.[3] Therefore the natural law is a habit.

Obj. 3. Further, the natural law abides in man always, as will be shown further on (A. 6). But man's reason, [which is involved in law],[a] does not always think about the natural law. Therefore the natural law is not an act, but a habit.

On the contrary, Augustine says that "a habit is that whereby something is done when necessary." [4] But such is not the natural

---

[a] D.F. Tr.: which the law regards.

42

law, since it is in infants and in the damned who cannot act by it. Therefore the natural law is not a habit.

I answer that, A thing may be called a habit in two ways. First, properly and essentially: and thus the natural law is not a habit. For it has been stated above (Q. 90, A. 1 *ad* 2) that the natural law is something appointed by reason, just as a proposition is a work of reason. Now that which a man does is not the same as that whereby he does it, for he makes a becoming speech by the habit of grammar. Since, then, a habit is that by which we act, a law cannot be a habit, properly and essentially.

Secondly, the term "habit" may be applied to that which we hold by a habit: thus faith may mean that which we hold by faith. And accordingly, since the precepts of the natural law are sometimes considered by reason actually, while sometimes they are in the reason only habitually, in this way the natural law may be called a habit. Thus, in speculative matters, the indemonstrable principles are not the habit itself whereby we hold those principles, but are the principles the habit of which we possess.

Reply Obj. 1. The Philosopher proposes there to discover the genus of virtue; and since it is evident that virtue is a principle of action, he mentions only those things which are principles of human acts, viz., powers, habits and passions. But there are other things in the soul besides these three: there are acts; thus to will is in the one that wills; again, things known are in the knower; moreover its own natural properties are in the soul, such as immortality and the like.

Reply Obj. 2. *Synderesis* is said to be the law of our mind, because it is a habit containing the precepts of the natural law, which are the first principles of human actions.

Reply Obj. 3. This argument proves that the natural law is held habitually; and this is granted.

To the argument advanced in the contrary sense we reply that sometimes a man is unable to make use of that which is in him habitually, on account of some impediment: thus, on account of sleep, a man is unable to use the habit of science. In like manner, through the deficiency of his age, a child cannot use the habit of understanding of principles, or the natural law, which is in him habitually.

SECOND ARTICLE

WHETHER THE NATURAL LAW CONTAINS SEVERAL PRECEPTS, OR ONE ONLY?

We proceed thus to the Second Article:

Objection 1. It would seem that the natural law contains, not several precepts, but one only. For law is a kind of precept, as stated above (Q. 92, A. 2). If therefore there were many precepts of the natural law, it would follow that there are also many natural laws.

Obj. 2. Further, the natural law is consequent to human nature. But human nature, as a whole, is one, though, as to its parts, it is manifold. Therefore, either there is but one precept of the law of nature, on account of the unity of nature as a whole, or there are many, by reason of the number of parts of human nature. The result would be that even things relating to the inclination of the concupiscible faculty belong to the natural law.

Obj. 3. Further, law is something pertaining to reason, as stated above (Q. 90, A. 1). Now reason is but one in man. Therefore there is only one precept of the natural law.

On the contrary, The precepts of the natural law in man stand in relation to practical matters, as the first principles to matters of demonstration. But there are several first indemonstrable principles. Therefore there are also several precepts of the natural law.

I answer that, As stated above (Q. 91, A. 3), the precepts of the natural law are to the practical reason what the first principles of demonstrations are to the speculative reason, because both are self-evident principles. Now a thing is said to be self-evident in two ways: first, in itself; secondly, in relation to us. Any proposition is said to be self-evident in itself if its predicate is contained in the notion of the subject, although to one who knows not the definition of the subject it happens that such a proposition is not self-evident. For instance, this proposition, "Man is a rational being," is, in its very nature, self-evident, since who says "man" says "a rational being"; and yet to one who knows not what a man is, this proposition is not self-evident. Hence it is that, as

Boethius says, certain axioms or propositions are universally self-evident to all; [5] and such are those propositions whose terms are known to all, as, "Every whole is greater than its part," and, "Things equal to one and the same are equal to one another." But some propositions are self-evident only to the wise who understand the meaning of the terms of such propositions; thus to one who understands that an angel is not a body, it is self-evident that an angel is not circumspectively in a place; but this is not evident to the unlearned, for they cannot grasp it.

Now a certain order is to be found in those things that are apprehended universally. For that which, before aught else, falls under apprehension, is "being," the notion of which is included in all things whatsoever a man apprehends. Wherefore the first indemonstrable principle is that *the same thing cannot be affirmed and denied at the same time,* which is based on the notion of "being" and "not-being"; and on this principle all others are based, as it is stated in *Metaphysics* iv. text. 9. Now as "being" is the first thing that falls under the apprehension simply, so "good" is the first thing that falls under the apprehension of the practical reason, which is directed to action, since every agent acts for an end under the aspect of good. Consequently the first principle in the practical reason is one founded on the notion of good, viz., that *good is that which all things seek after.* Hence this is the first precept of law, that *good is to be done and ensued, and evil is to be avoided.* All other precepts of the natural law are based upon this, so that whatever the practical reason naturally apprehends as man's good (or evil) belongs to the precepts of the natural law as something to be done or avoided.

Since, however, good has the nature of an end, and evil the nature of a contrary, hence it is that all those things to which man has a natural inclination are naturally apprehended by reason as being good and, consequently, as objects of pursuit, and their contraries as evil and objects of avoidance. Wherefore the order of the precepts of the natural law is according to the order of natural inclinations. Because in man there is first of all an inclination to good in accordance with the nature which he has in common with all substances, inasmuch as every substance seeks the

preservation of its own being, according to its nature; and by reason of this inclination, whatever is a means of preserving human
life and of warding off its obstacles belongs to the natural law.
Secondly, there is in man an inclination to things that pertain to
him more specially, according to that nature which he has in common with other animals; and in virtue of this inclination, those
things are said to belong to the natural law "which nature has
taught to all animals,"ᵇ such as sexual intercourse, education of
offspring, and so forth. Thirdly, there is in man an inclination to
good, according to the nature of his reason, which nature is proper
to him: thus man has a natural inclination to know the truth about
God and to live in society; and in this respect, whatever pertains
to this inclination belongs to the natural law, for instance, to shun
ignorance, to avoid offending those among whom one has to live,
and other such things regarding the above inclination.

Reply Obj. 1. All these precepts of the law of nature have the
character of one natural law, inasmuch as they flow from one first
precept.

Reply Obj. 2. All the inclinations of any parts whatsoever of
human nature, e.g., of the concupiscible and irascible parts, in so
far as they are ruled by reason, belong to the natural law and are
reduced to one first precept, as stated above, so that the precepts
of the natural law are many in themselves, but are based on one
common foundation.

Reply Obj. 3. Although reason is one in itself, yet it directs all
things regarding man, so that whatever can be ruled by reason is
contained under the law of reason.

Third Article

WHETHER ALL ACTS OF VIRTUE ARE PRESCRIBED BY THE NATURAL LAW?

We proceed thus to the Third Article:

Objection 1. It would seem that not all acts of virtue are prescribed by the natural law. Because, as stated above (Q. 90, A. 2),

ᵇ Justinian, *Digest* I, tit.i.

it is essential to a law that it be ordained to the common good. But some acts of virtue are ordained to the private good of the individual, as is evident especially in regard to acts of temperance. Therefore not all acts of virtue are the subject of natural law.

Obj. 2. Further, every sin is opposed to some virtuous act. If therefore all acts of virtue are prescribed by the natural law, it seems to follow that all sins are against nature, whereas this applies to certain special sins.

Obj. 3. Further, those things which are according to nature are common to all. But acts of virtue are not common to all, since a thing is virtuous in one, and vicious in another. Therefore not all acts of virtue are prescribed by the natural law.

On the contrary, Damascene says that "virtues are natural." [6] Therefore virtuous acts also are a subject of the natural law.

I answer that, We may speak of virtuous acts in two ways: first, under the aspect of virtuous; secondly, as such and such acts considered in their proper species. If then we speak of acts of virtue considered as virtuous, thus all virtuous acts belong to the natural law. For it has been stated (A. 2) that to the natural law belongs everything to which a man is inclined according to his nature. Now each thing is inclined naturally to an operation that is suitable to it according to its form: thus fire is inclined to give heat. Wherefore, since the rational soul is the proper form of man, there is in every man a natural inclination to act according to reason; and this is to act according to virtue. Consequently, considered thus, all acts of virtue are prescribed by the natural law, since each one's reason naturally dictates to him to act virtuously. But if we speak of virtuous acts considered in themselves, i.e., in their proper species, thus not all virtuous acts are prescribed by the natural law, the many things are done virtuously to which nature does not incline at first, but which, through the inquiry of reason, have been found by men to be conducive to well-living.

Reply Obj. 1. Temperance is about the natural concupiscences of food, drink, and sexual matters, which are indeed ordained to the natural common good, just as other matters of law [c] are ordained to the moral common good.

[c] [See Glossary under *legal.*]

Reply Obj. 2. By human nature we may mean either that which is proper to man—and in this sense all sins, as being against reason, are also against nature, as Damascene states [7]—or we may mean that nature which is common to man and other animals; and in this sense, certain special sins are said to be against nature: thus contrary to sexual intercourse, which is natural to all animals, is unisexual lust, which has received the special name of the unnatural crime.

Reply Obj. 3. This argument considers acts in themselves. For it is owing to the various conditions of men that certain acts are virtuous for some, as being proportionate and becoming to them, while they are vicious for others, as being out of proportion to them.

FOURTH ARTICLE

WHETHER THE NATURAL LAW IS THE SAME IN ALL MEN?

We proceed thus to the Fourth Article:

Objection 1. It would seem that the natural law is not the same in all. For it is stated in the *Decretals* that "the natural law is that which is contained in the Law and the Gospel." [8] But this is not common to all men because, as it is written, "all do not obey the gospel." [9] Therefore the natural law is not the same in all men.

Obj. 2. Further, "Things which are according to the law are said to be just," as stated in *Ethics* v. But it is stated in the same book that nothing is so universally just as not to be subject to change in regard to some men. Therefore, even the natural law is not the same in all men.

Obj. 3. Further, as stated above (AA. 2, 3), to the natural law belongs everything to which a man is inclined according to his nature. Now different men are naturally inclined to different things, some to the desire of pleasures, others to the desire of honors, and other men to other things. Therefore, there is not one natural law for all.

On the contrary, Isidore says: "The natural law is common to all nations." [10]

I answer that, As stated above (AA. 2, 3), to the natural law belong those things to which a man is inclined naturally; [and among these it is a special property of man to be inclined to act according to reason. Now reason proceeds from what is common, or general, to what is proper, or special, as stated in *Physics* i. But there is a difference in this regard between the speculative reason and practical reason. The speculative reason is concerned primarily with what is necessary, that is, with those things which cannot be other than they are; and therefore, in the case of speculative reason, both the common principles and the special conclusions are necessarily true. In the case of the practical reason, on the other hand, which is concerned with contingent matters, such as human actions, even though there be some necessary truth in the common principles, yet the more we descend to what is proper and peculiar, the more deviations we find. Therefore in speculative matters the same truth holds among all men both as to principles and as to conclusions, even though all men do not discern this truth in the conclusions but only in those principles which are called axiomatic notions. In active matters, on the other hand, all men do not hold to the same truth or practical rectitude in what is peculiar and proper, but only in what is common. And even among those who hold to the same line of rectitude in proper and peculiar matters, such rectitude is not equally known to all. It is clear, therefore, that as far as common principles are concerned in the case of speculative as well as of practical reason the same truth and the same rectitude exists among all and is equally known to all. In the case, however, of the proper or peculiar conclusions of speculative reason, the same truth obtains among all, even though it is not known equally to all. For it is true among all men that the three angles of a triangle are equal to two right angles, even though not all men know this. But in the case of the proper or peculiar conclusions of the practical reason there is neither the same truth and rectitude among all men, nor, where it does exist, is it equally known to all. Thus it is true and right among all men that action proceed in accordance with reason. From this principle there follows as a proper conclusion that deposits should be restored to the owner. This conclusion is indeed true in the majority of cases. But a case may possibly arise in which such restitution is harmful and consequently contrary to reason; so, for example, if things deposited were claimed so that they might be used against the fatherland. This uncertainty increases the more particular the cases become: as, for example, if it were laid down that the restitution should take place in a certain way, with certain *definite* precautions; for as the limiting particular conditions become more numerous, so do the possibilities decrease that render the principle normally applicable, with the result that neither the restitution nor the failure to do so can be rigorously presented as right.

It follows therefore that natural law in its first common principles is the same among all men, both as to validity and recognition (something is right for all and is so by all recognized). But as to certain proper or derived norms, which are, as it were, conclusions of these common principles, they are valid and are so recognized by all men only in the majority of cases. For in special cases they may prove defective both as to validity because of certain particular impediments (just as things of nature in the sphere of generation and corruption prove to be defective because of impediments) and also as to recognition. And this because some men have a reason that has been distorted by passion, or by evil habits, or by bad natural relations. Such was the case among the ancient Germans, who failed to recognize theft as contrary to justice, as Julius Caesar relates,[11] even though it is an explicit violation of natural law.] [d]

Reply Obj. 1. The meaning of the sentence quoted is not that whatever is contained in the Law and the Gospel belongs to the natural law, since they contain many things that are above nature, but that whatever belongs to the natural law is fully contained in them. Wherefore Gratian, after saying that "the natural law is what is contained in the Law and the Gospel," adds at once, by way of example, "by which everyone is commanded to do to others as he would be done by."

[d] The editor has retranslated the bracketed passage. For the Dominican Fathers' translation see Appendix, Note 12.

Reply Obj. 2. The saying of the Philosopher is to be understood of things that are naturally just, not as general principles, but as conclusions drawn from them, having rectitude in the majority of cases, but failing in a few.

Reply Obj. 3. As, in man, reason rules and commands the other powers, so all the natural inclinations belonging to the other powers must needs be directed according to reason. Wherefore it is universally right for all men that all their inclinations should be directed according to reason.

FIFTH ARTICLE

WHETHER THE NATURAL LAW CAN BE CHANGED?

We proceed thus to the Fifth Article:

Objection 1. It would seem that the natural law can be changed. Because on Ecclesiasticus xvii. 9, "He gave them instructions, and the law of life," the gloss says: "He wished the law of the letter to be written, in order to correct the law of nature." But that which is corrected is changed. Therefore the natural law can be changed.

Obj. 2. Further, the slaying of the innocent, adultery, and theft are against the natural law. But we find these things changed by God: as when God commanded Abraham to slay his innocent son; [13] and when He ordered the Jews to borrow and purloin the vessels of the Egyptians; [14] and when He commanded Osee to take to himself "a wife of fornications." [15] Therefore the natural law can be changed.

Obj. 3. Further, Isidore says that "the possession of all things in common and universal freedom are matters of natural law." [16] But these things are seen to be changed by human laws. Therefore it seems that the natural law is subject to change.

On the contrary, It is said in the *Decretals:* "The natural law dates from the creation of the rational creature. It does not vary according to time, but remains unchangeable." [17]

I answer that, A change in the natural law may be understood in two ways. First, by way of addition. In this sense nothing hinders the natural law from being changed, since many things, for the benefit of human life, have been added over and above the natural law, both by the divine law and by human laws.

Secondly, a change in the natural law may be understood by way of subtraction, so that what previously was according to the natural law ceases to be so. In this sense the natural law is altogether unchangeable in its first principles, but in its secondary principles, which, as we have said (A. 4), are certain [special] [e] conclusions drawn from the first principles, the natural law is not changed so that what it prescribes be not right in most cases. But it may be changed in some particular cases of rare occurrence, through some special causes hindering the observance of such precepts, as stated above (A. 4).

Reply Obj. 1. The written law is said to be given for the correction of the natural law, either because it supplies what was wanting to the natural law or because the natural law was perverted in the hearts of some men, as to certain matters, so that they esteemed those things good which are naturally evil; which perversion stood in need of correction.

Reply Obj. 2. All men alike, both guilty and innocent, die the death of nature; which death of nature is inflicted by the power of God on account of original sin, according to 1 Kings ii. 6: "The Lord killeth and maketh alive." Consequently, by the command of God, death can be inflicted on any man, guilty or innocent, without any injustice whatever.—In like manner adultery is intercourse with another's wife, who is allotted to him by the law emanating from God. Consequently intercourse with any woman, by the command of God, is neither adultery nor fornication.—The same applies to theft, which is the taking of another's property. For whatever is taken by the command of God, to Whom all things belong, is not taken against the will of its owner, whereas it is in this that theft consists. Nor is it only in human things that whatever is commanded by God is right, but also in natural things— whatever is done by God is, in some way, natural, as stated in the First Part.[18]

Reply Obj. 3. A thing is said to belong to the natural law in two

[e] D.F. Tr.: detailed proximate.

ways. First, because nature inclines thereto: e.g., that one should not do harm to another. Secondly, because nature did not bring in the contrary: thus we might say that for man to be naked is of the natural law because nature did not give him clothes, but art invented them. In this sense, "the possession of all things in common and universal freedom" are said to be of the natural law because, to wit, the distinction of possessions and slavery were not brought in by nature, but devised by human reason for the benefit of human life. Accordingly the law of nature was not changed in this respect, except by addition.

SIXTH ARTICLE

WHETHER THE LAW OF NATURE CAN BE ABOLISHED FROM THE HEART OF MAN?

We proceed thus to the Sixth Article:

Objection 1. It would seem that the natural law can be abolished from the heart of man. Because on Romans ii. 14, "When the Gentiles who have not the law," etc., a gloss says that "the law of righteousness, which sin had blotted out, is graven on the heart of man when he is restored by grace." But the law of righteousness is the law of nature. Therefore the law of nature can be blotted out.

Obj. 2. Further, the law of grace is more efficacious than the law of nature. But the law of grace is blotted out by sin. Much more therefore can the law of nature be blotted out.

Obj. 3. Further, that which is established by law is made just. But many things are [established by law] ᶠ which are contrary to the law of nature. Therefore the law of nature can be abolished from the heart of man.

On the contrary, Augustine says: "Thy law is written in the hearts of men, which iniquity itself effaces not." [19] But the law which is written in men's hearts is the natural law. Therefore the natural law cannot be blotted out.

I answer that, As stated above (AA. 4, 5), there belong to the

ᶠ D.F. Tr.: enacted by men.

natural law, first, certain most general precepts, that are known to all; and secondly, certain secondary and more detailed precepts, which are, as it were, conclusions following closely from first principles. As to those general principles, the natural law, in the abstract, can nowise be blotted out from men's hearts. But it is blotted out in the case of a particular action, in so far as reason is hindered from applying the general principle to a particular point of practice, on account of concupiscence or some other passion, as stated above.[20] But as to the other, i.e., the secondary precepts, the natural law can be blotted out from the human heart either by evil persuasions, just as in speculative matters errors occur in respect of necessary conclusions, or by vicious customs and corrupt habits, as among some men theft and even unnatural vices, as the Apostle states, were not esteemed sinful.[21]

Reply Obj. 1. Sin blots out the law of nature in particular cases, not universally, except perchance in regard to the secondary precepts of the natural law, in the way stated above.

Reply Obj. 2. Although grace is more efficacious than nature, yet nature is more essential to man and therefore more enduring.

Reply Obj. 3. The argument is true of the secondary precepts of the natural law, against which some legislators have framed certain enactments which are unjust.

QUESTION 95

OF HUMAN LAW

(*In Four Articles*)

WE must now consider human law, and (1) this law considered in itself, (2) its power, (3) its mutability. Under the first head there are four points of inquiry: (1) its utility; (2) its origin; (3) its quality; (4) its division.

FIRST ARTICLE

WHETHER IT WAS USEFUL FOR LAWS TO BE FRAMED BY MEN?

We proceed thus to the First Article:

Objection 1. It would seem that it was not useful for laws to be framed by men. Because the purpose of every law is that man be made good thereby, as stated above (Q. 92, A. 1). But men are more to be induced to be good willingly, by means of admonitions, than against their will, by means of laws. Therefore there was no need to frame laws.

Obj. 2. Further, as the Philosopher says, "men have recourse to a judge as to animate justice." [1] But animate justice is better than inanimate justice, which is contained in laws. Therefore it would have been better for the execution of justice to be entrusted to the decision of judges than to frame laws in addition.

Obj. 3. Further, every law is framed for the direction of human actions, as is evident from what has been stated above (Q. 90, AA. 1, 2). But since human actions are about singulars, which are infinite in number, matters pertaining to the direction of human actions cannot be taken into sufficient consideration except by a wise man, who looks into each one of them. Therefore it would have been better for human acts to be directed by the judgment

55

of wise men than by the framing of laws. Therefore there was no
need of human laws.

On the contrary, Isidore says: "Laws were made that in fear
thereof human audacity might be held in check, that innocence
might be safeguarded in the midst of wickedness, and that the
dread of punishment might prevent the wicked from doing harm." [2]
But these things are most necessary to mankind. Therefore it was
necessary that human laws should be made.

I answer that, As stated above (Q. 63, A. 1; Q. 94, A. 3), man
has a natural aptitude for virtue, but the perfection of virtue must
be acquired by man by means of some kind of training. Thus we
observe that man is helped by industry in his necessities, for instance, in food and clothing. Certain beginnings of these he has
from nature, viz., his reason and his hands, but he has not the full
complement, as other animals have to whom nature has given sufficiency of clothing and food. Now it is difficult to see how man
could suffice for himself in the matter of this training, since the
perfection of virtue consists chiefly in withdrawing man from un-
due pleasures, to which above all man is inclined, and especially
the young, who are more capable of being trained. Consequently
a man needs to receive this training from another, whereby to
arrive at the perfection of virtue. And as to those young people
who are inclined to acts of virtue, by their good natural disposition, or by custom, or rather by the gift of God, paternal training
suffices, which is by admonitions. But since some are found to be
depraved and prone to vice, and not easily amenable to words, it
was necessary for such to be restrained from evil by force and
fear, in order that, at least, they might desist from evil-doing and
leave others in peace, and that they themselves, by being habitu-
ated in this way, might be brought to do willingly what hitherto
they did from fear, and thus become virtuous. Now this kind of
training which compels through fear of punishment is the discipline
of laws. Therefore, in order that man might have peace and virtue,
it was necessary for laws to be framed, for, as the Philosopher says,
"as man is the most noble of animals if he be perfect in virtue, so
is he the lowest of all if he be severed from law and righteousness"; [3] because man can use his reason to devise means of satis-

fying his lusts and evil passions, which other animals are unable
to do.

Reply Obj. 1. Men who are well disposed are led willingly to
virtue by being admonished better than by coercion, but men who
are evilly disposed are not led to virtue unless they are compelled.

Reply Obj. 2. As the Philosopher says, "It is better that all
things be regulated by law than left to be decided by judges"; [4]
and this for three reasons. First, because it is easier to find a few
wise men competent to frame right laws than to find the many who
would be necessary to judge aright of each single case. Secondly,
because those who make laws consider long beforehand what laws
to make, whereas judgment on each single case has to be pronounced as soon as it arises; and it is easier for man to see what
is right by taking many instances into consideration than by considering one solitary fact. Thirdly, because lawgivers judge in the
abstract and of future events, whereas those who sit in judgment
judge of things present, toward which they are affected by love,
hatred, or some kind of cupidity; wherefore their judgment is
perverted.

Since then the animated justice of the judge is not found in
every man, and since it can be deflected, therefore it was necessary, whenever possible, for the law to determine how to judge,
and for very few matters to be left to the decision of men.

Reply Obj. 3. Certain individual facts which cannot be covered
by the law "have necessarily to be committed to judges," as the
Philosopher says in the same passage; for instance, "concerning
something that has happened or not happened," and the like.

SECOND ARTICLE

WHETHER EVERY HUMAN LAW IS DERIVED FROM THE NATURAL LAW?

We proceed thus to the Second Article:

Objection 1. It would seem that not every human law is derived
from the natural law. For the Philosopher says that "the legal just
is that which originally was a matter of indifference." [5] But those

things which arise from the natural law are not matters of indifference. Therefore the enactments of human laws are not all derived from the natural law.

Obj. 2. Further, positive law is contrasted with natural law, as stated by Isidore [6] and the Philosopher.[7] But those things which flow as conclusions from the general principles of the natural law belong to the natural law, as stated above (Q. 94, A. 4). Therefore that which is established by human law does not belong to the natural law.

Obj. 3. Further, the law of nature is the same for all, since the Philosopher says that "the natural just is that which is equally valid everywhere." [8] If, therefore, human laws were derived from the natural law, it would follow that they too are the same for all, which is clearly false.

Obj. 4. Further, it is possible to give a reason for things which are derived from the natural law. But "it is not possible to give the reason for all the legal enactments of the lawgivers," as the Jurist says.[9] Therefore not all human laws are derived from the natural law.

On the contrary, Cicero says: "Things which emanated from nature and were approved by custom were sanctioned by fear and reverence for the laws." [10]

I answer that, As Augustine says, "that which is not just seems to be no law at all";[11] wherefore the force of a law depends on the extent of its justice. Now in human affairs a thing is said to be just from being right according to the rule of reason. But the first rule of reason is the law of nature, as is clear from what has been stated above (Q. 91, A. 2 *ad* 2). Consequently, every human law has just so much of the nature of law as it is derived from the law of nature. But if in any point it deflects from the law of nature, it is no longer a law but a perversion of law.

But it must be noted that something may be derived from the natural law in two ways: first, as a conclusion from premises; secondly, by way of determination of certain generalities. The first way is like to that by which, in the sciences, demonstrated conclusions are drawn from the principles, while the second mode is likened to that whereby, in the arts, general forms are particularized as to details: thus the craftsman needs to determine the general form of a house to some particular shape. Some things are therefore derived from the general principles of the natural law, by way of conclusions, e.g., that "one must not kill" may be derived as a conclusion from the principle that "one should do harm to no man"; while some are derived therefrom by way of determination, e.g., the law of nature has it that the evildoer should be punished; but that he be punished in this or that way is not directly by natural law but is a derived determination of it.

Accordingly, both modes of derivation are found in the human law. But those things which are derived in the first way are contained in human law, not as emanating therefrom exclusively, but having some force from the natural law also. But those things which are derived in the second way have no other force than that of human law.

Reply Obj. 1. The Philosopher is speaking of those enactments which are by way of determination or specification of the precepts of the natural law.

Reply Obj. 2. This argument avails for those things that are derived from the natural law, by way of conclusions.

Reply Obj. 3. The general principles of the natural law cannot be applied to all men in the same way, on account of the great variety of human affairs, and hence arises the diversity of positive laws among various people.

Reply Obj. 4. These words of the Jurist are to be understood as referring to decisions of rulers in determining particular points of the natural law, on which determinations the judgment of expert and prudent men is based as on its principles, in so far, to wit, as they see at once what is the best thing to decide.

Hence the Philosopher says that in such matters "we ought to pay as much attention to the undemonstrated sayings and opinions of persons who surpass us in experience, age, and prudence as to their demonstrations." [12]

THIRD ARTICLE

WHETHER ISIDORE'S DESCRIPTION OF THE QUALITY OF POSITIVE LAW IS APPROPRIATE?

We proceed thus to the Third Article:

Objection 1. It would seem that Isidore's description of the quality of positive law is not appropriate, when he says: "Law shall be virtuous, just [possible, in agreement with nature, and in agreement with the customs of the country],ᵃ suitable to place and time, necessary, useful; clearly expressed, lest by its obscurity it lead to misunderstanding; framed for no private benefit, but for the common good." [13] Because he had previously expressed the quality of law in three conditions, saying that "law is anything founded on reason provided that it foster religion, be helpful to discipline, and further the common weal." Therefore it was needless to add any further conditions to these.

Obj. 2. Further, justice is included in [virtue], as Cicero says.[14] Therefore after saying ["virtuous"] ᵇ it was superfluous to add "just."

Obj. 3. Further, written law [is contrasted to] ᶜ custom, according to Isidore.[15] Therefore it should not be stated in the definition of law that it is "in agreement with the customs of the country."

Obj. 4. Further, a thing may be necessary in two ways. It may be necessary simply because it cannot be otherwise; and that which is necessary in this way is not subject to human judgment, wherefore human law is not concerned with necessity of this kind. Again a thing may be necessary for an end, and this necessity is the same as usefulness. Therefore it is superfluous to say both "necessary" and "useful."

On the contrary stands the authority of Isidore.

I answer that, Whenever a thing is for an end, its form must be determined proportionately to that end, as the form of a saw is

ᵃ D.F. Tr.: possible to nature, according to the custom of the country.

ᵇ D.F. Tr.: "honesty" and "honest," respectively.

ᶜ D.F. Tr.: is condivided with.

such as to be suitable for cutting (*Physics* ii. text. 88). Again, everything that is ruled and measured must have a form proportionate to its rule and measure. Now both these conditions are verified of human law, since it is both something ordained to an end and is a rule or measure ruled or measured by a higher measure. And this higher measure is twofold, viz., the divine law and the natural law, as explained above (A. 2; Q. 93, A. 3). Now the end of human law is to be useful to man, as the Jurist states.[16] Wherefore Isidore, in determining the nature of law, lays down, at first, three conditions: viz., that it "foster religion," inasmuch as it is proportionate to the divine law; that it be "helpful to discipline," inasmuch as it is proportionate to the natural law; and that it "further the common weal," inasmuch as it is proportionate to the utility of mankind.

All the other conditions mentioned by him are reduced to these three. For it is called "virtuous" because it fosters religion. And when he goes on to say that it should be "just, [possible, in accord with nature, and in accordance with the customs of the country,] [d] adapted to place and time," he implies that it should be helpful to discipline. For human discipline depends, first, on the order of reason, to which he refers by saying "just"; secondly, [it depends on the capacity of the agent, because discipline must be suitable to each one according to his possibility, taking into account also the possibility of nature] [e] (for the same burdens should be not laid on children as on adults), and should be according to human customs, since man cannot live alone in society, paying no heed to others; thirdly, it depends on certain circumstances, in respect of which he says, "adapted to place and time."—The remaining words, "necessary," "useful," etc., mean that law should further the common weal, so that "necessity" refers to the removal of evils, "usefulness" to the attainment of good, "clearness of expression" to the need of preventing any harm ensuing from the law itself.—And

[d] D.F. Tr.: possible to nature, according to the customs of the country.
[e] D.F. Tr.: it depends on the ability of the agent, because discipline should be adapted to each one according to his ability, taking also into account the ability of nature.

since, as stated above (Q. 90, A. 2), law is ordained to the common good this is expressed in the last part of the description.

This suffices for the *Replies* to the *Objections*.

Fourth Article

WHETHER ISIDORE'S DIVISION OF HUMAN LAWS IS APPROPRIATE?

We proceed thus to the Fourth Article:

Objection 1. It would seem that Isidore wrongly divided human statutes or human law. For under this law he includes the "law of nations," so called, because, as he says, "nearly all nations use it." But as he says, "natural law is that which is common to all nations." [17] Therefore the law of nations is not contained under positive human law, but rather under natural law.

Obj. 2. Further, those laws which have the same force seem to differ not formally but only materially. But "statutes, decrees of the commonalty, senatorial decrees," and the like which he mentions, all have the same force.[18] Therefore they do not differ except materially. But art takes no notice of such a distinction, since it may go on to infinity. Therefore this division of human laws is not appropriate.

Obj. 3. Further, just as, in the state, there are princes, priests, and soldiers, so are there other human offices. Therefore it seems that, as this division includes "military law," and "public law," referring to priests and magistrates, so also it should include other laws pertaining to other offices of the state.

Obj. 4. Further, those things that are accidental should be passed over. But it is accidental to law that it be framed by this or that man. Therefore it is unreasonable to divide laws according to the names of lawgivers, so that one be called the *Cornelian* law, another the *Falcidian* law, etc.

On the contrary, The authority of Isidore (*Objection* 1) suffices.

I answer that, A thing can of itself [f] be divided in respect of something contained in the notion of that thing. Thus a soul either

[f] [I.e., "essentially," as contrasted with "by accident."]

rational or irrational is contained in the notion of animal; and therefore animal is divided properly and of itself ᵍ in respect of its being rational or irrational, but not in the point of its being white or black, which are entirely beside the notion of animal. Now, in the notion of human law, many things are contained in respect of any of which human law can be divided properly and of itself.ᵍ For in the first place it belongs to the notion of human law to be derived from the law of nature, as explained above (A. 2). In this respect positive law is divided into the "law of nations" and "civil law," according to the two ways in which something may be derived from the law of nature, as stated above (A. 2). Because to the law of nations belong those things which are derived from the law of nature as conclusions from premises, e.g., just buyings and sellings, and the like, without which men cannot live together, which is a point of the law of nature, since man is by nature a social animal, as is proved in *Politics* i.2. But those things which are derived from the law of nature by way of particular determination belong to the civil law, according as each state decides on what is best for itself.

Secondly, it belongs to the notion of human law to be ordained to the common good of the state. In this respect human law may be divided according to the different kinds of men who work in a special way for the common good: e.g., priests, by praying to God for the people; princes, by governing the people; soldiers, by fighting for the safety of the people. Wherefore certain special kinds of law are adapted to these men.

Thirdly, it belongs to the notion of human law to be framed by that one who governs the community of the state, as shown above (Q. 90, A. 3). In this respect there are various human laws according to the various forms of government. Of these, according to the Philosopher,[19] one is *monarchy*, i.e., when the state is governed by one, and then we have "royal ordinances." Another form is *aristocracy*, i.e., government by the best men or men of highest rank, and then we have the "authoritative legal opinions" (*Responsa Prudentum*) and "decrees of the senate" (*Senatus consulta*). Another form is *oligarchy*, i.e., government by a few rich and power-

ᵍ [See p. 62, Note f.]

ful men, and then we have "Praetorian," also called "honorary," law. Another form of government is that of the people, which is called *democracy,* and there we have "decrees of the commonalty" (*Plebiscita*). There is also tyrannical government, which is altogether corrupt, which, therefore, has no corresponding law. Finally, there is a form of government made up of all these, and which is the best; and in this respect we have "law [(in its more proper sense) sanctioned by the Elders] [h] and Commons," as stated by Isidore.[20]

Fourthly, it belongs to the notion of human law to direct human actions. In this respect, according to the various matters of which the law treats, there are various kinds of laws, which are sometimes named after their authors: thus we have the *Lex Julia* about adultery, the *Lex Cornelia* concerning assassins, and so on, differentiated in this way, not on account of the authors, but on account of the matters to which they refer.

Reply Obj. 1. The law of nations is indeed, in some way, natural to man, in so far as he is a reasonable being, because it is derived from the natural law by way of a conclusion that is not very remote from its premises. Wherefore men easily agreed thereto. Nevertheless it is distinct from the natural law, especially from that natural law which is common to all animals.

The *Replies* to the other *Objections* are evident from what has been said.

[h] D.F. Tr.: sanctioned by the Lords.

QUESTION 96

OF THE POWER OF HUMAN LAW

(*In Six Articles*)

WE must now consider the power of human law. Under this head there are six points of inquiry: (1) Whether human law should be framed for the community? (2) Whether human law should repress all vices? (3) Whether human law is competent to direct all acts of virtue? (4) Whether it binds man in conscience? (5) Whether all men are subject to human law? (6) Whether those who are under the law may act beside the letter of the law?

FIRST ARTICLE

WHETHER HUMAN LAW SHOULD BE FRAMED FOR THE COMMUNITY RATHER THAN FOR THE INDIVIDUAL?

We proceed thus to the First Article:

Objection 1. It would seem that human law should be framed, not for the community, but rather for the individual. For the Philosopher says that "the legal just . . . includes all particular acts of legislation *. . .* and all those matters which are the subject of decrees,"[1] which are also individual matters, since decrees are framed about individual actions. Therefore law is framed not only for the community, but also for the individual.

Obj. 2. Further, law is the director of human acts, as stated above (Q. 90, AA. 1, 2). But human acts are about individual matters. Therefore human laws should be framed, not for the community, but rather for the individual.

Obj. 3. Further, law is a rule and measure of human acts, as stated above (Q. 90, AA. 1, 2). But a measure should be most certain, as stated in *Metaphysics* x. Since therefore in human acts no general proposition can be so certain as not to fail in some individual cases, it seems that laws should be framed not in general but for individual cases.

On the contrary, The Jurist says that "laws should be made to suit the majority of instances; and they are not framed according to what may possibly happen in an individual case." [2]

I answer that, Whatever is for an end should be proportionate to that end. Now the end of law is the common good; because, as Isidore says, "law should be framed, not for any private benefit, but for the common good of all the citizens." [3] Hence human laws should be proportionate to the common good. Now the common good comprises many things. Wherefore law should take account of many things, as to persons, as to [activities],[a] and as to times; because the community of the state is composed of many persons and its good is procured by many actions; nor is it established to endure for only a short time, but to last for all time by the citizens succeeding one another, as Augustine says.[4]

Reply Obj. 1. The Philosopher divides the "legal just," i.e., positive law, into three parts. For some things are laid down simply in a general way: [b] and these are the general laws. Of these he says that "the legal is that which originally was a matter of indifference, but which, when enacted, is so no longer," as the fixing of the ransom of a captive.—Some things affect the community in one respect and individuals in another.[c] These are called "privileges," i.e., "private laws," as it were, because they regard private persons, although their power extends to many matters; and in regard to these, he adds, "and further [any regulations enacted for particular cases."] [d]—Other matters are legal, not through being laws, but through being applications of general laws to particular cases, such are decrees which have the force of law; and in regard to these, he adds "all matters subject to decrees." [5]

Reply Obj. 2. A principle of direction should be applicable to many, wherefore the Philosopher says that all things belonging to

[a] D.F. Tr.: matters.

[b] [I.e., there are measures which are absolutely common (applicable to everybody in every way).]

[c] [I.e., some measures are common from one point of view and private from another.]

[d] D.F. Tr.: all particular acts of legislation.

one genus are measured by one which is the [first] e in that genus.[6] For if there were as many rules or measures as there are things measured or ruled, they would cease to be of use, since their use consists in being applicable to many things. Hence law would be of no use if it did not extend further than to one single act. Because the decrees of prudent men are made for the purpose of directing individual actions, whereas law is a general precept, as stated above (Q. 92, A. 2, Obj. 2).

Reply Obj. 3. "We must not seek the same degree of certainty in all things." [7] Consequently in contingent matters, such as natural and human things, it is enough for a thing to be certain, as being true in the greater number of instances, though at times and less frequently it fail.

Second Article

WHETHER IT BELONGS TO HUMAN LAW TO REPRESS ALL VICES?

We proceed thus to the Second Article:

Objection 1. It would seem that it belongs to human law to repress all vices. For Isidore says that "laws were made in order that, in fear thereof, man's audacity might be held in check." [8] But it would not be held in check sufficiently unless all evils were repressed by law. Therefore human law should repress all evils.

Obj. 2. Further, the intention of the lawgiver is to make the citizens virtuous. But a man cannot be virtuous unless he forbear from all kinds of vice. Therefore it belongs to human law to repress all vices.

Obj. 3. Further, human law is derived from the natural law, as stated above (Q. 95, A. 2). But all vices are contrary to the law of nature. Therefore human law should repress all vices.

On the contrary, We read in *De libero arbitrio* i. 5: "It seems to me that the law which is written for the governing of the people rightly permits these things, and that divine providence punishes them." But divine providence punishes nothing but vices. There-

e D.F. Tr.: principle.

fore human law rightly allows some vices, by not repressing them.

I answer that, As stated above (Q. 90, AA. 1, 2), law is framed as a rule or measure of human acts. Now a measure should be homogeneous with that which it measures, as stated in *Metaphysics* x. text. 3, 4, since different things are measured by different measures. Wherefore laws imposed on men should also be in keeping with their condition, for, as Isidore says,[9] law should be "possible both according to nature, and according to the customs of the country." [f] Now possibility or faculty of action is due to an interior habit or disposition, since the same thing is not possible to one who has not a virtuous habit as is possible to one who has. Thus the same is not possible to a child as to a full-grown man; for which reason the law for children is not the same as for adults, since many things are permitted to children which in an adult are punished by law or at any rate are open to blame. In like manner many things are permissible to men not perfect in virtue which would be intolerable in a virtuous man.

Now human law is framed for a number of human beings, the majority of whom are not perfect in virtue. Wherefore human laws do not forbid all vices from which the virtuous abstain, but only the more grievous vices from which it is possible for the majority to abstain; and chiefly those that are to the hurt of others, without the prohibition of which human society could not be maintained: thus human law prohibits murder, theft, and suchlike.

Reply Obj. 1. Audacity seems to refer to the assailing of others. Consequently it belongs to those sins chiefly whereby one's neighbor is injured; and these sins are forbidden by human law, as stated.

Reply Obj. 2. The purpose of human law is to lead men to virtue, not suddenly, but gradually. Wherefore it does not lay upon the multitude of imperfect men the burdens of those who are already virtuous, viz., that they should abstain from all evil. Otherwise these imperfect ones, being unable to bear such precepts, would break out into yet greater evils; thus it is written: "He that violently bloweth his nose, bringeth out blood"; [10] and that if "new wine," i.e., precepts of a perfect life, is "put into old

[f] [Cf. Note d on page 61.]

bottles," i.e., into imperfect men, "the bottles break, and the wine runneth out," i.e., the precepts are despised and those men, from contempt, break out into evils worse still.[11]

Reply Obj. 3. The natural law is a participation in us of the eternal law, while human law falls short of the eternal law. Now Augustine says: "The law which is framed for the government of states allows and leaves unpunished many things that are punished by divine providence. Nor, if this law does not attempt to do everything, is this a reason why it should be blamed for what it does." [12] Wherefore, too, human law does not prohibit everything that is forbidden by the natural law.

THIRD ARTICLE

WHETHER HUMAN LAW PRESCRIBES ACTS OF ALL THE VIRTUES?

We proceed thus to the Third Article:

Objection 1. It would seem that human law does not prescribe acts of all the virtues. For vicious acts are contrary to acts of virtue. But human law does not prohibit all vices, as stated above (A. 2). Therefore neither does it prescribe all acts of virtue.

Obj. 2. Further, a virtuous act proceeds from a virtue. But virtue is the end of law, so that whatever is from a virtue cannot come under a precept of law. Therefore human law does not prescribe all acts of virtue.

Obj. 3. Further, law is ordained to the common good, as stated above (Q. 90, A. 2). But some acts of virtue are ordained, not to the common good, but to private good. Therefore the law does not prescribe all acts of virtue.

On the contrary, The Philosopher says that the law "prescribes the performance of the acts of a brave man . . . and the acts of the temperate man . . . and the acts of the meek man; and in like manner as regards the other virtues and vices, prescribing the former, forbidding the latter." [13]

I answer that, The species of virtues are distinguished by their objects, as explained above.[14] Now all the objects of virtues can be referred either to the private good of an individual or to the common good of the multitude: thus matters of fortitude may be achieved either for the safety of the state or for upholding the rights of a friend, and in like manner with the other virtues. But law, as stated above (Q. 90, A. 2), is ordained to the common good. Wherefore there is no virtue whose acts cannot be prescribed by the law. Nevertheless human law does not prescribe concerning all the acts of every virtue, but only in regard to those that are ordainable to the common good—either immediately, as when certain things are done directly for the common good, or mediately, as when a lawgiver prescribes certain things pertaining to [proper instruction] g whereby the citizens are directed in the upholding of the common good of justice and peace.

Reply Obj. 1. Human law does not forbid all vicious acts by the obligation of a precept, as neither does it prescribe all acts of virtue. But it forbids certain acts of each vice, just as it prescribes some acts of each virtue.

Reply Obj. 2. An act is said to be an act of virtue in two ways. First, from the fact that a man does something virtuous; thus the act of justice is to do what is right, and an act of fortitude is to do brave things—and in this way law prescribes certain acts of virtue. Secondly, an act of virtue is when a man does a virtuous thing in a way in which a virtuous man does it. Such an act always proceeds from virtue, and it does not come under a precept of law, but is the end at which every lawgiver aims.

Reply Obj. 3. There is no virtue whose act is not ordainable to the common good, as stated above, either mediately or immediately.

Fourth Article

WHETHER HUMAN LAW BINDS A MAN IN CONSCIENCE?

We proceed thus to the Fourth Article:

Objection 1. It would seem that human law does not bind a man in conscience. For an inferior power has no jurisdiction in a court of higher power. But the power of man which frames human

g D.F. Tr.: good order.

law is beneath the divine power. Therefore human law cannot impose its precept in a divine court, such as is the court of conscience.

Obj. 2. Further, the judgment of conscience depends chiefly on the commandments of God. But sometimes God's commandments are made void by human laws, according to Matthew xv. 6: "You have made void the commandment of God for your tradition." Therefore human law does not bind a man in conscience.

Obj. 3. Further, human laws often bring loss of character and injury on man, according to Isaias x. 1 ff.: "Woe to them that make wicked laws, and when they write, write injustice; to oppress the poor in judgment, and do violence to the cause of the humble of My people." But it is lawful for anyone to avoid oppression and violence. Therefore human laws do not bind man in conscience.

On the contrary, It is written: "This is thanksworthy, if for conscience . . . a man endure sorrows, suffering wrongfully." [15]

I answer that, Laws framed by man are either just or unjust. If they be just, they have the power of binding in conscience, from the eternal law whence they are derived, according to Proverbs viii. 15: "By Me kings reign, and lawgivers decree just things." Now laws are said to be just—from the end, when, to wit, they are ordained to the common good—and from their author, that is to say, when the law that is made does not exceed the power of the lawgiver—and from their form, when, to wit, burdens are laid on the subjects, according to an equality of proportion and with a view to the common good. For, since one man is a part of the community, each man, in all that he is and has, belongs to the community, just as a part, in all that it is, belongs to the whole; wherefore nature inflicts a loss on the part in order to save the whole, so that on this account such laws as these which impose proportionate burdens are just and binding in conscience and are legal laws.[h]

On the other hand, laws may be unjust in two ways: first, by being contrary to human good, through being opposed to the things mentioned above—either in respect of the end, as when an authority imposes on his subjects burdensome laws, conducive, not to the common good, but rather to his own cupidity or vainglory; or

[h] [See Glossary under *legal*.]

in respect of the author, as when a man makes a law that goes beyond the power committed to him; or in respect of the form, as when burdens are imposed unequally on the community, although with a view to the common good. The like are acts of violence rather than laws, because, as Augustine says, "A law that is not just, seems to be no law at all." [16] Wherefore such laws do not bind in conscience, except perhaps in order to avoid scandal or disturbance, for which cause a man should even yield his right, according to Matthew v. 40, 41: "If a man . . . take away thy coat, let go thy cloak also unto him; and whosoever will force thee one mile, go with him other two."

Secondly, laws may be unjust through being opposed to the divine good: such are the laws of tyrants inducing to idolatry or to anything else contrary to the divine law; and laws of this kind must nowise be observed because, as stated in Acts v. 29, "we ought to obey God rather than men."

Reply Obj. 1. As the Apostle says, all human power is from God . . . "therefore he that resisteth the power" in matters that are within its scope "resisteth the ordinance of God"; so that he becomes guilty according to his conscience.[17]

Reply Obj. 2. This argument is true of laws that are contrary to the commandments of God, which is beyond the scope of (human) power. Wherefore in such matters human law should not be obeyed.

Reply Obj. 3. This argument is true of a law that inflicts unjust hurt on its subjects. The power that man holds from God does not extend to this, wherefore neither in such matters is man bound to obey the law, provided he avoid giving scandal or inflicting a more grievous hurt.

Fifth Article

WHETHER ALL ARE SUBJECT TO THE LAW?

We proceed thus to the Fifth Article:

Objection 1. It would seem that not all are subject to the law. For those alone are subject to a law for whom a law is made. But the Apostle says: "The law is not made for the just man." [18] Therefore the just are not subject to the law.

Obj. 2. Further, Pope Urban says: "He that is guided by a private law need not for any reason be bound by the public law." [19] Now all spiritual men are led by the private law of the Holy Ghost, for they are the sons of God, of whom it is said: "Whosoever are led by the Spirit of God, they are the sons of God." [20] Therefore not all men are subject to human law.

Obj. 3. Further, the Jurist says that "the sovereign is exempt from the laws." [21] But he that is exempt from the law is not bound thereby. Therefore not all are subject to the law.

On the contrary, The Apostle says: "Let every soul be subject to the higher powers." [22] But subjection to a power seems to imply subjection to the laws framed by that power. Therefore all men should be subject to human law.

I answer that, As stated above (Q. 90, AA. 1, 2; A. 3 *ad* 2), the notion of law contains two things: first, that it is a rule of human acts; secondly, that it has coercive power. Wherefore a man may be subject to law in two ways. First, as the regulated is subject to the regulator; and, in this way, whoever is subject to a power is subject to the law framed by that power. But it may happen in two ways that one is not subject to a power. In one way, by being altogether free from its authority; hence the subjects of one city or kingdom are not bound by the laws of the sovereign of another city or kingdom, since they are not subject to his authority. In another way, by being under a yet higher law; thus the subject of a proconsul should be ruled by his command, but not in those matters in which the subject receives his orders from the emperor, for in these matters he is not bound by the mandate of the lower authority, since he is directed by that of a higher. In this way one who is simply subject to a law may not be subject thereto in certain matters in respect of which he is ruled by a higher law.

Secondly, a man is said to be subject to a law as the coerced is subject to the coercer. In this way the virtuous and righteous are not subject to the law, but only the wicked. Because coercion and violence are contrary to the will, but the will of the good is in harmony with the law, whereas the will of the wicked is discordant from it. Wherefore in this sense the good are not subject to the law, but only the wicked.

Reply Obj. 1. This argument is true of subjection by way of coercion, for, in this way, "the law is not made for the just men: because they are a law to themselves," since they "show the work of the law written in their hearts," as the Apostle says.[23] Consequently the law does not enforce itself upon them as it does on the wicked.

Reply Obj. 2. The law of the Holy Ghost is above all law framed by man; and therefore spiritual men, in so far as they are led by the law of the Holy Ghost, are not subject to the law in those matters that are inconsistent with the guidance of the Holy Ghost. Nevertheless the very fact that spiritual men are subject to law is due to the leading of the Holy Ghost, according to 1 Peter ii. 13: "Be ye subject . . . to every human creature for God's sake."

Reply Obj. 3. The sovereign is said to be "exempt from the law," as to its coercive power, since, properly speaking, no man is coerced by himself, and law has no coercive power save from the authority of the sovereign. Thus then is the sovereign said to be exempt from the law, because none is competent to pass sentence on him if he acts against the law. Wherefore on Psalm L. 6: "To Thee only have I sinned," a gloss says that "there is no man who can judge the deeds of a king."—But as to the directive force of law, the sovereign is subject to the law by his own will, according to the statement that "whatever law a man makes for another, he should keep himself." [24] And a wise authority says: "Obey the law that thou makest thyself." [25] Moreover the Lord reproaches those who "say and do not"; and who "bind heavy burdens and lay them on men's shoulders, but with a finger of their own they will not move them." [26] Hence, in the judgment of God, the sovereign is not exempt from the law as to its directive force, but he should fulfill it of his own free will and not of constraint.—Again the sovereign is above the law in so far as, when it is expedient, he can change the law and dispense in it according to time and place.

SIXTH ARTICLE

WHETHER HE WHO IS UNDER A LAW MAY ACT BESIDE THE LETTER OF THE LAW?

We proceed thus to the Sixth Article:

Objection 1. It seems that he who is subject to a law may not act beside the letter of the law. For Augustine says: "Although men judge about temporal laws when they make them, yet when once they are made they must pass judgment not on them, but according to them." [27] But if anyone disregard the letter of the law, saying that he observes the intention of the lawgiver, he seems to pass judgment on the law. Therefore it is not right for one who is under a law to disregard the letter of the law in order to observe the intention of the lawgiver.

Obj. 2. Further, he alone is competent to interpret the law who can make the law. But those who are subject to the law cannot make the law. Therefore they have no right to interpret the intention of the lawgiver, but should always act according to the letter of the law.

Obj. 3. Further, every wise man knows how to explain his intention by words. But those who framed the laws should be reckoned wise, for Wisdom says: "By Me kings reign, and lawgivers decree just things." [28] Therefore we should not judge of the intention of the lawgiver otherwise than by the words of the law.

On the contrary, Hilary says: "The meaning of what is said is according to the motive for saying it, because things are not subject to speech, but speech to things." [29] Therefore we should take account of the motive of the lawgiver rather than to his very words.

I answer that, As stated above (A. 4), every law is directed to the common weal of men and derives the force and nature of law accordingly [but in so far as it falls short, it possesses no binding power]. Hence the Jurist says: "By no reason of law or favor of equity is it allowable for us to interpret harshly and render burdensome those useful measures which have been enacted for the welfare of man." [30] Now it happens often that the observance of some point of law conduces to the common weal in the majority of instances, and yet, in some cases, is very hurtful. Since, then, the lawgiver cannot have in view every single case, he shapes the law according to what happens most frequently, by directing his attention to the common good. Wherefore, if a case arise wherein the observance of that law would be hurtful to the general welfare, it should not be observed. For instance, suppose that in a besieged city it be an established law that the gates of the city are to be kept closed, this is good for public welfare as a general rule, but if it were to happen that the enemy are in pursuit of certain citizens who are defenders of the city, it would be a great loss to the city if the gates were not opened to them; and so in that case the gates ought to be opened, contrary to the letter of the law, in order to maintain the common weal, which the lawgiver had in view.

Nevertheless it must be noted that if the observance of the law according to the letter does not involve any sudden risk needing instant remedy, it is not competent for everyone to expound what is useful and what is not useful to the state; those alone can do this who are in authority and who, on account of suchlike cases, have the power to dispense from the laws. If, however, the peril be so sudden as not to allow of the delay involved by referring the matter to authority, the mere necessity brings with it a dispensation, since necessity knows no law.

Reply Obj. 1. He who in a case of necessity acts beside the letter of the law does not judge of the law, but of a particular case in which he sees that the letter of the law is not to be observed.

Reply Obj. 2. He who follows the intention of the lawgiver does not interpret the law [as a general rule, except][1] in a case in which it is evident, by reason of the manifest harm, that the lawgiver intended otherwise. For if it be a matter of doubt, he must either act according to the letter of the law or consult those in power.

Reply Obj. 3. No man is so wise as to be able to take account of every single case, wherefore he is not able sufficiently to express in words all those things that are suitable for the end he has

[1] D.F. Tr.: simply, but.

in view. And even if a lawgiver were able to take all the cases into consideration, he ought not to mention them all in order to avoid confusion, but should frame the law according to that which is of most common occurrence.

QUESTION 97

OF CHANGE IN LAWS

(*In Four Articles*)

WE must now consider change in laws, under which head there are four points of inquiry: (1) Whether human law is changeable? (2) Whether it should always be changed whenever something better occurs? (3) Whether it is abolished by custom, and whether custom obtains the force of law? (4) Whether the application of human law should be changed by dispensation of those in authority?

FIRST ARTICLE

WHETHER HUMAN LAW SHOULD BE CHANGED IN ANY WAY?

We proceed thus to the First Article:

Objection 1. It would seem that human law should not be changed in any way at all. Because human law is derived from the natural law, as stated above (Q. 95, A. 2). But the natural law endures unchangeably. Therefore human law should also remain without any change.

Obj. 2. Further, as the Philosopher says, a measure should be absolutely stable.[1] But human law is the measure of human acts, as stated above (Q. 90, AA. 1, 2). Therefore it should remain without change.

Obj. 3. Further, it is of the essence of law to be just and right, as stated above (Q. 95, A. 2). But that which is right once is right always. Therefore that which is law once should be always law.

On the contrary, Augustine says: "A temporal law, however just, may be justly changed in course of time." [2]

78

I answer that, As stated above (Q. 92, A. 3), human law is a dictate of reason whereby human acts are directed. Thus there may be two causes for the just change of human law: one on the part of reason, the other on the part of man whose acts are regulated by law. The cause on the part of reason is that it seems natural to human reason to advance gradually from the imperfect to the perfect. Hence, in speculative sciences, we see that the teaching of the early philosophers was imperfect, and that it was afterward perfected by those who succeeded them. So also in practical matters; for those who first endeavored to discover something useful for the human community, not being able by themselves to take everything into consideration, set up certain institutions which were deficient in many ways, and these were changed by subsequent lawgivers who made institutions that might prove less frequently deficient in respect of the common weal.

On the part of man whose acts are regulated by law the law can be rightly changed on account of the changed condition of man, to whom different things are expedient according to the difference of his condition. An example is proposed by Augustine: "If the people have a sense of moderation and responsibility and are most careful guardians of the common weal, it is right to enact a law allowing such a people to choose their own magistrates for the government of the commonwealth. But if, as time goes on, the same people become so corrupt as to sell their votes and entrust the government to scoundrels and criminals, then the right of appointing their public officials is rightly forfeit to such a people, and the choice devolves to a few good men." [3]

Reply Obj. 1. The natural law is a participation of the eternal law, as stated above (Q. 91, A. 2), and therefore endures without change, owing to the unchangeableness and perfection of the divine reason, the Author of nature. But the reason of man is changeable and imperfect, wherefore his law is subject to change.— Moreover the natural law contains certain universal precepts which are everlasting, whereas human law contains certain particular precepts, according to various emergencies.

Reply Obj. 2. A measure should be as enduring as possible. But nothing can be absolutely unchangeable in things that are subject to change. And therefore human law cannot be altogether unchangeable.

Reply Obj. 3. [In material things, straight (right)] [a] is predicated absolutely and therefore, as far as itself is concerned, always remains right. But right is predicated of law with reference to the common weal, to which one and the same thing is not always adapted, as stated above; wherefore rectitude of this kind is subject to change.

SECOND ARTICLE

WHETHER HUMAN LAW SHOULD ALWAYS BE CHANGED WHENEVER SOMETHING BETTER OCCURS?

We proceed thus to the Second Article:

Objection 1. It would seem that human law should be changed whenever something better occurs. Because human laws are devised by human reason, like other arts. But in the other arts, the tenets of former times give place to others if something better occurs. Therefore the same should apply to human laws.

Obj. 2. Further, by taking note of the past we can provide for the future. Now unless human laws had been changed when it was found possible to improve them, considerable inconvenience would have ensued because the laws of old were crude in many points. Therefore it seems that laws should be changed whenever anything better occurs to be enacted.

Obj. 3. Further, human laws are enacted about single acts of man. But we cannot acquire perfect knowledge in singular matters except by experience, which "requires time," as stated in *Ethics* ii. Therefore it seems that as time goes on it is possible for something better to occur for legislation.

On the contrary, It is stated in the *Decretals:* "It is absurd and a detestable shame that we should suffer those traditions to be changed which we have received from the fathers of old." [4]

I answer that, As stated above (A. 1), human law is rightly changed in so far as such change is conducive to the common

[a] D.F. Tr.: In corporal things, right.

weal. But, to a certain extent, the mere change of law is of itself prejudicial to the common good because custom avails much for the observance of laws, seeing that what is done contrary to general custom, even in slight matters, is looked upon as grave. Consequently, when a law is changed, the binding power of the law is diminished in so far as custom is abolished. Wherefore human law should never be changed unless, in some way or other, the common weal be compensated according to the extent of the harm done in this respect. Such compensation may arise either from some very great and very evident benefit conferred by the new enactment or from the extreme urgency of the case, due to the fact that either the existing law is clearly unjust or its observance extremely harmful. Wherefore the Jurist says that "in establishing new laws, there should be evidence of the benefit to be derived, before departing from a law which has long been considered just." [5]

Reply Obj. 1. Rules of art derive their force from reason alone, and therefore, whenever something better occurs, the rule followed hitherto should be changed. But "laws derive very great force from custom," as the Philosopher states; [6] consequently they should not be quickly changed.

Reply Obj. 2. This argument proves that laws ought to be changed, not in view of any improvement, but for the sake of a great benefit or in a case of great urgency, as stated above. This answer applies also to the *Third Objection.*

THIRD ARTICLE

WHETHER CUSTOM CAN OBTAIN FORCE OF LAW?

We proceed thus to the Third Article:

Objection 1. It would seem that custom cannot obtain force of law, nor abolish a law. Because human law is derived from the natural law and from the divine law, as stated above (Q. 93, A. 3; Q. 95, A. 2). But human custom cannot change either the law of nature or the divine law. Therefore neither can it change human law.

Obj. 2. Further, many evils cannot make one good. But he who first acted against the law did evil. Therefore by multiplying such acts nothing good is the result. Now a law is something good, since it is a rule of human acts. Therefore law is not abolished by custom, so that the mere custom should obtain force of law.

Obj. 3. Further, the framing of laws belongs to those public men whose business it is to govern the community; wherefore private individuals cannot make laws. But custom grows by the acts of private individuals. Therefore custom cannot obtain force of law, so as to abolish the law.

On the contrary, Augustine says: "The customs of God's people and the institutions of our ancestors are to be considered as laws. And those who throw contempt on the customs of the Church ought to be punished as those who disobey the law of God." [7]

I answer that, All law proceeds from the reason and will of the lawgiver: the divine and natural laws from the reasonable will of God, the human law from the will of man regulated by reason. Now just as human reason and will, in practical matters, may be made manifest by speech, so may they be made known by deeds, since seemingly a man chooses as good that which he carries into execution. But it is evident that by human speech law can be both changed and expounded in so far as it manifests the interior movement and thought of human reason. Wherefore by actions also, especially if they be repeated so as to make a custom, law can be changed and expounded; and also something can be established which obtains force of law in so far as by repeated external actions the inward movement of the will and concepts of reason are most effectually declared, for when a thing is done again and again, it seems to proceed from a deliberate judgment of reason. Accordingly custom has the force of law, abolishes law, and is the interpreter of law.

Reply Obj. 1. The natural and divine laws proceed from the divine will, as stated above. Wherefore they cannot be changed by a custom proceeding from the will of man, but only by divine authority. Hence it is that no custom can prevail over the divine or natural laws, for Isidore says: "Let custom yield to authority; evil customs should be eradicated by law and reason." [8]

Reply Obj. 2. As stated above (Q. 96, A. 6), human laws fail in some cases, wherefore it is possible sometimes to act beside the law—namely, in a case where the law fails, yet the act will not be evil. And when such cases are multiplied, by reason of some change .in man, then custom shows that the law is no longer useful, just as it might be declared by the verbal promulgation of a law to the contrary. If, however, the same reason remains for which the law was useful hitherto, then it is not the custom that prevails against the law, but the law that overcomes the custom, unless perhaps the sole reason for the law seeming useless be that it is not "possible according to the custom of the country," [b] which has been stated to be one of the conditions of law. For it is not easy to set aside the custom of a whole people.

Reply Obj. 3. The people among whom a custom is introduced may be of two conditions. For if they are free and able to make their own laws, the consent of the whole people expressed by a custom counts far more in favor of a particular observance than does the authority of the sovereign, who has not the power to frame laws except as representing the people. Wherefore, although [a single individual] [c] cannot make laws, yet the whole people can. If however the people have not the free power to make their own laws or to abolish a law made by a higher authority, nevertheless with such a people a prevailing custom obtains force of law in so far as it is tolerated by those to whom it belongs to make laws for that people; because by the very fact that they tolerate it they seem to approve of that which is introduced by custom.

FOURTH ARTICLE

WHETHER THE RULERS OF THE PEOPLE CAN DISPENSE FROM HUMAN LAWS?

We proceed thus to the Fourth Article:

Objection 1. It would seem that the rulers of the people cannot dispense from human laws. For the law is established for the

[b] Cf. I-II, O. 95, A. 3.   [c] D.F. Tr.: each individual.

"common weal," as Isidore says.[9] But the common good should not be set aside for the private convenience of an individual, because, as the Philosopher says, "the good of the nation is more godlike than the good of one man." [10] Therefore it seems that a man should not be dispensed from acting in compliance with the general law.

Obj. 2. Further, those who are placed over others are commanded as follows: "You shall hear the little as well as the great; neither shall you respect any man's person, because it is the judgment of God." [11] But to allow one man to do that which is equally forbidden to all seems to be respect of persons. Therefore the rulers of a community cannot grant such dispensations, since this is against a precept of the divine law.

Obj. 3 Further, human law, in order to be just, should accord with the natural and divine laws, else it would not *foster religion,* nor be *helpful to discipline* [which is a requisite of law],[d] as laid down by Isidore.[12] But no man can dispense from the divine and natural laws. Neither, therefore, can he dispense from the human law.

On the contrary, The Apostle says: "A dispensation is committed to me." [13]

I answer that, Dispensation, properly speaking, denotes a measuring out to individuals of some common goods: thus the head of a household is called a dispenser because to each member of the household he distributes work and necessaries of life in due weight and measure. Accordingly in every community a man is said to dispense, from the very fact that he directs how some general precept is to be fulfilled by each individual. Now it happens at times that a precept which is conducive to the common weal as a general rule is not good for a particular individual or in some particular case, either because it would hinder some greater good or because it would be the occasion of some evil, as explained above (Q. 96, A. 6). But it would be dangerous to leave this to the discretion of each individual, except perhaps by reason of an evident and sudden emergency, as stated above (*ibid.*). Consequently he who is placed over a community is empowered to dispense in a human

d D.F. Tr.: which is requisite to the nature of a law.

law that rests upon his authority, so that, when the law fails in its application to persons or circumstances, he may allow the precept of the law not to be observed. If however he grant this permission without any such reason and of his mere will, he will be an unfaithful or an imprudent dispenser: unfaithful, if he has not the common good in view; imprudent, if he ignores the reasons for granting dispensations. Hence our Lord says: "Who, thinkest thou, is the faithful and wise dispenser,[e] whom his lord setteth over his family?" [14]

Reply Obj. 1. When a person is dispensed from observing the general law, this should not be done to the prejudice of, but with the intention of benefiting, the common good.

Reply Obj. 2. It is not "respect of persons" if unequal measures are served out to those who are themselves unequal. Wherefore when the condition of any person requires that he should reasonably receive special treatment, it is not "respect of persons" if he be the object of special favor.

Reply Obj. 3. Natural law, so far as it contains general precepts, which never fail, does not allow of dispensation. In the other precepts, however, which are as conclusions of the general precepts, man sometimes grants a dispensation: for instance, that a loan should not be paid back to the betrayer of his country, or something similar. But to the divine law each man stands as a private person to the public law to which he is subject. Wherefore just as none can dispense from public human law, except the man from whom the law derives its authority, or his delegate, so, in the precepts of the divine law, which are from God, none can dispense but God or the man to whom He may give special power for that purpose.

[e] Douay: steward.

QUESTION 105 [a]

OF THE REASON FOR THE JUDICIAL PRECEPTS

FIRST ARTICLE

WHETHER THE OLD LAW ENJOINED FITTING PRECEPTS CONCERNING RULERS?

We proceed thus to the First Article:

Objection 1. It would seem that the Old Law made unfitting precepts concerning rulers. Because, as the Philosopher says, "the ordering of the people depends mostly on the chief ruler." [1] But the Law contains no precept relating to the institution of the chief ruler, and yet we find therein prescriptions concerning the inferior rulers; firstly: "Provide out of all the people wise [b] men," [2] etc.; again: "Gather unto Me seventy men of the ancients of Israel"; [3] and again: "Let Me have from among you wise and understanding men," [4] etc. Therefore the Law provided insufficiently in regard to the rulers of the people.

Obj. 2. Further, "The best gives of the best," as Plato states [5] (*Timaeus* ii). Now the best ordering of a state or of any nation is to be ruled by a king, because this kind of government approaches nearest in resemblance to the divine government, whereby God rules the world from the beginning. Therefore the Law should have set a king over the people, and they should not have been allowed a choice in the matter, as indeed they were allowed: "When thou . . . shalt say: I will set a king over me . . . thou shalt set him," [6] etc.

Obj. 3. Further, according to Matthew xii. 25: "Every kingdom divided against itself shall be made desolate"—a saying which was verified in the Jewish people, whose destruction was

[a] [Q. 105 consists of four articles, of which only the first article is here reprinted.]
[b] Vulg.: able.

brought about by the division of the kingdom. But the Law should aim chiefly at things pertaining to the general well-being of the people. Therefore it should have forbidden the kingdom to be divided under two kings, nor should this have been introduced even by divine authority, as we read of its being introduced by the authority of the prophet Ahias the Silonite.[7]

Obj. 4. Further, just as priests are instituted for the benefit of the people in things concerning God, as stated in Hebrews v. 1, so are rulers set up for the benefit of the people in human affairs. But certain things were allotted as a means of livelihood for the priests and Levites of the Law, such as the tithes and first-fruits, and many like things. Therefore, in like manner, certain things should have been determined for the livelihood of the rulers of the people, the more that they were forbidden to accept presents, as is clearly stated in Exodus xxiii. 8: "You shall not [c] take bribes, which even blind the wise, and pervert the words of the just."

Obj. 5. Further, as a kingdom is the best form of government, so is tyranny the most corrupt. But when the Lord appointed the king, He established a tyrannical law, for it is written: "This will be the right of the king, that shall reign over you: He will take your sons," [8] etc. Therefore the Law made unfitting provision with regard to the institution of rulers.

On the contrary, The people of Israel is commended for the beauty of its order: "How beautiful are thy tabernacles, O Jacob, and thy tents, O Israel." [9] But the beautiful ordering of a people depends on the right establishment of its rulers. Therefore the Law made right provision for the people with regard to its rulers.

I answer that, Two points are to be observed concerning the right ordering of rulers in a state or nation. One is that all should take some share in the government, for this form of constitution ensures peace among the people, commends itself to all, and is most enduring,[d] as stated in *Politics* ii. 6. [The other point is one which has to do with the kind of regime, or, in other words, with the forms of government. Of these there are indeed several, as the Philosopher says,[10] but the best ones are two, viz., the *kingdom,*

c Vulg.: Neither shalt thou.
d [I.e., all men love and protect such a regime.]

in which one man rules on the strength of his virtue (prudence), and *aristocracy*, that is, the rule of the best, in which few govern, again on the strength of their virtue. Accordingly, the best form of government is to be found in a city or in a kingdom in which one man is placed at the head to rule over all because of the pre-eminence of his virtue, and under him a certain number of men have governing power also on the strength of their virtue]; [e] and yet a government of this kind is shared by all, both because all are eligible to govern and because the rulers are chosen by all. For this is the best form of polity, being partly kingdom, since there is one at the head of all; partly aristocracy, in so far as a number of persons are set in authority; partly democracy, i.e., government by the people, in so far as the rulers can be chosen from the people and the people have the right to choose their rulers.

Such was the form of government established by the divine Law. For Moses and his successors governed the people in such a way that each of them was ruler over all, so that there was a kind of kingdom. Moreover, seventy-two men were chosen, who were elders in virtue; for it is written: "I took out of your tribes men wise and honourable, and appointed them rulers," [11] so that there was an element of aristocracy. But it was a democratical government in so far as the rulers were chosen from all the people; for it is written: "Provide out of all the people wise [f] men," [12] etc.; and, again, in so far as they were chosen by the people; wherefore it is written: "Let me have from among you wise [g] men," [13] etc. Consequently it is evident that [the ordering of the rulers provided for by the Law was the best.] [h]

[e] D.F. Tr.: The other point is to be observed in respect of the kinds of government, or the different ways in which the constitutions are established. For whereas these differ in kind, as the Philosopher states (*Politics* iii.5), nevertheless the first place is held by the *kingdom,* where the power of government is vested in one; and *aristocracy,* which signifies government by the best, where the power of government is vested in a few. Accordingly, the best form of government is in a state or kingdom, wherein one is given the power to preside over all; while under him are others having governing powers.

[f] Vulg.: able.   [g] Vulg.: able.

[h] D.F. Tr.: the ordering of the rulers was well provided for by the Law.

Reply Obj. 1. This people was governed under the special care of God; wherefore it is written: "The Lord thy God hath chosen thee to be His peculiar people"; [14] and this is why the Lord reserved to Himself the institution of the chief ruler. For this, too, did Moses pray: "May the Lord the God of the spirits of all the flesh provide a man, that may be over this multitude." [15] Thus by God's orders Josue was set at the head [to succeed Moses]; [1] and we read about each of the judges who succeeded Josue that God "raised . . . up a saviour" for the people and that "the spirit of the Lord was" in them.[16] Hence the Lord did not leave the choice of a king to the people, but reserved this to Himself, as appears from Deuteronomy xvii. 15: "Thou shalt set him whom the Lord thy God shall choose."

Reply Obj. 2. A kingdom is the best form of government of the people, so long as it is not corrupt. But since the power granted to a king is so great, it easily degenerates into tyranny unless he to whom this power is given be a very virtuous man; for it is only the virtuous man that conducts himself well in the midst of prosperity, as the Philosopher observes.[17] Now perfect virtue is to be found in few; and especially were the Jews inclined to cruelty and avarice, which vices above all turn men into tyrants. Hence from the very first the Lord did not set up the kingly authority with full power, but gave them judges and governors to rule them. But afterwards when the people asked Him to do so, being indignant with them, so to speak, He granted them a king, as is clear from His words to Samuel: "They have not rejected thee, but Me, that I should not reign over them." [18]

Nevertheless, as regards the appointment of a king, He did establish the manner of election from the very beginning,[19] and then He determined two points: first, that in choosing a king they should wait for the Lord's decision, and that they should not make a man of another nation king, because such kings are wont to take little interest in the people they are set over, and consequently to have no care for their welfare. Secondly, He prescribed how the king, after his appointment, should behave in regard to himself—namely, that he should not accumulate chariots and

¹ D.F. Tr.: in place of Moses.

horses, nor wives, nor immense wealth, because through craving
for such things princes become tyrants and forsake justice. He also
appointed the manner in which they were to conduct themselves
toward God—namely, that they should continually read and pon-
der on God's Law, and should ever fear and obey God. Moreover,
He decided how they should behave toward their subjects—
namely, that they should not proudly despise them, or ill-treat
them, and that they should not depart from the paths of justice.

Reply Obj. 3. The division of the kingdom and a number of
kings was rather a punishment inflicted on that people for their
many dissensions, specially against the just rule of David, than a
benefit conferred on them for their profit. Hence it is written: "I
will give thee a king in My wrath"; [20] and: "They have reigned,
but not by Me: they have been princes, and I knew not." [21]

Reply Obj. 4. The priestly office was bequeathed by succession
from father to son; and this in order that it might be held in
greater respect if not any man from the people could become a
priest, since honor was given to them out of reverence for the
divine worship. Hence it was necessary to put aside certain things
for them both as to tithes and as to first-fruits, and, again, as to
oblations and sacrifices, that they might be afforded a means of
livelihood. On the other hand, the rulers, as stated above, were
chosen from the whole people, wherefore they had their own possessions from which to derive a living, and so much the more
since the Lord forbade even a king to have superabundant wealth
or to make too much show of magnificence; both because he
could scarcely avoid the excesses of pride and tyranny arising
from such things and because, if the rulers were not very rich
and if their office involved much work and anxiety, it would not
tempt the ambition of the common people and would not become
an occasion of sedition.

Reply Obj. 5. That right was not given to the king by divine
institution, rather was it foretold that kings would usurp that
right by framing unjust laws and by degenerating into tyrants
who preyed on their subjects. This is clear from the context that
follows: "And you shall be his slaves," [j] which is significative of

j Douay: servants.

tyranny, since a tyrant rules his subjects as though they were his slaves. Hence Samuel spoke these words to deter them from asking for a king, since the narrative continues: "But the people would not hear the voice of Samuel."—It may happen, however, that even a good king, without being a tyrant, may take away the sons and make them tribunes and centurions, and may take many things from his subjects in order to secure the common weal.

THE SUMMA THEOLOGICA

[Second Part of the Second Part]

QUESTION 42

OF SEDITION

(*In Two Articles*)

WE must now consider sedition, under which head there are two points of inquiry: (1) Whether it is a special sin? (2) Whether it is a mortal sin?

FIRST ARTICLE

WHETHER SEDITION IS A SPECIAL SIN DISTINCT FROM OTHER SINS?

We proceed thus to the First Article:

Objection 1. It would seem that sedition is not a special sin distinct from other sins. For, according to Isidore, "a seditious man is one who sows dissent among minds and begets discord." [1] Now by provoking the commission of a sin a man sins by no other kind of sin than that which he provoked. Therefore it seems that sedition is not a special sin distinct from discord.

Obj. 2. Further, sedition denotes a kind of division. Now schism takes its name from scission, as stated above.[2] Therefore, seemingly, the sin of sedition is not distinct from that of schism.

Obj. 3. Further, every special sin that is distinct from other sins is either a capital vice or arises from some capital vice. Now sedition is reckoned neither among the capital vices nor among those vices which arise from them, as appears from *Moralium* xxxi. 45, where both kinds of vice are enumerated. Therefore sedition is not a special sin, distinct from other sins.

On the contrary, Seditions are mentioned as distinct from other sins.[3]

I answer that, Sedition is a special sin, having something in common with war and strife and differing somewhat from them. It has something in common with them in so far as it implies a certain antagonism, and it differs from them in two points. First, because war and strife denote actual aggression on either side, whereas sedition may be said to denote either actual aggression or the preparation for such aggression. Hence a gloss on II Corinthians xii. 20 says that "seditions are tumults tending to fight," when, to wit, a number of people make preparations with the intention of fighting. Secondly, they differ in that war is, properly speaking, carried on against external foes, being as it were between one people and another; whereas strife is between one individual and another or between few people on one side and few on the other, while sedition, in its proper sense, is between the mutually dissentient parts of one people, as when one part of the state rises in tumult against another part. Wherefore since sedition is opposed to a special kind of good, namely, the unity and peace of a people, it is a special kind of sin.

Reply Obj. 1. A seditious man is one who incites others to sedition, and since sedition denotes a kind of discord it follows that a seditious man is one who creates discord, not of any kind, but between the parts of a multitude. And the sin of sedition is not only in him who sows discord, but also in those who dissent from one another inordinately.

Reply Obj. 2. Sedition differs from schism in two respects. First, because schism is opposed to the spiritual unity of the multitude, viz., ecclesiastical unity, whereas sedition is contrary to the temporal or secular unity of the multitude, for instance, of a city or kingdom. Secondly, schism does not imply any preparation for a material fight as sedition does, but only a spiritual dissent.

Reply Obj. 3. Sedition, like schism, is contained under discord since each is a kind of discord, not between individuals, but between the parts of a multitude.

SECOND ARTICLE

WHETHER SEDITION IS ALWAYS A MORTAL SIN?

We proceed thus to the Second Article:

Objection 1. It would seem that sedition is not always a mortal sin. For sedition denotes "a tumult tending to fight, according to the gloss quoted above (A. 1). But fighting is not always a mortal sin; indeed it is sometimes just and lawful, as stated above.[4] Much more, therefore, can sedition be without a mortal sin.

Obj. 2. Further, sedition is a kind of discord, as stated above (A. 1 *ad* 3). Now discord can be without mortal sin, and sometimes without any sin at all. Therefore sedition can be also.

Obj. 3. Further, it is praiseworthy to deliver a multitude from a tyrannical rule. Yet this cannot easily be done without some dissension in the multitude, if one part of the multitude seeks to retain the tyrant while the rest strive to dethrone him. Therefore there can be sedition without mortal sin.

On the contrary, The Apostle forbids seditions together with other things that are mortal sins.[5]

I answer that, As stated above (A. 1 *ad* 2), sedition is contrary to the unity of the multitude, viz., the people of a city or kingdom. Now Augustine says that "wise men understand the word people to designate not any crowd of persons, but the assembly of those who are united together in fellowship recognized by law and for the common good." [6] Wherefore it is evident that the unity to which sedition is opposed is the unity of law and common good; whence it follows manifestly that sedition is opposed to justice and the common good. Therefore by reason of its genus it is a mortal sin, and its gravity will be all the greater according as the common good which it assails surpasses the private good which is assailed by strife.

Accordingly the sin of sedition is first and chiefly in its authors, who sin most grievously; and secondly, it is in those who are led by them to disturb the common good. Those, however, who defend the common good and withstand the seditious party are not themselves seditious, even as neither is a man to be called quarrelsome because he defends himself, as stated above.[7]

Reply Obj. 1. It is lawful to fight, provided it be for the common good, as stated above.[8] But sedition runs counter to the common good of the multitude, so that it is always a mortal sin.

Reply Obj. 2. Discord from what is not evidently good may be without sin, but discord from what is evidently good cannot be without sin; and sedition is discord of this kind, for it is contrary to the unity of the multitude, which is a manifest good.

Reply Obj. 3. A tyrannical government is not just, because it is directed not to the common good, but to the private good of the ruler, as the Philosopher states.[9] Consequently there is no sedition in disturbing a government of this kind, unless indeed the tyrant's rule be disturbed so inordinately that his subjects suffer greater harm from the consequent disturbance than from the tyrant's government. Indeed it is the tyrant rather that is guilty of sedition, since he encourages discord and sedition among his subjects that he may lord over them more securely; for this is tyranny, being conducive to the private good of the ruler and to the injury of the multitude.

QUESTION 57

OF RIGHT

(*In Four Articles*)

AFTER considering prudence we must in due sequence consider justice, the consideration of which will be fourfold: (1) of justice, (2) of it parts, (3) of the corresponding gift, (4) of the precepts relating to justice.

Four points will have to be considered about justice: (1) right; (2) justice itself; (3) injustice; (4) judgment.

Under the first head there are four points of inquiry: (1) Whether right is the object of justice? (2) Whether right is fittingly divided into natural and positive right? (3) Whether the right of nations is the same as natural right? (4) Whether right of dominion and paternal right are distinct species?

FIRST ARTICLE

WHETHER RIGHT IS THE OBJECT OF JUSTICE?

We proceed thus to the First Article:

Objection 1. It would seem that right is not the object of justice. For the jurist Celsus says that "right is the art of goodness and equality." [1] Now art is not the object of justice, but is by itself an intellectual virtue. Therefore right is not the object of justice.

Obj. 2. Further, "Law," according to Isidore, "is a kind of right." [2] Now law is the object not of justice but of prudence, wherefore the Philosopher reckons "legislative" as one of the parts of prudence. [3] Therefore right is not the object of justice.

Obj. 3. Further, justice, before all, subjects man to God; for Augustine says that "justice is love serving God alone and consequently governing aright all things subject to man." [4] Now right (*ius*) does not pertain to divine things, but only to human affairs, for Isidore says that "*fas* is the divine law, and *ius* the human law." [5] Therefore right is not the object of justice.

On the contrary, Isidore says that "*ius* (right) is so called because it is just." [6] Now the "just" is the object of justice, for the Philosopher declares that "all are agreed in giving the name of justice to the habit which makes men capable of doing just actions." [7]

I answer that, It is proper to justice, as compared with the other virtues, to direct man in his relations with others, because it denotes a kind of equality, as its very name implies; indeed we are wont to say that things are adjusted when they are made equal, for equality is in reference of one thing to some other. On the other hand, the other virtues perfect man in those matters only which befit him in relation to himself. Accordingly that which is right in the works of the other virtues, and to which the intention of the virtue tends as to its proper object, depends on its relation to the agent only, whereas the right in a work of justice, besides its relation to the agent, is set up by its relation to others. Because a man's work is said to be just when it is related to some other by way of some kind of equality; for instance, the payment of the wage due for a service rendered. And so a thing is said to be just, as having the rectitude of justice, when it is the term of an act of justice, without taking into account the way in which it is done by the agent; whereas in the other virtues nothing is declared to be right unless it is done in a certain way by the agent. For this reason justice has its own special proper object over and above the other virtues, and this object is called the "just," which is the same as "right." Hence it is evident that right is the object of justice.

Reply Obj. 1. It is usual for words to be distorted from their original signification so as to mean something else: thus the word "medicine" was first employed to signify a remedy used for curing a sick person, and then it was drawn to signify the art by which this is done. In like manner the word *ius* (right) was first of all used to denote the just thing itself, but afterwards it was transferred to designate the art whereby it is known what is just, and further to denote the place where justice is administered: thus a man is said to appear *in jure*,[a] and yet further, we say even that a man who has the office of exercising justice administers the *ius* even if his sentence be unjust.

Reply Obj. 2. Just as there pre-exists in the mind of the crafts-man an expression of the things to be made externally by his craft, which expression is called the rule of his craft, so, too, there pre-exists in the mind an expression of the particular just work which the reason determines, and which is a kind of rule of prudence. If this rule be expressed in writing, it is called a "law," which, according to Isidore, is "a written decree," [8] and so law is not the same as right, but an expression of right.

Reply Obj. 3. Since justice implies equality and since we can-not offer God an equal return, it follows that we cannot make Him a perfectly just repayment. For this reason the divine law is not properly called *ius* but *fas*, because, to wit, God is satisfied if we accomplish what we can. Nevertheless justice tends to make man repay God as much as he can, by subjecting his mind to Him entirely.

SECOND ARTICLE

WHETHER RIGHT IS FITTINGLY DIVIDED INTO NATURAL RIGHT AND POSITIVE RIGHT?

We proceed thus to the Second Article:

Objection 1. It would seem that right is not fittingly divided into natural right and positive right. For that which is natural is unchangeable, and is the same for all. Now nothing of the kind is to be found in human affairs, since all the rules of human right fail in certain cases, nor do they obtain force everywhere. There-fore there is no such thing as natural right.

Obj. 2. Further, a thing is called "positive" when it proceeds from the human will. But a thing is not just simply because it proceeds from the human will, else a man's will could not be un-

[a] [In English we speak of a court of law, a barrister at law, etc.]

just. Since then the "just" and the "right" are the same, it seems that there is no positive right.

Obj. 3. Further, divine right is not natural right, since it transcends human nature. In like manner, neither is it positive right, since it is based not on human but on divine authority. Therefore right is unfittingly divided into natural and positive.

On the contrary, The Philosopher says that "political justice is partly natural and partly legal," [9] i.e., established by law.

I answer that, As stated above (A. 1), the "right" or the "just" is a work that is adjusted to another person according to some kind of equality. Now a thing can be adjusted to a man in two ways: first, by its very nature, as when a man gives so much that he may receive equal value in return, and this is called "natural right." In another way, a thing is adjusted or commensurated to another person by agreement or by common consent, when, to wit, a man deems himself satisfied if he receives so much. This can be done in two ways: first, by private agreement, as that which is confirmed by an agreement between private individuals; secondly, by public agreement, as when the whole community agrees that something should be deemed as though it were adjusted and commensurated to another person, or when this is decreed by the prince who is placed over the people and acts in its stead, and this is called "positive right."

Reply Obj. 1. That which is natural to one whose nature is unchangeable must needs be such always and everywhere. But man's nature is changeable, wherefore that which is natural to man may sometimes fail. Thus the restitution of a deposit to the depositor is in accordance with natural equality, and if human nature were always right, this would always have to be observed; but since it happens sometimes that man's will is unrighteous, there are cases in which a deposit should not be restored, lest a man of unrighteous will make evil use of the thing deposited: as when a madman or an enemy of the common weal demands the return of his weapons.

Reply Obj. 2. The human will can, by common agreement, make a thing to be just provided it be not, of itself, contrary to natural justice, and it is in such matters that positive right has its place. Hence the Philosopher says that "in the case of the legal just, it does not matter in the first instance whether it takes one form or another, it only matters when once it is laid down." [10] If, however, a thing is, of itself, contrary to natural right, the human will cannot make it just, for instance, by decreeing that it is lawful to steal or to commit adultery. Hence it is written: "Woe to them that make wicked laws." [11]

Reply Obj. 3. The divine right is that which is promulgated by God. Such things are partly those that are naturally just, yet their justice is hidden to man, and partly are made just by God's decree. Hence also divine right may be divided in respect of these two things, even as human right is. For the divine law commands certain things because they are good, and forbids others because they are evil, while others are good because they are prescribed, and others evil because they are forbidden.

THIRD ARTICLE

WHETHER THE RIGHT OF NATIONS IS THE SAME AS THE NATURAL RIGHT?

We proceed thus to the Third Article:

Objection 1. It would seem that the right of nations is the same as the natural right. For all men do not agree save in that which is natural to them. Now all men agree in the right of nations, since the Jurist says that "the right of nations is that which is in use among all nations." [12] Therefore the right of nations is the natural right.

Obj. 2. Further, slavery among men is natural, for some are naturally slaves, according to the Philosopher. [13] Now "slavery belongs to the right of nations," as Isidore states. [14] Therefore the right of nations is a natural right.

Obj. 3. Further, right, as stated above (A. 2), is divided into natural and positive. Now the right of nations is not a positive right, since all nations never agreed to decree anything by common agreement. Therefore the right of nations is a natural right.

On the contrary, Isidore says that "right is either natural, or civil, or right of nations,"[15] and consequently the right of nations is distinct from natural right.

I answer that, as stated above (A. 2), the natural right or just is that which by its very nature is adjusted to or commensurate with another person. Now this may happen in two ways: first, according as it is considered absolutely; thus a male by his very nature is commensurate with the female to beget offspring by her, and a parent is commensurate with the offspring to nourish it. Secondly, a thing is naturally commensurate with another person, not according as it is considered absolutely, but according to something resultant from it, for instance, the possession of property. For if a particular piece of land be considered absolutely, it contains no reason why it should belong to one man more than to another, but if it be considered in respect of its adaptability to cultivation and the unmolested use of the land, it has a certain commensuration to be the property of one and not of another man, as the Philosopher shows.[16]

Now it belongs not only to man but also to other animals to apprehend a thing absolutely; wherefore the right which we call natural is common to us and other animals according to the first kind of commensuration. But the right of nations falls short of natural right in this sense, as the Jurist says, because "the latter is common to all animals, while the former is common to men only."[17] On the other hand, to consider a thing by comparing it with what results from it is proper to reason, wherefore this same is natural to man in respect of natural reason which dictates it. Hence the jurist Gaius says: "Whatever natural reason decrees among all men is observed by all equally, and is called the right of nations."[18] This suffices for the *Reply* to the *First Objection.*

Reply Obj. 2. Considered absolutely, the fact that this particular man should be a slave rather than another man is based, not on natural reason, but on some resultant utility, in that it is useful to this man to be ruled by a wiser man, and to the latter to be helped by the former, as the Philosopher states.[19] Wherefore slavery which belongs to the right of nations is natural in the second way, but not in the first.

Reply Obj. 3. Since natural reason dictates matters which are according to the right of nations as implying a proximate equality, it follows that they need no special institution, for they are instituted by natural reason itself, as stated by the authority quoted above.

Fourth Article

WHETHER PATERNAL RIGHT AND RIGHT OF DOMINION SHOULD BE DISTINGUISHED AS SPECIAL SPECIES?

We proceed thus to the Fourth Article:

Objection 1. It would seem that "paternal right" and "right of dominion" should not be distinguished as special species. For it belongs to justice to render to each one what is his, as Ambrose states.[20] Now right is the object of justice, as stated above (A. 1). Therefore right belongs to each one equally; and we ought not to distinguish the rights of fathers and masters as distinct species.

Obj. 2. Further, the law is an expression of what is just, as stated above (A. 1 *ad* 2). Now a law looks to the common good of a city or kingdom, as stated above (I-II, Q. 90, A. 2), but not to the private good of an individual or even of one household. Therefore there is no need for a special right of dominion or paternal right, since the master and the father pertain to a household, as stated in *Politics* i. 2.

Obj. 3. Further, there are many other differences of degrees among men, for instance some are soldiers, some are priests, some are princes. Therefore some special kind of right should be allotted to them.

On the contrary, The Philosopher distinguishes right of dominion, paternal right, and so on, as species distinct from civil right.[21]

I answer that, Right or just depends on commensuration with another person. Now "another" has a twofold signification. First, it may denote something that is other simply, as that which is altogether distinct; as, for example, two men neither of whom is subject to the other and both of whom are subjects of the ruler of the state, and between these, according to the Philosopher, there is the "just" simply.[22] Secondly, a thing is said to be other from something else, not simply, but as belonging in some way to that something else; and in this way, as regards human affairs, a son belongs to his father, since he is part of him somewhat, as stated in *Ethics* viii. 12, and a slave belongs to his master, because he is his instrument, as stated in *Politics* i. 2.[23] Hence a father is not compared to his son as to another simply, and so between them there is not the just simply, but a kind of just called "paternal." In like manner neither is there the just simply between master and servant, but that which is called "dominative." A wife, though she is something belonging to the husband, since she stands related to him as to her own body, as the Apostle declares, is nevertheless more distinct from her husband than a son from his father, or a slave from his master; for she is received into a kind of social life, that of matrimony; [24] wherefore, according to the Philosopher, there is more scope for justice between husband and wife than between father and son, or master and slave,[25] because, as husband and wife have an immediate relation to the community of the household, as stated in *Politics* i. 2, 5, it follows that between them there is *domestic justice* rather than *civic*.

Reply Obj. 1. It belongs to justice to render to each one his right, the distinction between individuals being presupposed; for if a man gives himself his due, this is not strictly called "just." And since what belongs to the son is his father's, and what belongs to the slave is his master's, it follows that, properly speaking, there is not justice of father to son or of master to slave.

Reply Obj. 2. A son, as such, belongs to his father, and a slave, as such, belongs to his master; yet each, considered as a man, is something having separate existence and distinct from others. Hence in so far as each of them is a man, there is justice toward them in a way; and for this reason, too, there are certain laws regulating the relations of a father to his son and of a master to his slave; but in so far as each is something belonging to another, the perfect idea of "right" or "just" is wanting to them.

Reply Obj. 3. All other differences between one person and another in a state have an immediate relation to the community of the state and to its ruler, wherefore there is "just" toward them in the perfect sense of justice. This "just" however is distinguished according to various offices; hence when we speak of "military," or "magisterial," or "priestly" right, it is not as though such rights fell short of the simply right, as when we speak of "paternal" right, or right of "dominion," but for the reason that something proper is due to each class or person in respect of his particular office.

QUESTION 58

OF JUSTICE

(In Twelve Articles)

WE must now consider justice. Under this head there are twelve points of inquiry: (1) What is justice? (2) Whether justice is always toward another? (3) Whether it is a virtue? (4) Whether it is in the will as its subject? (5) Whether it is a general virtue? (6) Whether, as a general virtue, it is essentially the same as every virtue? (7) Whether there is a particular justice? (8) Whether particular justice has a matter of its own? (9) Whether it is about passions or about operations only? (10) Whether the mean of justice is the real mean? (11) Whether the act of justice is to render to everyone his own? (12) Whether justice is the chief of the moral virtues?

FIRST ARTICLE

WHETHER JUSTICE IS FITTINGLY DEFINED AS BEING THE PERPETUAL AND CONSTANT WILL TO RENDER TO EACH ONE HIS RIGHT?

We proceed thus to the First Article:

Objection 1. It would seem that lawyers have unfittingly defined justice as being "the perpetual and constant will to render to each one his right." [1] For, according to the Philosopher, justice is a habit which makes a man "capable of doing what is just, and of being just in action and in intention." [2] Now "will" denotes a power or also an act. Therefore justice is unfittingly defined as being a will.

Obj. 2. Further, rectitude of the will is not the will; else if the will were its own rectitude, it would follow that no will is unright-

105

eous. Yet, according to Anselm, justice is rectitude.[3] Therefore justice is not the will.

Obj. 3. Further, no will is perpetual save God's. If therefore justice is a perpetual will, in God alone will there be justice.

Obj. 4. Further, whatever is perpetual is constant, since it is unchangeable. Therefore it is needless, in defining justice, to say that it is both "perpetual" and "constant."

Obj. 5. Further, it belongs to the sovereign to give each one his right. Therefore, if justice gives each one his right, it follows that it is in none but the sovereign, which is absurd.

Obj. 6. Further, Augustine says that "justice is love serving God alone." [4] Therefore it does not render to each one his right.

I answer that, The aforesaid definition of justice is fitting if understood aright. For since every virtue is a habit which is the principle of a good act, a virtue must needs be defined by means of the good act bearing on the matter proper to that virtue. Now the proper matter of justice consists of those things that belong to our intercourse with other men, as shall be shown further on (A. 2). Hence the act of justice in relation to its proper matter and object is indicated in the words, "Rendering to each one his right," since, as Isidore says, "a man is said to be just because he respects the rights (*ius*) of others." [5]

Now in order that an act bearing upon any matter whatever be virtuous, it requires to be voluntary, stable, and firm, because the Philosopher says that in order for an act to be virtuous it needs first of all to be done "knowingly," secondly to be done "by choice" and "for a due end," thirdly to be done "immovably." [6] Now the first of these is included in the second, since "what is done through ignorance is involuntary." [7] Hence the definition of justice mentions first the "will," in order to show that the act of justice must be voluntary; and mention is made afterwards of its "constancy" and "perpetuity" in order to indicate the firmness of the act.

Accordingly this is a complete definition of justice, save that the act is mentioned instead of the habit which takes its species from that act, because habit implies relation to act. And if any-one would reduce it to the proper form of a definition, he might say that *justice is a habit whereby a man renders to each one his due by a constant and perpetual will;* and this is about the same definition as that given by the Philosopher, who says that "justice is a habit whereby a man is said to be capable of doing just actions in accordance with his choice." [8]

Reply Obj. 1: Will here denotes the act, not the power, and it is customary among writers to define habits by their acts: thus Augustine says that "faith is to believe what one sees not." [9]

Reply Obj. 2. Justice is the same as rectitude, not essentially but causally; for it is a habit which rectifies the deed and the will.

Reply Obj. 3. The will may be called perpetual in two ways. First, on the part of the will's act which endures forever, and thus God's will alone is perpetual. Secondly, on the part of the subject, because, to wit, a man wills to do a certain thing always, and this is a necessary condition of justice. For it does not satisfy the conditions of justice that one wish to observe justice in some particular matter for the time being, because one could scarcely find a man willing to act unjustly in every case; and it is requisite that one should have the will to observe justice at all times and in all cases.

Reply Obj. 4. Since "perpetual" does not imply perpetuity of the act of the will, it is not superfluous to add "constant"; for while the "perpetual will" denotes the purpose of observing justice always, "constant" signifies a firm perseverance in this purpose.

Reply Obj. 5. A judge renders to each one what belongs to him by way of command and direction, because a judge is the "personification of justice," and "the sovereign is its guardian." [10] On the other hand, the subjects render to each one what belongs to him by way of execution.

Reply Obj. 6. Just as love of God includes love of our neighbor, as stated above,[11] so, too, the service of God includes rendering to each one his due.

SECOND ARTICLE

WHETHER JUSTICE IS ALWAYS TOWARD ANOTHER?

We proceed thus to the Second Article:

Objection 1. It would seem that justice is not always toward another. For the Apostle says that "the justice of God is by faith of Jesus Christ." [12] Now faith does not concern the dealings of one man with another. Neither therefore does justice.

Obj. 2. Further, according to Augustine, "it belongs to justice that man should direct to the service of God his authority over the things that are subject to him." [13] Now the sensitive appetite is subject to man, according to Genesis iv. 7, where it is written: "The lust thereof," viz., of sin, "shall be under thee, and thou shalt have dominion over it." Therefore it belongs to justice to have dominion over one's own appetite, so that justice is toward oneself.

Obj. 3. Further, the justice of God is eternal. But nothing else is coeternal with God. Therefore justice is not essentially toward another.

Obj. 4. Further, man's dealings with himself need to be rectified no less than his dealings with another. Now man's dealings are rectified by justice; according to Proverbs xi. 5, "The justice of the upright shall make his way prosperous." Therefore justice is about our dealings not only with others, but also with ourselves.

On the contrary, Cicero says that "the object of justice is to keep men together in society and mutual intercourse." [14] Now this implies relationship of one man to another. Therefore justice is concerned only about our dealings with others.

I answer that, As stated above (Q. 57, A. 1), since justice by its name implies equality, it denotes essentially relation to another, for a thing is equal, not to itself, but to another. And forasmuch as it belongs to justice to rectify human acts, as stated above (Q. 57, A. 1; I-II, Q. 93, A. 1), this otherness which justice demands must needs be between beings capable of action. Now actions belong to supposits [a] and wholes and, properly speaking, not to parts and forms or powers, for we do not say prop-

[a] [See Glossary.]

erly that the hand strikes, but a man with his hand, nor that heat makes a thing hot, but fire by heat, although such expressions may be employed metaphorically. Hence, justice, properly speaking, demands a distinction of supposits and consequently is only in one man toward another. Nevertheless in one and the same man we may speak metaphorically of his various principles of action, such as the reason, the irascible, and the concupiscible, as though they were so many agents; so that metaphorically in one and the same man there is said to be justice in so far as the reason commands the irascible and concupiscible and these obey reason, and in general in so far as to each part of man is ascribed what is becoming to it. Hence the Philosopher calls this "metaphorical justice." [15]

Reply Obj. 1. The justice which faith works in us is that whereby the ungodly is justified; it consists in the due co-ordination of the parts of the soul, as stated above (I-II, Q. 93, A. 1) where we were treating of the justification of the ungodly.[16] Now this belongs to metaphorical justice, which may be found even in a man who lives all by himself.

This suffices for the *Reply* to the *Second Objection*.

Reply Obj. 3. God's justice is from eternity in respect of the eternal will and purpose (and it is chiefly in this that justice consists), although it is not eternal as regards its effect, since nothing is coeternal with God.

Reply Obj. 4. Man's dealings with himself are sufficiently rectified by the rectification of the passions by the other moral virtues. But his dealings with others need a special rectification, not only in relation to the agent, but also in relation to the person to whom they are directed. Hence about such dealings there is a special virtue, and this is justice.

THIRD ARTICLE

WHETHER JUSTICE IS A VIRTUE?

We proceed thus to the Third Article:

Objection 1. It would seem that justice is not a virtue. For it is written: "When you shall have done all these things that are

commanded you, say: 'We are unprofitable servants; we have
done that which we ought to do.' " [17] Now it is not unprofitable
to do a virtuous deed, for Ambrose says: "We look to a profit
that is estimated not by pecuniary gain but by the acquisition of
godliness." [18] Therefore to do what one ought to do is not a virtuous deed. And yet it is an act of justice. Therefore justice is not
a virtue.

Obj. 2. Further, that which is done of necessity is not meritorious. But to render to a man what belongs to him, as justice requires, is of necessity. Therefore it is not meritorious. Yet it is
by virtuous actions that we gain merit. Therefore justice is not
a virtue.

Obj. 3. Further [every moral virtue deals with inherent activities
(*agibilia*). Those things, on the other hand, which are made outside of the doer are not *agibilia* but *factibilia*,[b] according to the
Philosopher.[19] Now, since it pertains to justice to produce, externally, a deed which is just in itself, it follows that justice is not
a moral virtue.] [c]

On the contrary, Gregory says that "the entire structure of
good works is built on four virtues," [20] viz., temperance, prudence,
fortitude and justice.

I answer that, A human virtue is one "which renders a human
act and man himself good," [21] and this can be applied to justice.
For a man's act is made good through attaining the rule of reason, which is the rule whereby human acts are regulated. Hence,
since justice regulates human operations, it is evident that it
renders man's operations good; and, as Cicero declares, good men
are so called chiefly from their justice, wherefore, as he says again,
"the luster of virtue appears above all in justice." [22]

Reply Obj. 1. When a man does what he ought, he brings no
gain to the person to whom he does what he ought, but only ab-

---

[b] [See Glossary under *art.*]

[c] D.F. Tr.: every moral virtue is about matters of action. Now those things
which are wrought externally are not things concerning behavior but concerning handicraft, according to the Philosopher.[19] Therefore, since it belongs
to justice to produce externally a deed that is just in itself, it seems that
justice is not a moral virtue.

stains from doing him a harm. He does, however, profit himself, in so far as he does what he ought spontaneously and readily, and this is to act virtuously. Hence it is written that divine wisdom "teacheth temperance, and prudence, and justice, and fortitude, which are such things as men (i.e. *virtuous men*) can have nothing more profitable in life." [23]

Reply Obj. 2. Necessity is twofold. One arises from *constraint*, and this removes merit, since it runs counter to the will. The other arises from the obligation of a *command* or from the necessity of obtaining an end when, to wit, a man is unable to achieve the end of virtue without doing some particular thing. The latter necessity does not remove merit when a man does voluntarily that which is necessary in this way. It does however exclude the credit of supererogation; according to 1 Corinthians ix. 16, "If I preach the Gospel, it is no glory to me, for a necessity lieth upon me."

Reply Obj. 3. Justice is concerned about external things, not by making them, which pertains to art, but by using them in our dealings with other men.

Fourth Article

WHETHER JUSTICE IS IN THE WILL AS ITS SUBJECT?

We proceed thus to the Fourth Article:

Objection 1. It would seem that justice is not in the will as its subject. For justice is sometimes called truth. But truth is not in the will, but in the intellect. Therefore justice is not in the will as its subject.

Obj. 2. Further, justice is about our dealings with others. Now it belongs to the reason to direct one thing in relation to another. Therefore justice is not in the will as its subject but in the reason.

Obj. 3. Further, justice is not an intellectual virtue, since it is not directed to knowledge; wherefore it follows that it is a moral virtue. Now the subject of moral virtue is the faculty which is "rational by participation," viz. the irascible and the concupiscible, as the Philosopher declares.[24] Therefore justice is not in the will as its subject, but in the irascible and concupiscible.

On the contrary, Anselm says that "justice is rectitude of the will observed for its own sake." [25]

I answer that, The subject of a virtue is the power whose act that virtue aims at rectifying. Now justice does not aim at directing an act of the cognitive power, for we are not said to be just through knowing something aright. Hence the subject of justice is not the intellect or reason, which is a cognitive power. But since we are said to be just through doing something aright, and because the proximate principle of action is the appetitive power, justice must needs be in some appetitive power as its subject.

Now the appetite is twofold; namely, the will which is in the reason, and the sensitive appetite which follows on sensitive apprehension, and is divided into the irascible and the concupiscible, as stated in the First Part.[26] Again the act of rendering his due to each man cannot proceed from the sensitive appetite, because sensitive apprehension does not go so far as to be able to consider the relation of one thing to another; but this is proper to the reason. Therefore justice cannot be in the irascible or concupiscible as its subject, but only in the will; hence the Philosopher defines justice by an act of the will,[27] as may be seen above (A. 1).

Reply Obj. 1. Since the will is the rational appetite, when the rectitude of the reason which is called truth is imprinted on the will on account of its nighness to the reason, this imprint retains the name of truth; and hence it is that justice sometimes goes by the name of truth.

Reply Obj. 2. The will is borne toward its object consequently on the apprehension of reason; wherefore, since the reason directs one thing in relation to another, the will can will one thing in relation to another, and this belongs to justice.

Reply Obj. 3. Not only the irascible and concupiscible parts are "rational by participation," but the entire "appetitive" faculty, as stated in *Ethics* i. 13, because all appetite is subject to reason. Now the will is contained in the appetitive faculty, wherefore it can be the subject of moral virtue.

FIFTH ARTICLE

WHETHER JUSTICE IS A GENERAL VIRTUE?

We proceed thus to the Fifth Article:

Objection 1. It would seem that justice is not a general virtue. For justice is specified with the other virtues, according to Wisdom viii. 7: "She teacheth temperance, and prudence, and justice, and fortitude." Now the "general" is not specified or reckoned together with the species contained under the same "general." Therefore justice is not a general virtue.

Obj. 2. Further, as justice is accounted a cardinal virtue, so are temperance and fortitude. Now neither temperance nor fortitude is reckoned to be a general virtue. Therefore neither should justice in any way be reckoned a general virtue.

Obj. 3. Further, justice is always toward others, as stated above (A. 2). But a sin committed against one's neighbor cannot be a general sin, because it is condivided with sin committed against oneself. Therefore neither is justice a general virtue.

On the contrary, The Philosopher says that "justice is every virtue." [28]

I answer that, Justice, as stated above (A. 2), directs man in his relations with other men. Now this may happen in two ways: first, as regards his relations with individuals; secondly, as regards his relations with others in general, in so far as a man who serves a community serves all those who are included in that community. Accordingly justice in its proper acceptation can be directed to another in both these senses. Now it is evident that all who are included in a community stand in relation to that community as parts to a whole; while a part, as such, belongs to a whole, so that whatever is the good of a part can be directed to the good of the whole. It follows, therefore, that the good of any virtue, whether such virtue direct man in relation to himself or in relation to certain other individual persons, is referable to the common good to which justice directs; so that all acts of virtue can pertain to justice, in so far as it directs man to the common good. It is in this sense that justice is called a general virtue. And since it belongs to the law to direct to the common good, as stated above (I-II, Q. 90, A. 2), it follows that the justice which is in this way styled general, is called "legal justice," because thereby man is in harmony with the law which directs the acts of all the virtues to the common good.

Reply Obj. 1. Justice is specified or enumerated with the other virtues, not as a general but as a special virtue, as we shall state further on (AA. 7, 12).

Reply Obj. 2. Temperance and fortitude are in the sensitive appetite, viz. in the concupiscible and irascible. Now these powers are appetitive of certain particular goods, even as the senses are cognitive of particulars. On the other hand justice is in the intellective appetite as its subject, which can have the universal good as its object, knowledge whereof belongs to the intellect. Hence justice can be a general virtue rather than temperance or fortitude.

Reply Obj. 3. Things referable to oneself are referable to another, especially in regard to the common good. Wherefore legal justice, in so far as it directs to the common good, may be called a general virtue, and in like manner injustice may be called a general sin; hence it is written that all "sin is iniquity." [29]

Sixth Article

WHETHER JUSTICE, AS A GENERAL VIRTUE, IS ESSENTIALLY THE SAME AS ALL VIRTUE?

We proceed thus to the Sixth Article:

Objection 1. It would seem that justice, as a general virtue, is essentially the same as all virtue. For the Philosopher says that "virtue and legal justice are the same as all virtue, but differ in their mode of being." [30] Now things that differ merely in their mode of being or [subjectively] [d] do not differ essentially. Therefore justice is essentially the same as every virtue.

Obj. 2. Further, every virtue that is not essentially the same as all virtue is a part of virtue. Now the aforesaid justice, accord-

[d] D.F. Tr.: logically.

ing to the Philosopher, "is not a part but the whole of virtue." [31]
Therefore the aforesaid justice is essentially the same as all virtue.

Obj. 3. Further, the essence of a virtue does not change through
that virtue directing its act to some higher end, even as the habit
of temperance remains essentially the same even though its act
be directed to a divine good. Now it belongs to legal justice that
the acts of all the virtues are directed to a higher end, namely,
the common good of the multitude, which transcends the good of
one single individual. Therefore it seems that legal justice is essentially all virtue.

Obj. 4. Further, every good of a part can be directed to the
good of the whole, so that if it be not thus directed it would seem
without use or purpose. But that which is in accordance with virtue cannot be so. Therefore it seems that there can be no act of
any virtue that does not belong to general justice, which directs
to the common good; and so it seems that general justice is essentially the same as all virtue.

On the contrary, The Philosopher says that "many are able to
be virtuous in matters affecting themselves, but are unable to be
virtuous in matters relating to others," [32] and that "the virtue of
the good man is not strictly the same as the virtue of the good
citizen." [33] Now the virtue of a good citizen is general justice,
whereby a man is directed to the common good. Therefore general justice is not the same as virtue in general, and it is possible
to have one without the other.

I answer that, A thing is said to be "general" in two ways. First,
by "predication": thus "animal" is general in relation to man and
horse and the like; and in this sense that which is general must
needs be essentially the same as the things in relation to which it
is general, for the reason that the genus belongs to the essence of
the species and forms part of its definition. Secondly, a thing is
said to be general [in accordance with its power]: [e] thus a universal cause is general in relation to all its effects—the sun, for instance, in relation to all bodies that are illumined or transmuted by
its power; and in this sense there is no need for that which is
"general" to be essentially the same as those things in relation to

[e] D.F. Tr.: virtually.

which it is general, since cause and effect are not essentially the same. Now it is in the latter sense that, according to what has been said (A. 5), legal justice is said to be a general virtue, inasmuch, to wit, as it directs the acts of the other virtues to its own end, and this is to move all the other virtues by its command; for just as charity may be called a general virtue in so far as it directs the acts of all the virtues to the divine good, so, too, is legal justice in so far as it directs the acts of all the virtues to the common good. Accordingly, just as charity which regards the divine good as its proper object is a special virtue in respect of its essence, so, too, legal justice is a special virtue in respect of its essence in so far as it regards the common good as its proper object. And thus it is in the sovereign principally and by way of a master-craft, while it is secondarily and administratively in his subjects.

However the name of legal justice can be given to every virtue in so far as every virtue is directed to the common good by the aforesaid legal justice, which though special essentially is nevertheless [general in accordance with its efficacy].^f Speaking in this way, legal justice is essentially the same as all virtue, but differs therefrom logically; and it is in this sense that the Philosopher speaks.

Wherefore the *Replies* to the *First* and *Second Objections* are manifest.

Reply Obj. 3. This argument again takes legal justice for the virtue commanded by legal justice.

Reply Obj. 4. Every virtue, strictly speaking, directs its act to that virtue's proper end; that it should happen to be directed to a further end either always or sometimes does not belong to that virtue considered strictly, for it needs some higher virtue to direct it to that end. Consequently there must be one supreme virtue essentially distinct from every other virtue, which directs all the virtues to the common good; and this virtue is legal justice.

^f D.F. Tr.: virtually general.

SEVENTH ARTICLE

WHETHER THERE IS A PARTICULAR BESIDES A GENERAL JUSTICE?

We proceed thus to the Seventh Article:

Objection 1. It would seem that there is not a particular besides a general justice. For there is nothing superfluous in the virtues, as neither is there in nature. Now general justice directs man suf‹ ficiently in all his relations with other men. Therefore there is no need for a particular justice.

Obj. 2. Further, the species of a virtue does not vary according to "one" and "many." But legal justice directs one man to another in matters relating to the multitude, as shown above (AA. 5, 6). Therefore there is not another species of justice directing one man to another in matters relating to the individual.

Obj. 3. Further, between the individual and the general public stands the household community. Consequently, if in addition to general justice there is a particular justice corresponding to the individual, for the same reason there should be a domestic justice directing man to the common good of a household; and yet this is not the case. Therefore neither should there be a particular besides a legal justice.

On the contrary, Chrysostom in his commentary on Matthew v. 6, "Blessed are they that hunger and thirst after justice," says: "By justice He signifies either the general virtue or the particular virtue which is opposed to covetousness." [34]

I answer that, As stated above (A. 6), legal justice is not essentially the same as every virtue, and besides legal justice, which directs man immediately to the common good, there is need for other virtues to direct him immediately in matters relating to particular goods; and these virtues may be relative to himself or to another individual person. Accordingly, just as in addition to legal justice there is a need for particular virtues to direct man in relation to himself, such as temperance and fortitude, so, too, besides legal justice there is need for particular justice to direct man in his relations to other individuals.

Reply Obj. 1. Legal justice does indeed direct man sufficiently in his relations toward others. As regards the common good it does so immediately, but as to the good of the individual, it does so mediately. Wherefore there is need for particular justice to direct a man immediately to the good of another individual.

Reply Obj. 2. The common good of the realm and the particular good of the individual differ not only in respect of the "many" and the "few," but also under a formal [essence].ᵍ For the essence of the "common" good differs from the essence of the "individual" good, even as the essence of "whole" differs from that of "part." Wherefore the Philosopher says that "they are wrong who maintain that the State and the home and the like differ only as many and few and not specifically." [85]

Reply Obj. 3. The household community, according to the Philosopher, differs in respect of a threefold fellowship; namely, "of husband and wife, father and son, master and slave," [36] in each of which one person is, as it were, part of the other. Wherefore between such persons there is not justice simply, but a species of justice, viz. "domestic" justice, as stated in *Ethics* v. 6.

EIGHTH ARTICLE

WHETHER PARTICULAR JUSTICE HAS A SPECIAL MATTER?

We proceed thus to the Eighth Article:

Objection 1. It would seem that particular justice has no special matter. Because a gloss on Genesis ii. 14, "The fourth river is Euphrates," says: "Euphrates signifies 'fruitful'; nor is it stated through what country it flows, because justice pertains to all the parts of the soul." Now this would not be the case if justice had a special matter, since every special matter belongs to a special power. Therefore particular justice has no special matter.

Obj. 2. Further, Augustine says that "the soul has four virtues whereby, in this life, it lives spiritually, viz. temperance, prudence, fortitude and justice"; and he says that "the fourth is justice,

ᵍ D.F. Tr.: "aspect" throughout *Reply Obj.* 2.

which pervades all the virtues." [37] Therefore particular justice, which is one of the four cardinal virtues, has no special matter.

Obj. 3. Further, justice directs man sufficiently in matters relating to others. Now a man can be directed to others in all matters relating to this life. Therefore the matter of justice is general and not special.

On the contrary, The Philosopher reckons particular justice to be specially about those things which belong to social life.[38]

I answer that, Whatever can be rectified by reason is the matter of moral virtue, for this is defined in reference to right reason, according to the Philosopher.[39] Now the reason can rectify not only the internal passions of the soul, but also external actions, and also those external things of which man can make use. And yet it is in respect of external actions and external things by means of which men can communicate with one another that the relation of one man to another is to be considered; whereas it is in respect of internal passions that we consider man's rectitude in himself. Consequently, since justice is directed to others, it is not about the entire matter of moral virtue, but only about external actions and things, under a certain special aspect of the object, in so far as one man is related to another through them.

Reply Obj. 1. It is true that justice belongs essentially to one part of the soul, where it resides as in its subject; and this is the will which moves by its command all the other parts of the soul; and, accordingly, justice belongs to all the parts of the soul, not directly but by a kind of diffusion.

Reply Obj. 2. As stated above,[40] the cardinal virtues may be taken in two ways: first, as special virtues, each having a determinate matter; secondly, as certain general modes of virtue. In this latter sense Augustine speaks in the passage quoted; for he says that "prudence is knowledge of what we should seek and avoid, temperance is the curb on the lust for fleeting pleasures, fortitude is strength of mind in bearing with passing trials, justice is the love of God and our neighbor which pervades the other virtues, that is to say, is the common principle of the entire order between one man and another."

Reply Obj. 3. A man's internal passions which are a part of moral matter are not in themselves directed to another man, which belongs to the specific nature of justice; yet their effects, i.e., external actions, are capable of being directed to another man. Consequently it does not follow that the matter of justice is general.

NINTH ARTICLE

WHETHER JUSTICE IS ABOUT THE PASSIONS?

We proceed thus to the Ninth Article:

Objection 1. It would seem that justice is about the passions. For the Philosopher says that "moral virtue is about pleasure and pain." [41] Now pleasure or delight, and pain are passions, as stated above [42] when we were treating of the passions. Therefore justice, being a moral virtue, is about the passions.

Obj. 2. Further, justice is the means of rectifying a man's operations in relation to another man. Now suchlike operations cannot be rectified unless the passions be rectified, because it is owing to disorder of the passions that there is disorder in the aforesaid operations; thus sexual lust leads to adultery, and overmuch love of money leads to theft. Therefore justice must needs be about the passions.

Obj. 3. Further, even as particular justice is toward another person, so is legal justice. Now legal justice is about the passions, else it would not extend to all the virtues, some of which are evidently about the passions. Therefore justice is about the passions.

On the contrary, The Philosopher says that justice is about operations.[43]

I answer that, The true answer to this question may be gathered from a twofold source. First from the subject of justice, i.e. from the will, whose movements or acts are not passions, as stated above,[44] for it is only the sensitive appetite whose movements are called passions. Hence justice is not about the passions, as are temperance and fortitude, which are in the irascible and concupiscible parts. Secondly, on the part of the matter, because justice is about a man's relations with another, and we are not directed immediately to another by the internal passions. Therefore justice is not about the passions.

Reply Obj. 1. Not every moral virtue is about pleasure and pain as its proper matter, since fortitude is about fear and daring; but every moral virtue is directed to pleasure and pain, as to ends to be acquired, for, as the Philosopher says, "pleasure and pain are the principal end in respect of which we say that this is an evil and that a good," [45] and in this way, too, they belong to justice, since "a man is not just unless he rejoice in just actions." [46]

Reply Obj. 2. External operations are, as it were, between external things which are their matter and internal passions which are their origin. Now it happens sometimes that there is a defect in one of these, without there being a defect in the other. Thus a man may steal another's property, not through the desire to have the thing, but through the will to hurt the man; or vice versa, a man may covet another's property without wishing to steal it. Accordingly, the directing of operations in so far as they tend toward external things belongs to justice, but in so far as they arise from the passions it belongs to the other moral virtues which are about the passions. Hence justice hinders theft of another's property in so far as stealing is contrary to the equality that should be maintained in external things, while liberality hinders it as resulting from an immoderate desire for wealth. Since, however, external operations take their species, not from the internal passions, but from external things as being their objects, it follows that external operations are essentially the matter of justice rather than of the other moral virtues.

Reply Obj. 3. The common good is the end of each individual member of a community, just as the good of the whole is the end of each part. On the other hand the good of one individual is not the end of another individual; wherefore legal justice which is directed to the common good is more capable of extending to the internal passions whereby man is disposed in some way or other in himself, than particular justice which is directed to the good of another individual; although legal justice extends chiefly to other virtues in the point of their external operations, in so far, to wit, as "the law commands us to perform the actions of a courageous person . . . the actions of a temperate person . . . and the actions of a gentle person." [47]

WHETHER THE MEAN OF JUSTICE IS THE REAL MEAN?

We proceed thus to the Tenth Article:

Objection 1. [It would seem that the mean of justice is not the mean of the thing. For the nature of genus is to be found in all its species. Now moral virtue (which is a genus) is defined as "an elective habit existing in a mean, which mean is to be found (not in things but) in relation to us, so determined by reason." [48] Therefore justice is the mean of reason, not of the thing.] [h]

Obj. 2. Further, in things that are good simply, there is neither excess nor defect, and consequently neither is there a mean, as is clearly the case with the virtues, according to *Ethics* ii. 6. Now justice is about things that are good simply, as stated in *Ethics* v. Therefore justice does not observe the real mean.

Obj. 3. Further, the reason why the other virtues are said to observe the rational and not the real mean is because in their case the mean varies according to different persons, since what is too much for one is too little for another.[49] Now this is also the case in justice; for one who strikes a prince does not receive the same punishment as one who strikes a private individual. Therefore justice also observes, not the real, but the rational mean.

On the contrary, The Philosopher says that the mean of justice is to be taken according to "arithmetical" proportion,[50] so that it is the real mean.

I answer that, As stated above (A. 9; I-II, Q. 59, A. 4), the other moral virtues are chiefly concerned with the passions, the regulation of which is gauged entirely by a comparison with the very man who is the subject of those passions, in so far as his

---

[h] D.F. Tr.: It would seem that the mean of justice is not the real mean. For the generic nature remains entire in each species. Now moral virtue is defined to be "an elective habit which observes the mean fixed, in our regard, by reason." [48] Therefore justice observes the rational and not the real mean.

anger and desire are vested with their various due circumstances. Hence the mean in suchlike virtues is measured not by the proportion of one thing to another, but merely by comparison with the virtuous man himself, so that with them the mean is only that which is fixed by reason in our regard.

On the other hand, the matter of justice is external operation in so far as an operation or the thing used in that operation is duly proportionate to another person; wherefore the mean of justice consists in a certain proportion of equality between the external thing and the external person. Now equality is the real mean between greater and less, as stated in *Metaphysics* x; [51] wherefore justice observes the real mean.

Reply Obj. 1. This real mean is also the rational mean, wherefore justice satisfies the conditions of a moral virtue.

Reply Obj. 2. We may speak of a thing being good simply in two ways. First, a thing may be good in every way: thus the virtues are good, and there is neither mean nor extremes in things that are good simply in this sense. Secondly, a thing is said to be good simply through being good absolutely, i.e. in its nature, although it may become evil through being abused. Such are riches and honors; and in the like it is possible to find excess, deficiency, and mean, as regards men who can use them well or ill; and it is in this sense that justice is about things that are good simply.

Reply Obj. 3. The injury inflicted bears a different proportion to a prince from that which it bears to a private person; wherefore each injury requires to be equalized by vengeance in a different way, and this implies a real and not merely a rational diversity.

ELEVENTH ARTICLE

WHETHER THE ACT OF JUSTICE IS TO RENDER TO
EACH ONE HIS OWN?

We proceed thus to the Eleventh Article:

Objection 1. It would seem that the act of justice is not to render to each one his own. For Augustine ascribes to justice the act of succoring the needy.[52] Now in succoring the needy we give them what is not theirs but ours. Therefore the act of justice does not consist in rendering to each one his own.

Obj. 2. Further, Cicero says that "beneficence, which we may call kindness or liberality, belongs to justice." [53] Now it pertains to liberality to give to another of one's own, not of what is his. Therefore the act of justice does not consist in rendering to each one his own.

Obj. 3. Further, it belongs to justice not only to distribute things duly, but also to repress injurious actions, such as murder, adultery, and so forth. But the rendering to each one of what is his seems to belong solely to the distribution of things. Therefore the act of justice is not sufficiently described by saying that it consists in rendering to each one his own.

On the contrary, Ambrose says: "It is justice that renders to each one what is his, and claims not another's property; it disregards its own profit in order to preserve the common equity." [54]

I answer that, As stated above (AA. 8, 10), the matter of justice is an external operation in so far as either it or the thing we use by it is made proportionate to some other person to whom we are related by justice. Now each man's own is that which is due to him according to equality of proportion. Therefore the proper act of justice is nothing else than to render to each one his own.

Reply Obj. 1. Since justice is a cardinal virtue, other secondary virtues, such as mercy, liberality, and the like, are connected with it, as we shall state further on.[55] Wherefore to succor the needy, which belongs to mercy or pity, and to be liberally beneficent, which pertains to liberality, are by a kind of reduction ascribed to justice as to their principal virtue.

This suffices for the *Reply* to the *Second Objection.*

Reply Obj. 3. As the Philosopher states, in matters of justice the name of "profit" is extended to whatever is excessive, and whatever is deficient is called "loss." [56] The reason for this is that justice is first of all and more commonly exercised in voluntary interchanges of things, such as buying and selling, wherein those expressions are properly employed; and yet they are transferred to

all other matters of justice. The same applies to the rendering to
each one of what is his own.

WHETHER JUSTICE STANDS FOREMOST AMONG ALL MORAL VIRTUES?

We proceed thus to the Twelfth Article:

Objection 1. It would seem that justice does not stand foremost
among all the moral virtues. Because it belongs to justice to render
to each one what is his, whereas it belongs to liberality to give of
one's own, and this is more virtuous. Therefore liberality is a
greater virtue than justice.

Obj. 2. Further, nothing is adorned by a less excellent thing than
itself. Now magnanimity is the ornament both of justice and of
all the virtues, according to *Ethics* iv. 3. Therefore magnanimity is
more excellent than justice.

Obj. 3. Further, virtue is about that which is "difficult" and
"good," as stated in *Ethics* ii. 3. But fortitude is about more difficult things than justice is, since it is about dangers of death,
according to *Ethics* iii. 6. Therefore fortitude is more excellent
than justice.

On the contrary, Cicero says: "Justice is the most resplendent
of the virtues and gives its name to a good man." [57]

I answer that, If we speak of legal justice, it is evident that it
stands foremost among all the moral virtues, for as much as the
common good transcends the individual good of one person. In
this sense the Philosopher declares that "the most excellent of the
virtues would seem to be justice, and more glorious than either the
evening or the morning star." [58] But even if we speak of particular
justice, it excels the other moral virtues for two reasons. The first
reason may be taken from the subject, because justice is in the
more excellent part of the soul, viz. the rational appetite or will,
whereas the other moral virtues are in the sensitive appetite,
whereunto appertain the passions which are the matter of the other

moral virtues. The second reason is taken from the object, because the other virtues are commendable in respect of the sole good of the virtuous person himself, whereas justice is praiseworthy in respect of the virtuous person being well disposed toward another, so that justice is somewhat the good of another person, as stated in *Ethics* v. 1. Hence the Philosopher says: "The greatest virtues must needs be those which are most profitable to other persons, because virtue is a faculty of doing good to others. For this reason the greatest honors are accorded the brave and the just, since bravery is useful to others in warfare, and justice is useful to others both in warfare and in time of peace." [59]

Reply Obj. 1. Although the liberal man gives of his own, yet he does so in so far as he takes into consideration the good of his own virtue, while the just man gives to another what is his, through consideration of the common good. Moreover justice is observed toward all, whereas liberality cannot extend to all. Again liberality which gives of a man's own is based on justice, whereby one renders to each man what is his.

Reply Obj. 2. When magnanimity is added to justice it increases the latter's goodness; and yet without justice it would not even be a virtue.

Reply Obj. 3. Although fortitude is about the most difficult things, it is not about the best, for it is only useful in warfare, whereas justice is useful both in war and in peace, as stated above.

QUESTION 66

OF THEFT AND ROBBERY

(*In Nine Articles*)

WE must now consider the sins opposed to justice whereby a man injures his neighbor in his belongings, namely, theft and robbery.

Under this head there are nine points of inquiry: (1) Whether it is natural to man to possess external things? (2) Whether it is lawful for a man to possess something as his own? (3) Whether theft is the secret taking of another's property? (4) Whether robbery is a species of sin distinct from theft? (5) Whether every theft is a sin? (6) Whether theft is a mortal sin? (7) Whether it is lawful to thieve in a case of necessity? (8) Whether every robbery is a mortal sin? (9) Whether robbery is a more grievous sin than theft?

FIRST ARTICLE

WHETHER IT IS NATURAL FOR MAN TO POSSESS EXTERNAL THINGS?

We proceed thus to the First Article:

Objection 1. It would seem that it is not natural for man to possess external things. For no man should ascribe to himself that which is God's. Now the dominion over all creatures is proper to God, according to Psalm xxiii. 1, "The earth is the Lord's," etc. Therefore it is not natural for man to possess external things.

Obj. 2. Further, Basil, in expounding the words of the rich man, "I will gather all things that are grown to me, and my goods," [1] says: "Tell me; which are thine? where did you take them from and bring them into being?" [2] Now whatever man possesses naturally, he can fittingly call his own. Therefore man does not naturally possess external things.

127

Obj. 3. Further, according to Ambrose [3] ["the word 'owner' is a term implying power."] [a] But man has no power over external things, since he can work no change in their nature. Therefore the possession of external things is not natural to man.

On the contrary, It is written: "Thou hast subjected all things under his feet." [4]

I answer that, External things can be considered in two ways. First, as regards their nature, and this is not subject to the power of man, but only to the power of God, Whose mere will all things obey. Secondly, as regards their use, and in this way man has a natural dominion over external things, because, by his reason and will, he is able to use them for his own profit, as they were made on his account, for the imperfect is always for the sake of the perfect, as stated above. [5] It is by this argument that the Philosopher proves that the possession of external things is natural to man. [6] Moreover, this natural dominion of man over other creatures, which is competent to man in respect of his reason, wherein God's image resides, is shown forth in man's creation by the words: "Let Us make man to Our image and likeness, and let him have dominion over the fishes of the sea," [7] etc.

Reply Obj. 1. God has sovereign dominion over all things; and He, according to His providence, directed certain things to the sustenance of man's body. For this reason man has a natural dominion over things, as regards the power to make use of them.

Reply Obj. 2. The rich man is reproved for deeming external things to belong to him principally, as though he had not received them from another, namely, from God.

Reply Obj. 3. This argument considers the dominion over external things as regards their nature. Such a dominion belongs to God alone, as stated above.

[a] D.F. Tr.: "dominion denotes power."

SECOND ARTICLE

WHETHER IT IS LAWFUL FOR A MAN TO POSSESS A THING AS HIS OWN?

We proceed thus to the Second Article:

Objection 1. It would seem unlawful for a man to possess a thing as his own. For whatever is contrary to the natural law is unlawful. Now according to the natural law all things are common property, and the possession of property is contrary to this community of goods. Therefore it is unlawful for any man to appropriate any external thing to himself.

Obj. 2. Further, Basil, in expounding the words of the rich man quoted above (A. 1, *Obj.* 2), says: "The rich who deem as their own property the common goods they have seized upon are like to those who by going beforehand to the play prevent others from coming, and appropriate to themselves what is intended for common use." Now it would be unlawful to prevent others from obtaining possession of common goods. Therefore it is unlawful to appropriate to oneself what belongs to the community.

Obj. 3. Further, Ambrose says,[8] and his words are quoted in the *Decretals:* "Let no man call his own that which is common property,"[9] and by "common" he means external things, as is clear from the context. Therefore it seems unlawful for a man to appropriate an external thing to himself.

On the contrary,. Augustine says: "The 'Apostolici' are those who with extreme arrogance have given themselves that name, because they do not admit into their communion persons who are married or possess anything of their own, such as both monks and clerics who in considerable number are to be found in the Catholic Church."[10] Now the reason why these people are heretics is because, severing themselves from the Church, they think that those who enjoy the use of the above things, which they themselves lack, have no hope of salvation. Therefore it is erroneous to maintain that it is unlawful for a man to possess property.

I answer that, Two things are competent to man in respect of exterior things. One is the power to procure and dispense them, and in this regard it is lawful for man to possess property. More-over this is necessary to human life for three reasons. First, be-cause every man is more careful to procure what is for himself alone than that which is common to many or to all; since each one would shirk the labor and leave to another that which concerns the com-munity, as happens where there is a great number of servants. Secondly, because human affairs are conducted in more orderly fashion if each man is charged with taking care of some particular thing himself, whereas there would be confusion if everyone had to look after any one thing indeterminately. Thirdly, because a more peaceful state is insured to man if each one is contented with his own. Hence it is to be observed that quarrels arise more frequently where there is no division of the things possessed.

The second thing that is competent to man with regard to ex-ternal things is their use. In this respect man ought to possess external things, not as his own, but as common, so that, to wit, he is ready to communicate them to others in their need. Hence the Apostle says: "Charge the rich of this world . . . to give easily, to communicate to others," etc.[11]

Reply Obj. 1. Community of goods is ascribed to the natural law, not that the natural law dictates that all things should be possessed in common and that nothing should be possessed as one's own, but because the division of possessions is not according to the natural law, but rather arose from human agreement, which belongs to positive law, as stated above (Q. 57, AA. 2, 3). Hence the ownership of possessions is not contrary to the natural law, but an addition thereto devised by human reason.

Reply Obj. 2. A man would not act unlawfully if by going be-forehand to the play he prepared the way for others, but he acts unlawfully if by so doing he hinders others from going. In like manner a rich man does not act unlawfully if he anticipates some-one in taking possession of something which at first was common property and gives others a share, but he sins if he excludes others indiscriminately from using it. Hence Basil says: "Why are you rich while another is poor, unless it be that you may have the merit of a good stewardship and he the reward of patience?" [12]

Reply Obj. 3. When Ambrose says: "Let no man call his own that which is common," he is speaking of ownership as regards use, wherefore he adds: "He who spends too much is a robber."

THIRD ARTICLE

WHETHER THE ESSENCE OF THEFT CONSISTS IN TAKING ANOTHER'S THING SECRETLY?

We proceed thus to the Third Article:

Objection 1. It would seem that it is not essential to theft to take another's thing secretly. For that which diminishes a sin does not, apparently, belong to the essence of a sin. Now to sin secretly tends to diminish a sin, just as, on the contrary, it is written as indicating an aggravating circumstance of the sin of some: "They have proclaimed abroad their sin as Sodom, and they have not hid it." [13] Therefore it is not essential to theft that it should consist in taking another's thing secretly.

Obj. 2. Further, Ambrose says,[14] and his words are embodied in the *Decretals:* "It is no less a crime to take from him that has than to refuse to succor the needy when you can and are well off." [15] Therefore, just as theft consists in taking another's thing, so does it consist in keeping it back.

Obj. 3. Further, a man may take by stealth from another even that which is his own, for instance, a thing that he has deposited with another, or that has been taken away from him unjustly. Therefore, it is not essential to theft that it should consist in taking another's thing secretly.

On the contrary, Isidore says: "*Fur* (thief) is derived from *furvus* and so from *fuscus* (dark), because he takes advantage of the night." [16]

I answer that, Three things combine together to constitute theft. The first belongs to theft as being contrary to justice, which gives to each one that which is his, so that it belongs to theft to take possession of what is another's. The second thing belongs to theft as distinct from those sins which are committed against the person, such as murder and adultery, and in this respect it belongs to theft to be about a thing possessed; for if a man takes what is another's, not as a possession but as a part (for instance, if he amputates a limb), or as a person connected with him (for instance, if he carry off his daughter or his wife), it is not, strictly speaking, a case of theft. The third difference is that which completes the nature of theft and consists in a thing being taken secretly, and in this respect it belongs properly to theft that it consists in "taking another's thing secretly."

Reply Obj. 1. Secrecy is sometimes a cause of sin, as when a man employs secrecy in order to commit a sin, for instance in fraud and guile. In this way it does not diminish sin, but constitutes a species of sin, and thus it is in theft. In another way secrecy is merely a circumstance of sin, and thus it diminishes sin, both because it is a sign of shame and because it removes scandal.

Reply Obj. 2. To keep back what is due to another inflicts the same kind of injury as taking a thing unjustly, wherefore an unjust detention is included in an unjust taking.

Reply Obj. 3. Nothing prevents that which belongs to one person simply from belonging to another in some respect: thus a deposit belongs simply to the depositor, but with regard to its custody it is the depositary's, and the thing stolen is the thief's, not simply, but as regards its custody.

Fourth Article

WHETHER THEFT AND ROBBERY ARE SINS OF DIFFERENT SPECIES?

We proceed thus to the Fourth Article:

Objection 1. It would seem that theft and robbery are not sins of different species. For theft and robbery differ as "secret" and "manifest"; because theft is taking something secretly, while robbery is to take something violently and openly. Now in the other kinds of sins the secret and the manifest do not differ specifically. Therefore theft and robbery are not different species of sin.

Obj. 2. Further, moral actions take their species from the end, as stated above.[17] Now theft and robbery are directed to the same end, viz., the possession of another's property. Therefore they do not differ specifically.

Obj. 3. Further, just as a thing is taken by force for the sake of possession, so is a woman taken by force for pleasure; wherefore Isidore says that "he who commits a rape is called a corrupter, and the victim of the rape is said to be corrupted." [18] Now it is a case of rape whether the woman be carried off publicly or secretly. Therefore, the thing appropriated is said to be taken by force, whether it be done secretly or publicly. Therefore, theft and robbery do not differ.

On the contrary, The Philosopher distinguishes theft from robbery, and states that theft is done in secret, but that robbery is done openly.[19]

I answer that, Theft and robbery are vices contrary to justice inasmuch as one man does another an injustice. Now "no man suffers an injustice willingly," as stated in *Ethics* v. 9. Wherefore theft and robbery derive their sinful nature through the taking being involuntary on the part of the person from whom something is taken. Now the involuntary is twofold, namely, through violence and through ignorance, as stated in *Ethics* iii. 1. Therefore the sinful aspect of robbery differs from that of theft, and consequently they differ specifically.

Reply Obj. 1. In the other kinds of sin the sinful nature is not derived from something involuntary, as in the sins opposed to justice; and so, where there is a different kind of involuntary, there is a different species of sin.

Reply Obj. 2. The remote end of robbery and theft is the same. But this is not enough for identity of species, because there is a difference of proximate ends, since the robber wishes to take a thing by his own power, but the thief by cunning.

Reply Obj. 3. The robbery of a woman cannot be secret on the part of the woman who is taken; wherefore, even if it be secret as regards the others from whom she is taken, the nature of robbery remains on the part of the woman to whom violence is done.

FIFTH ARTICLE

WHETHER THEFT IS ALWAYS A SIN?

We proceed thus to the Fifth Article:

Objection 1. It would seem that theft is not always a sin. For no sin is commanded by God, since it is written: "He hath commanded no man to do wickedly." [20] Yet we find that God commanded theft, for it is written: "And the children of Israel did as the Lord had commanded Moses [b] . . . and they stripped the Egyptians." [21] Therefore theft is not always a sin.

Obj. 2. Further, if a man finds a thing that is not his and takes it, he seems to commit a theft, for he takes another's property. Yet this seems lawful according to natural equity, as the jurists hold.[22] Therefore it seems that theft is not always a sin.

Obj. 3. Further, he that takes what is his own does not seem to sin, because he does not act against justice, since he does not destroy its equality. Yet a man commits a theft even if he secretly take his own property that is detained by or in the safekeeping of another. Therefore it seems that theft is not always a sin.

On the contrary, It is written: "Thou shalt not steal." [23]

I answer that, If anyone consider what is meant by theft, he will find that it is sinful on two counts. First, because of its opposition to justice, which gives to each one what is his, so that for this reason theft is contrary to justice, through being a taking of what belongs to another. Secondly, because of the guile or fraud committed by the thief, by laying hands on another's property secretly and cunningly. Wherefore it is evident that every theft is a sin.

Reply Obj. 1. It is no theft for a man to take another's property either secretly or openly by order of a judge who has commanded him to do so, because it becomes his due by the very fact that it is adjudicated to him by the sentence of the court. Hence still less was it a theft for the Israelites to take away the spoils of the Egyptians at the command of the Lord, Who ordered this to be done on account of the ill-treatment accorded to them by the

[b] Vulg.: as Moses had commanded.

Egyptians without any cause; wherefore it is written significantly: "The just took the spoils of the wicked." [24]

Reply Obj. 2. With regard to treasure-trove a distinction must be made. For some there are that were never in anyone's possession, for instance precious stones and jewels found on the seashore, and such the finder is allowed to keep.[25] The same applies to treasure hidden underground long since and belonging to no man, except that according to civil law the finder is bound to give half to the owner of the land if the treasure-trove be in the land of another person.[26] Hence in the parable of the gospel it is said of the finder of the treasure hidden in a field that he bought the field, as though he purposed thus to acquire the right of possessing the whole treasure.[27] On the other hand the treasure-trove may be nearly in someone's possession; and then if anyone take it with the intention, not of keeping it, but of returning it to the owner who does not look upon such things as unappropriated, he is not guilty of theft. In like manner, if the thing found appears to be unappropriated and if the finder believes it to be so, although he keep it, he does not commit a theft.[28] In any other case the sin of theft is committed,[29] wherefore Augustine says in a homily: "If thou hast found a thing and not returned it, thou hast stolen it." [30]

Reply Obj. 3. He who by stealth takes his own property, which is deposited with another man, burdens the depositary, who is bound either to restitution or to prove himself innocent. Hence he is clearly guilty of sin and is bound to ease the depositary of his burden. On the other hand he who by stealth takes his own property, if this be unjustly detained by another, he sins indeed; yet not because he burdens the retainer, and so he is not bound to restitution or compensation; but he sins against general justice by disregarding the order of justice and usurping judgment concerning his own property. Hence he must make satisfaction to God and endeavor to allay whatever scandal he may have given his neighbor by acting in this way.

Sixth Article

WHETHER THEFT IS A MORTAL SIN?

We proceed thus to the Sixth Article:

Objection 1. It would seem that theft is not a mortal sin. For it is written: "The fault is not so great when a man hath stolen." [31] But every mortal sin is a great fault. Therefore theft is not a mortal sin.

Obj. 2. Further, mortal sin deserves to be punished with death. But in the Law theft is punished not by death but by indemnity, according to Exodus xxii. 1: "If any man steal an ox or a sheep . . . he shall restore five oxen for one ox, and four sheep for one sheep." Therefore theft is not a mortal sin.

Obj. 3. Further, theft can be committed in small even as in great things. But it seems unreasonable for a man to be punished with eternal death for the theft of a small thing such as a needle or a quill. Therefore theft is not a mortal sin.

On the contrary, No man is condemned by the divine judgment save for a mortal sin. Yet a man is condemned for theft, according to Zacharias v. 3: "This is the curse that goeth forth over the face of the earth; for every thief shall be judged as is there written." Therefore theft is a mortal sin.

I answer that, As stated above,[32] a mortal sin is one that is contrary to charity as the spiritual life of the soul. Now charity consists principally in the love of God, and secondarily in the love of our neighbor, which is shown in our wishing and doing him well. But theft is a means of doing harm to our neighbor in his belongings; and if men were to rob one another habitually, human society would be undone. Therefore theft, as being opposed to charity, is a mortal sin.

Reply Obj. 1. The statement that theft is not a great fault is in view of two cases. First, when a person is led to thieve through necessity. This necessity diminishes or entirely removes sin, as we shall show further on (A. 7). Hence the text continues: "For he stealeth to fill his hungry soul." Secondly, theft is stated not to be a great fault in comparison with the guilt of adultery, which is punished with death. Hence the text goes on to say of the thief that "if he be taken, he shall restore sevenfold . . . but he that is an adulterer . . . shall destroy his own soul."

Reply Obj. 2. The punishments of this life are medicinal rather than retributive. For retribution is reserved to the divine judgment which is pronounced against sinners "according to truth." [33] Wherefore, according to the judgment of the present life, the death punishment is inflicted, not for every mortal sin, but only for such as inflict an irreparable harm, or again for such as contain some horrible deformity. Hence, according to the present judgment, the pain of death is not inflicted for theft which does not inflict an irreparable harm, except when it is aggravated by some grave circumstance, as in the case of sacrilege, which is the theft of a sacred thing, of peculation, which is theft of common property, as Augustine states,[34] and of kidnapping, which is stealing a man, for which the pain of death is inflicted.[35]

Reply Obj. 3. Reason accounts as nothing that which is little; so that a man does not consider himself injured in very little matters, and the person who takes such things can presume that this is not against the will of the owner. And if a person take suchlike very little things, he may be proportionately excused from mortal sin. Yet if his intention is to rob and injure his neighbor, there may be a mortal sin even in these very little things, even as there may be through consent in a mere thought.

SEVENTH ARTICLE

WHETHER IT IS LAWFUL TO STEAL THROUGH STRESS OF NEED?

We proceed thus to the Seventh Article:

Objection 1. It would seem unlawful to steal through stress of need. For penance is not imposed except on one who has sinned. Now it is stated: "If anyone, through stress of hunger or nakedness, steal food, clothing, or beast, he shall do penance for three weeks." [36] Therefore it is not lawful to steal through stress of need.

Obj. 2. Further, the Philosopher says that "there are some actions whose very name implies wickedness," [37] and among these he reckons theft. Now that which is wicked in itself may not be done for a good end. Therefore a man cannot lawfully steal in order to remedy a need.

Obj. 3. Further, a man should love his neighbor as himself. Now, according to Augustine, it is unlawful to steal in order to succor one's neighbor by giving him an alms.[38] Therefore neither is it lawful to steal in order to remedy one's own needs.

On the contrary, In cases of need all things are common property, so that there would seem to be no sin in taking another's property, for need has made it common.

I answer that, Things which are of human right cannot derogate from natural right or divine right. Now, according to the natural order established by divine providence, inferior things are ordained for the purpose of succoring man's needs by their means. Wherefore the division and appropriation of things which are based on human law do not preclude the fact that man's needs have to be remedied by means of these very things. Hence whatever certain people have in superabundance is due, by natural law, to the purpose of succoring the poor. For this reason Ambrose says,[39] and his words are embodied in the *Decretals:* "It is the hungry man's bread that you withhold, the naked man's cloak that you store away, the money that you bury in the earth is the price of the poor man's ransom and freedom." [40]

Since, however, there are many who are in need, while it is impossible for all to be succored by means of the same thing, each one is entrusted with the stewardship of his own things, so that out of them he may come to the aid of those who are in need. Nevertheless, if the need be so manifest and urgent that it is evident that the present need must be remedied by whatever means be at hand (for instance when a person is in some imminent danger, and there is no other possible remedy), then it is lawful for a man to succor his own need by means of another's property, by taking it either openly or secretly; nor is this, properly speaking, theft or robbery.

Reply Obj. 1. This decretal considers cases where there is no urgent need.

Reply Obj. 2. It is not theft, properly speaking, to take secretly and use another's property in a case of extreme need; because that which he takes for the support of his life becomes his own property by reason of that need.

Reply Obj. 3. In a case of a like need a man may also take secretly another's property in order to succor his neighbor in need.

EIGHTH ARTICLE

WHETHER ROBBERY MAY BE COMMITTED WITHOUT SIN?

We proceed thus to the Eighth Article:

Objection 1. It would seem that robbery may be committed without sin. For spoils are taken by violence, and this seems to belong to the essence of robbery, according to what has been said (A. 4). Now it is lawful to take spoils from the enemy; for Ambrose says: "When the conqueror has taken possession of the spoils, military discipline demands that all should be reserved for the sovereign," [41] in order, to wit, that he may distribute them. Therefore in certain cases robbery is lawful.

Obj. 2. Further, it is lawful to take from a man what is not his. Now the things which unbelievers have are not theirs, for Augustine says: "You falsely call things your own, for you do not possess them justly, and according to the laws of earthly kings you are commanded to forfeit them." [42] Therefore it seems that one may lawfully rob unbelievers.

Obj. 3. Further, earthly princes violently extort many things from their subjects, and this seems to savor of robbery. Now it would seem a grievous matter to say that they sin in acting thus, for in that case nearly every prince would be damned. Therefore in some cases robbery is lawful.

On the contrary, Whatever is taken lawfully may be offered to God in sacrifice and oblation. Now this cannot be done with the proceeds of robbery, according to Isaias lxi. 8: "I am the Lord that love judgment and hate robbery in a holocaust." Therefore it is not lawful to take anything by robbery.

I answer that, Robbery implies a certain violence and coercion employed in taking unjustly from a man that which is his. Now in human society no man can exercise coercion except through public authority; and, consequently, if a private individual not having public authority takes another's property by violence, he acts unlawfully and commits a robbery, as burglars do. As regards princes, the public power is entrusted to them that they may be the guardians of justice; hence it is unlawful for them to use violence or coercion save within the bounds of justice—either by fighting against the enemy, or against the citizens by punishing evildoers: and whatever is taken by violence of this kind is not the spoils of robbery, since it is not contrary to justice. On the other hand, to take other people's property violently and against justice, in the exercise of public authority, is to act unlawfully and to be guilty of robbery; and whoever does so is bound to restitution.

Reply Obj. 1. A distinction must be made in the matter of spoils. For if they who take spoils from the enemy are waging a just war, such things as they seize in the war become their own property. This is no robbery, so that they are not bound to restitution. Nevertheless even they who are engaged in a just war may sin in taking spoils through cupidity arising from an evil intention, if, to wit, they fight chiefly not for justice but for spoil. For Augustine says that "it is a sin to fight for booty." [43] If, however, those who take the spoil are waging an unjust war, they are guilty of robbery and are bound to restitution.

Reply Obj. 2. Unbelievers possess their goods unjustly in so far as they are ordered by the laws of earthly princes to forfeit those goods. Hence these may be taken violently from them, not by private but by public authority.

Reply Obj. 3. It is no robbery if princes exact from their subjects that which is due to them for the safeguarding of the common good, even if they use violence in so doing; but if they extort something unduly by means of violence, it is robbery even as burglary is. Hence Augustine says: "If justice be disregarded what is a king but a mighty robber? since what is a robber but a little king?" [44] And it is written: "Her princes in the midst of her are like wolves ravening the prey." [45] Wherefore they are bound to restitution, just as robbers are, and by so much do they sin more grievously than robbers as their actions are fraught with greater and more universal danger to public justice, whose wardens they are.

NINTH ARTICLE

WHETHER THEFT IS A MORE GRIEVOUS SIN THAN ROBBERY?

We proceed thus to the Ninth Article:

Objection 1. It would seem that theft is a more grievous sin than robbery. For theft adds fraud and guile to the taking of another's property, and these things are not found in robbery. Now fraud and guile are sinful in themselves, as stated above. [46] Therefore theft is a more grievous sin than robbery.

Obj. 2. Further, shame is fear about a wicked deed, as stated in *Ethics* iv. 9. Now men are more ashamed of theft than of robbery. Therefore theft is more wicked than robbery.

Obj. 3. Further, the more persons a sin injures the more grievous it would seem to be. Now the great and the lowly may be injured by theft, whereas only the weak can be injured by robbery, since it is possible to use violence toward them. Therefore the sin of theft seems to be more grievous than the sin of robbery.

On the contrary, According to the laws robbery is more severely punished than theft.

I answer that, Robbery and theft are sinful, as stated above (AA. 4, 6), on account of the involuntariness on the part of the person from whom something is taken; yet so that in theft the involuntariness is due to ignorance, whereas in robbery it is due to violence. Now a thing is more involuntary through violence than through ignorance, because violence is more directly opposed to the will than ignorance. Therefore robbery is a more grievous sin than theft. There is also another reason, since robbery not only inflicts a loss on a person in his things, but also conduces to the ignominy and injury of his person, and this is of graver import than fraud or guile, which belong to theft. Hence the *Reply* to the *First Objection* is evident.

Reply Obj. 2. Men who adhere to sensible things think more of external strength which is evidenced in robbery than of internal virtue which is forfeit through sin, wherefore they are less ashamed of robbery than of theft.

Reply Obj. 3. Although more persons may be injured by theft than by robbery, yet more grievous injuries may be inflicted by robbery than by theft, for which reason also robbery is more odious.

QUESTION 77 [a]

OF CHEATING, WHICH IS COMMITTED IN BUYING AND SELLING

FIRST ARTICLE

WHETHER IT IS LAWFUL TO SELL A THING FOR MORE THAN ITS WORTH?

We proceed thus to the First Article:

Objection 1. It would seem that it is lawful to sell a thing for more than its worth. In the commutations of human life civil laws determine that which is just. Now according to these laws it is just for buyer and seller to deceive one another,[1] and this occurs by the seller selling a thing for more than its worth and the buyer buying a thing for less than its worth. Therefore it is lawful to sell a thing for more than its worth.

Obj. 2. Further, that which is common to all would seem to be natural and not sinful. Now Augustine relates that the saying of a certain jester was accepted by all, "You wish to buy for a song and to sell at a premium," [1a] which agrees with the saying of Proverbs xx. 14: "It is naught, it is naught, saith every buyer; and when he is gone away, then he will boast." Therefore it is lawful to sell a thing for more than its worth.

Obj. 3. Further, it does not seem unlawful if that which honesty demands be done by mutual agreement. Now, according to the Philosopher, in the friendship which is based on utility the amount of the recompense for a favor received should depend on the utility accruing to the receiver;[2] and this utility sometimes is worth more than the thing given, for instance if the receiver be in great need of that thing, whether for the purpose of avoiding a danger or of deriving some particular benefit. Therefore, in contracts of buying

[a] [Q. 77 consists of four articles, of which only the first article is here reprinted.]

and selling, it is lawful to give a thing in return for more than its worth.

On the contrary, It is written: "[In] all things . . . whatsoever you would that men should do to you, do you also to them."[3] But no man wishes to buy a thing for more than its worth. Therefore no man should sell a thing to another man for more than its worth.

I answer that, It is altogether sinful to have recourse to deceit in order to sell a thing for more than its just price, because this is to deceive one's neighbor so as to injure him. Hence Cicero says: "Contracts should be entirely free from double-dealing; the seller must not impose upon the bidder, nor the buyer upon one that bids against him."[4]

But, apart from fraud, we may speak of buying and selling in two ways. First, as considered in themselves, and from this point of view buying and selling seem to be established for the common advantage of both parties, one of whom requires that which belongs to the other, and vice versa, as the Philosopher states.[5] Now whatever is established for the common advantage should not be more of a burden to one party than to another, and consequently all contracts between them should observe equality of thing and thing. Again, the [quantity][b] of a thing that comes into human use is measured by the price given for it, for which purpose money was invented, as stated in *Ethics* v. 5. Therefore if either the price exceed the quantity of the thing's worth, or, conversely, the thing exceed the price, there is no longer the equality of justice; and consequently, to sell a thing for more than its worth, or to buy it for less than its worth, is in itself unjust and unlawful.

Secondly, we may speak of buying and selling considered as accidentally tending to the advantage of one party and to the disadvantage of the other; for instance, when a man has great need of a certain thing, while another man will suffer if he be without it. In such a case the just price will depend not only on the thing sold, but on the loss which the sale brings on the seller. And thus it will be lawful to sell a thing for more than it is worth in itself, though the price paid be not more than it is worth to the owner. Yet if the one man derive a great advantage by becoming possessed

[b] D.F. Tr.: quality.

of the other man's property and the seller be not at a loss through being without that thing, the latter ought not to raise the price, because the advantage accruing to the buyer is not due to the seller, but to a circumstance affecting the buyer. Now no man should sell what is not his, though he may charge for the loss he suffers.

On the other hand, if a man find that he derives great advantage from something he has bought, he may, of his own accord, pay the seller something over and above; and this pertains to his honesty.

Reply Obj. 1. As stated above (I-II, Q. 96, A. 2), human law is given to the people among whom there are many lacking virtue, and it is not given to the virtuous alone. Hence human law was unable to forbid all that is contrary to virtue; and it suffices for it to prohibit whatever is destructive of human intercourse, while it treats other matters as though they were lawful, not by approving of them, but by not punishing them. Accordingly, if without employing deceit the seller disposes of his goods for more than their worth, or the buyer obtains them for less than their worth, the law looks upon this as licit and provides no punishment for so doing unless the excess be too great, because then even human law demands restitution to be made, for instance, if a man be deceived in regard of more than half the amount of the just price of a thing.[6]

On the other hand the divine law leaves nothing unpunished that is contrary to virtue. Hence, according to the divine law, it is reckoned unlawful if the equality of justice be not observed in buying and selling; and he who has received more than he ought must make compensation to him that has suffered loss, if the loss be considerable. I add this condition, because the just price of things is not fixed with mathematical precision, but depends on a kind of estimate, so that a slight addition or subtraction would not seem to destroy the equality of justice.

Reply Obj. 2. As Augustine says, "this jester, either by looking into himself or by his experience of others, thought that all men were inclined to wish to buy for a song and sell at a premium. But since in reality this is wicked, it is in every man's power to acquire that justice whereby he may resist and overcome this inclination." [7] And then he gives the example of a man who gave the just price for a book to a man who through ignorance asked a low price for it.

Hence it is evident that this common desire is not from nature but from vice, wherefore it is common to many who walk along the broad road of sin.

Reply Obj. 3. In commutative justice we consider chiefly real equality. On the other hand, in friendship based on utility we consider equality of usefulness, so that the recompense should depend on the usefulness accruing, whereas in buying it should be equal to the thing bought.

QUESTION 78

OF THE SIN OF USURY

(*In Four Articles*)

WE must now consider the sin of usury, which is committed in loans; and under this head there are four points of inquiry: (1) Whether it is a sin to take money as a price for money lent, which is to receive usury? (2) Whether it is lawful to lend money for any other kind of consideration, by way of payment for the loan? (3) Whether a man is bound to restore just gains derived from money taken in usury? (4) Whether it is lawful to borrow money under a condition of usury?

FIRST ARTICLE

WHETHER IT IS A SIN TO TAKE USURY FOR MONEY LENT?

We proceed thus to the First Article:

Objection 1. It would seem that it is not a sin to take usury for money lent. For no man sins through following the example of Christ. But our Lord said of Himself: "At My coming I might have exacted it," i.e. the money lent, "with usury." [1] Therefore it is not a sin to take usury for lending money.

Obj. 2. Further, according to Psalm xviii. 8, "The law of the Lord is unspotted," because, to wit, it forbids sin. Now usury of a kind is allowed in the divine law, according to Deuteronomy xxiii. 19-20, "Thou shalt not fenerate [a] to thy brother money, nor corn, nor any other thing, but to the stranger"; nay more, it is even promised as a reward for the observance of the Law, according to Deuteronomy xxviii. 12: "Thou shalt fenerate to many

---

[a] *Faeneraberis:* Thou shalt lend upon usury. The Douay version has simply "lend." The objection lays stress on the word *faeneraberis;* hence the necessity of rendering it by "fenerate."—D.F.

nations and shalt not borrow of any one." Therefore it is not a sin to take usury.

Obj. 3. Further, in human affairs justice is determined by civil laws. Now civil law allows usury to be taken. Therefore it seems to be lawful.

Obj. 4. Further, the counsels are not binding under sin. But, among other counsels we find: "Lend, hoping for nothing thereby." [2] Therefore it is not a sin to take usury.

Obj. 5. Further, it does not seem to be in itself sinful to accept a price for doing what one is not bound to do. But one who has money is not bound in every case to lend it to his neighbor. Therefore it is lawful for him sometimes to accept a price for lending it.

Obj. 6. Further, silver made into coins does not differ specifically from silver made into vessels. But it is lawful to accept a price for the loan of a silver vessel. Therefore it is also lawful to accept a price for the loan of a silver coin. Therefore usury is not in itself a sin.

Obj. 7. Further, anyone may lawfully accept a thing which its owner freely gives him. Now he who accepts the loan freely gives the usury. Therefore he who lends may lawfully take the usury.

On the contrary, It is written: "If thou lend money to any of [my] [b] people that is poor, that dwelleth with thee, thou shalt not be hard upon them as an extortioner, nor oppress them with usuries." [3]

I answer that, To take usury for money lent is unjust in itself, because this is to sell what does not exist, and this evidently leads to inequality which is contrary to justice.

In order to make this evident, we must observe that there are certain things the use of which consists in their consumption: thus we consume wine when we use it for drink, and we consume wheat when we use it for food. Wherefore in suchlike things the use of the thing must not be reckoned apart from the thing itself, and whoever is granted the use of the thing is granted the thing itself; and for this reason, to lend things of this kind is to transfer the ownership. Accordingly, if a man wanted to sell wine separately from the use of the wine, he would be selling the same

[b] D.F. Tr.: thy.

thing twice, or he would be selling what does not exist, wherefore he would evidently commit a sin of injustice. In like manner he commits an injustice who lends wine or wheat and asks for double payment, viz. one, the return of the thing in equal measure, the other, the price of the use, which is called usury.

On the other hand there are things the use of which does not consist in their consumption: thus to use a house is to dwell in it, not to destroy it. Wherefore in such things both may be granted; for instance, one man may hand over to another the ownership of his house while reserving to himself the use of it for a time, or vice versa, he may grant the use of the house while retaining the ownership. For this reason a man may lawfully make a charge for the use of his house and, besides this, revendicate the house from the person to whom he has granted its use, as happens in renting and letting a house.

Now money, according to the Philosopher,[4] was invented chiefly for the purpose of exchange, and consequently the proper and principal use of money is its consumption or alienation whereby it is sunk in exchange. Hence it is by its very nature unlawful to take payment for the use of money lent, which payment is known as usury; and just as a man is bound to restore other ill-gotten goods, so is he bound to restore the money which he has taken in usury.

Reply Obj. 1. In this passage usury must be taken figuratively for the increase of spiritual goods which God exacts from us, for He wishes us ever to advance in the goods which we receive from Him; and this is for our own profit, not for His.

Reply Obj. 2. The Jews were forbidden to take usury from their brethren, i.e. from other Jews. By this we are given to understand that to take usury from any man is evil simply, because we ought to treat every man as our neighbor and brother, especially in the state of the Gospel, whereto all are called. Hence it is said without any distinction in Psalm xiv. 5: "He that hath not put out his money to usury," and:[5] "Who hath not taken usury."[c] They were permitted, however, to take usury from for-

[c] Vulg.: If a man . . . hath not lent upon money, nor taken any increase . . . he is just.

eigners, not as though it were lawful, but in order to avoid a greater
evil, lest, to wit, through avarice to which they were prone according to Isaias lvi. 11, they should take usury from the Jews
who were worshippers of God.

Where we find it promised to them as a reward, "Thou shalt
fenerate to many nations," etc., fenerating is to be taken in a
broad sense for lending, as in Ecclesiasticus xxix. 10, where we
read: "Many have refused to fenerate, not out of wickedness,"
i.e. they would not lend. Accordingly the Jews are promised in reward an abundance of wealth, so that they would be able to lend
to others.

Reply Obj. 3. Human laws leave certain things unpunished, on
account of the condition of those who are imperfect and who would
be deprived of many advantages if all sins were strictly forbidden
and punishments appointed for them. Wherefore human law has
permitted usury, not that it looks upon usury as harmonizing with
justice, but lest the advantage of many should be hindered. Hence
it is that in civil law it is stated that "those things, according to
natural reason and civil law, which are consumed by being used
do not admit of usufruct," and that "the senate did not (nor could
it) appoint a usufruct to such things, but established a quasi-
usufruct," 6 namely, by permitting usury. Moreover the Philosopher, led by natural reason, says that "to make money by usury
is exceedingly unnatural." 7

Reply Obj. 4. A man is not always bound to lend, and for this
reason it is placed among the counsels. Yet it is a matter of precept not to seek profit by lending, although it may be called a
matter of counsel in comparison with the maxims of the Pharisees,
who deemed some kinds of usury to be lawful, just as love of one's
enemies is a matter of counsel. Or again, He speaks here not of
the hope of usurious gain, but of the hope which is put in man.
For we ought not to lend or do any good deed through hope in
man, but only through hope in God.

Reply Obj. 5. He that is not bound to lend may accept repayment for what he has done, but he must not exact more. Now he
is repaid according to equality of justice if he is repaid as much
as he has lent. Wherefore if he exacts more for the usufruct of a

thing which has no other use but the consumption of its substance, he exacts a price of something non-existent, and so his exaction is unjust.

Reply Obj. 6. The principal use of a silver vessel is not its consumption, and so one may lawfully sell its use while retaining one's ownership of it. On the other hand the principal use of silver money is sinking it in exchange, so that it is not lawful to sell its use and at the same time expect the restitution of the amount lent. It must be observed, however, that the secondary use of silver vessels may be an exchange, and such use may not be lawfully sold. In like manner there may be some secondary use of silver money; for instance, a man might lend coins for show, or to be used as security [and the use of such money may lawfully be sold].

Reply Obj. 7. He who gives usury does not give it voluntarily simply, but under a certain necessity in so far as he needs to borrow money which the owner is unwilling to lend without usury.

SECOND ARTICLE

WHETHER IT IS LAWFUL TO ASK FOR ANY OTHER KIND OF CONSIDERATION FOR MONEY LENT?

We proceed thus to the Second Article:

Objection 1. It would seem that one may ask for some other kind of consideration for money lent. For everyone may lawfully seek to indemnify himself. Now sometimes a man suffers loss through lending money. Therefore he may lawfully ask for or even exact something else besides the money lent.

Obj. 2. Further, as stated in *Ethics* v. 5, one is in duty bound by a point of honor to repay anyone who has done us a favor. Now to lend money to one who is in straits is to do him a favor for which he should be grateful. Therefore the recipient of a loan is bound by a natural debt to repay something. Now it does not seem unlawful to bind oneself to an obligation of the natural law. Therefore it is not unlawful, in lending money to anyone, to demand some sort of compensation as a condition of the loan.

Obj. 3. Further, just as there is real remuneration, so is there verbal remuneration and remuneration by service, as a gloss says on Isaias xxxiii. 15, "Blessed is he that shaketh his hands from all bribes." d Now it is lawful to accept service or praise from one to whom one has lent money. Therefore in like manner it is lawful to accept any other kind of remuneration.

Obj. 4. Further, seemingly the relation of gift to gift is the same as of loan to loan. But it is lawful to accept money for money given. Therefore it is lawful to accept repayment by loan in return for a loan granted.

Obj. 5. Further, the lender, by transferring his ownership of a sum of money, removes the money further from himself than he who entrusts it to a merchant or craftsman. Now it is lawful to receive interest for money entrusted to a merchant or craftsman. Therefore it is also lawful to receive interest for money lent.

Obj. 6. Further, a man may accept a pledge for money lent, the use of which pledge he might sell for a price, as when a man mortgages his land or the house wherein he dwells. Therefore it is lawful to receive interest for money lent.

Obj. 7. Further, it sometimes happens that a man raises the price of his goods under guise of loan, or buys another's goods at a low figure, or raises his price through delay in being paid, and lowers his price that he may be paid the sooner. Now in all these cases there seems to be payment for a loan of money, nor does it appear to be manifestly illicit. Therefore it seems to be lawful to expect or exact some consideration for money lent.

On the contrary, Among other conditions requisite in a just man it is stated that he "hath not taken usury and increase." 8

I answer that, According to the Philosopher, a thing is reckoned as money "if its value can be measured by money." 9 Consequently, just as it is a sin against justice to take money, by tacit or express agreement, in return for lending money or anything else that is consumed by being used, so also is it a like sin by tacit or express agreement to receive anything whose price can be measured by money. Yet there would be no sin in receiving something of the kind, not as exacting it, nor yet as though it were due on

d Vulg.: Which of you shall dwell with everlasting burnings? . . . He that shaketh his hands from all bribes.

account of some agreement tacit or expressed, but as a gratuity; since, even before lending the money, one could accept a gratuity, nor is one in a worse condition through lending.

On the other hand, it is lawful to exact compensation for a loan in respect of such things as are not appreciated by a measure of money, for instance, benevolence, and love for the lender, and so forth.

Reply Obj. 1. A lender may without sin enter an agreement with the borrower for compensation for the loss he incurs of something he ought to have, for this is not to sell the use of money but to avoid a loss. It may also happen that the borrower avoids a greater loss than the lender incurs, wherefore the borrower may repay the lender with what he has gained. But the lender cannot enter an agreement for compensation through the fact that he makes no profit out of his money; because he must not sell that which he has not yet and may be prevented in many ways from having.

Reply Obj. 2. Repayment for a favor may be made in two ways. In one way, as a debt of justice; and to such a debt a man may be bound by a fixed contract, and its amount is measured according to the favor received. Wherefore the borrower of money or any such thing the use of which is its consumption is not bound to repay more than he received in loan; and consequently it is against justice if he be obliged to pay back more. In another way a man's obligation to repayment for favor received is based on a debt of friendship, and the nature of this debt depends more on the feeling with which the favor was conferred than on the greatness of the favor itself. This debt does not carry with it a civil obligation involving a kind of necessity that would exclude the spontaneous nature of such a repayment.

Reply Obj. 3. If a man were, in return for money lent, as though there had been an agreement tacit or expressed, to expect or exact repayment in the shape of some remuneration of service or words, it would be the same as if he expected or exacted some real remuneration, because both can be priced at a money value, as may be seen in the case of those who offer for hire the labor which they exercise by work or by tongue. If on the other hand the remuneration by service or words be given, not as an obligation, but as a favor which is not to be appreciated at a money value, it is lawful to take, exact, and expect it.

Reply Obj. 4. Money cannot be sold for a greater sum than the amount lent, which has to be paid back; nor should the loan be made with a demand or expectation of aught else but of a feeling of benevolence, which cannot be priced at a pecuniary value, and which can be the basis of a spontaneous loan. Now the obligation to lend in return at some future time is repugnant to such a feeling, because again an obligation of this kind has its pecuniary value. Consequently it is lawful for the lender to borrow something else at the same time, but it is unlawful for him to bind the borrower to grant him a loan at some future time.

Reply Obj. 5. He who lends money transfers the ownership of the money to the borrower. Hence the borrower holds the money at his own risk and is bound to pay it all back; wherefore the lender must not exact more. On the other hand, he that entrusts his money to a merchant or craftsman so as to form a kind of society does not transfer the ownership of his money to them, for it remains his, so that at his risk the merchant speculates with it, or the craftsman uses it for his craft, and consequently he may lawfully demand, as something belonging to him, part of the profits derived from his money.

Reply Obj. 6. If a man in return for money lent to him pledges something that can be valued at a price, the lender must allow for the use of that thing toward the repayment of the loan. Else if he wishes the gratuitous use of that thing in addition to repayment, it is the same as if he took money for lending, and that is usury; unless perhaps it were such a thing as friends are wont to lend to one another gratis, as in the case of the loan of a book.

Reply Obj. 7. If a man wish to sell his goods at a higher price than that which is just, so that he may wait for the buyer to pay, it is manifestly a case of usury; because this waiting for the payment of the price has the character of a loan, so that whatever he demands beyond the just price in consideration of this delay is like a price for a loan, which pertains to usury. In like manner if a buyer wishes to buy goods at a lower price than what is just, for the reason that he pays for the goods before they can be delivered, it is a sin of usury; because again this anticipated payment of money has the character of a loan, the price of which is the rebate on the just price of the goods sold. On the other hand, if a man wishes to allow a rebate on the just price in order that he may have his money sooner, he is not guilty of the sin of usury.

THIRD ARTICLE

WHETHER A MAN IS BOUND TO RESTORE WHATEVER PROFITS HE HAS MADE OUT OF MONEY GOTTEN BY USURY?

We proceed thus to the Third Article:

Objection 1. It would seem that a man is bound to restore whatever profits he has made out of money gotten by usury. For the Apostle says: "If the root be holy, so are the branches." [10] Therefore, likewise, if the root be rotten, so are the branches. But the root was infected with usury. Therefore whatever profit is made therefrom is infected with usury. Therefore he is bound to restore it.

Obj. 2. Further, it is laid down: "Property accruing from usury must be sold, and the price repaid to the persons from whom the usury was extorted." [11] Therefore, likewise, whatever else is acquired from usurious money must be restored.

Obj. 3. Further, that which a man buys with the proceeds of usury is due to him by reason of the money he paid for it. Therefore he has no more right to the thing purchased than to the money he paid. But he was bound to restore the money gained through usury. Therefore he is also bound to restore what he acquired with it.

On the contrary, A man may lawfully hold what he has lawfully acquired. Now that which is acquired by the proceeds of usury is sometimes lawfully acquired. Therefore it may be lawfully retained.

I answer that, As stated above (A. 1), there are certain things whose use is their consumption, and which do not admit of usufruct according to law (*ibid., ad* 3). Wherefore if suchlike things be extorted by means of usury, for instance, money, wheat, wine, and so forth, the lender is not bound to restore more than he received (since what is acquired by such things is the fruit not of the thing but of human industry), unless indeed the other party by losing some of his own goods be injured through the lender retaining them, for then he is bound to make good the loss.

On the other hand, there are certain things whose use is not their consumption; such things admit of usufruct, for instance house or land property, and so forth. Wherefore if a man has by usury extorted from another his house or land, he is bound to restore not only the house or land but also the fruits accruing to him therefrom, since they are the fruits of things owned by another man and consequently are due to him.

Reply Obj. 1. The root has not only the character of matter, as money made by usury has, but has also somewhat the character of an active cause in so far as it adminsters nourishment. Hence the comparison fails.

Reply Obj. 2. Further, property acquired from usury does not belong to the person who paid usury, but to the person who bought it. Yet he that paid usury has a certain claim on that property just as he has on the other goods of the usurer. Hence it is not prescribed that such property should be assigned to the persons who paid usury, since the property is perhaps worth more than what they paid in usury, but it is commanded that the property be sold and the price be restored, of course according to the amount taken in usury.

Reply Obj. 3. The proceeds of money taken in usury are due to the person who acquired them, not by reason of the usurious money as instrumental cause, but on account of his own industry as principal cause. Wherefore he has more right to the goods acquired with usurious money than to the usurious money itself.

FOURTH ARTICLE

WHETHER IT IS LAWFUL TO BORROW MONEY UNDER A CONDITION OF USURY?

We proceed thus to the Fourth Article:

Objection 1. It would seem that it is not lawful to borrow money under a condition of usury. For the Apostle says that they "are worthy of death . . . not only they that do" these sins, "but they also that consent to them that do them." [12] Now he that borrows money under a condition of usury consents in the sin of the usurer and gives him an occasion of sin. Therefore he sins also.

Obj. 2. Further, for no temporal advantage ought one to give another an occasion of committing a sin, for this pertains to active scandal, which is always sinful, as stated above. [13] Now he that seeks to borrow from a usurer gives him an occasion of sin. Therefore he is not to be excused on account of any temporal advantage.

Obj. 3. Further, it seems no less necessary sometimes to deposit one's money with a usurer than to borrow from him. Now it seems altogether unlawful to deposit one's money with a usurer, even as it would be unlawful to deposit one's sword with a madman, a maiden with a libertine, or food with a glutton. Neither therefore is it lawful to borrow from a usurer.

On the contrary, He that suffers injury does not sin, according to the Philosopher, [14] wherefore justice is not a mean between two vices, as stated in the same book. [15] Now a usurer sins by doing an injury to the person who borrows from him under a condition of usury. Therefore he that accepts a loan under a condition of usury does not sin.

I answer that, It is by no means lawful to induce a man to sin, yet it is lawful to make use of another's sin for a good end, since even God uses all sin for some good since He draws some good from every evil, as stated in the *Enchiridion* (xi).[e] Hence when Publicola asked whether it were lawful to make use of an oath taken by a man swearing by false gods (which is a manifest sin, for he gives divine honor to them), Augustine answered that he

[e] [St. Augustine.]

who uses, not for a bad but for a good purpose, the oath of a man that swears by false gods is a party, not to his sin of swearing by demons, but to his good compact whereby he kept his word. [16] If however he were to induce him to swear by false gods, he would sin.

Accordingly we must also answer to the question in point that it is by no means lawful to induce a man to lend under a condition of usury; yet it is lawful to borrow for usury from a man who is ready to do so and is a usurer by profession, provided the borrower have a good end in view, such as the relief of his own or another's need. Thus, too, it is lawful for a man who has fallen among thieves to point out his property to them (which they sin in taking) in order to save his life, after the example of the ten men who said to Ismahel: "Kill us not; for we have stores in the field." [17]

Reply Obj. 1. He who borrows for usury does not consent to the usurer's sin but makes use of it. Nor is it the usurer's acceptance of usury that pleases him, but his lending, which is good.

Reply Obj. 2. He who borrows for usury gives the usurer an occasion, not for taking usury, but for lending; it is the usurer who finds an occasion of sin in the malice of his heart. Hence there is passive scandal on his part, while there is no active scandal on the part of the person who seeks to borrow. Nor is this passive scandal a reason why the other person should desist from borrowing if he is in need, since this passive scandal arises not from weakness or ignorance but from malice.

Reply Obj. 3. If one were to entrust one's money to a usurer lacking other means of practicing usury, or [with the intention of affording the usurer the possibility of making greater profits by his usury],ᶠ one would be giving a sinner matter for sin, so that one would be a participator in his guilt. If, on the other hand, the usurer to whom one entrusts one's money has other means of practicing usury, there is no sin in entrusting it to him that it may be in safer keeping, since this is to use a sinner for a good purpose.

ᶠ D.F. Tr.: with the intention of making a greater profit from his money by reason of the usury.

QUESTION 104

OF OBEDIENCE

(*In Six Articles*)

WE must now consider obedience, under which head there are six points of inquiry: (1) Whether one man is bound to obey another? (2) Whether obedience is a special virtue? (3) Of its comparison with other virtues? (4) Whether God must be obeyed in all things? (5) Whether subjects are bound to obey their superiors in all things? (6) Whether the faithful are bound to obey the secular power?

FIRST ARTICLE

WHETHER ONE MAN IS BOUND TO OBEY ANOTHER?

We proceed thus to the First Article:

Objection 1. It seems that one man is not bound to obey another. For nothing should be done contrary to the divine ordinance. Now God has so ordered that man is ruled by his own counsel, according to Ecclesiasticus xv. 14: "God made man from the beginning, and left him in the hand of his own counsel." Therefore one man is not bound to obey another.

Obj. 2. Further, if one man were bound to obey another, he would have to look upon the will of the person commanding him as being his rule of conduct. Now God's will alone, which is always right, is a rule of human conduct. Therefore man is bound to obey none but God.

Obj. 3. Further, the more gratuitous the service the more is it acceptable. Now what a man does out of duty is not gratuitous. Therefore if a man were bound in duty to obey others in doing good deeds, for this very reason his good deeds would be rendered less acceptable through being done out of obedience. Therefore one man is not bound to obey another.

159

On the contrary, It is prescribed: "Obey your prelates and be subject to them." [1]

I answer that, Just as the actions of natural things proceed from natural powers, so do human actions proceed from the human will. In natural things it behooved the higher to move the lower to their actions by the excellence of the natural power bestowed on them by God; and so in human affairs also the higher must move the lower by their will in virtue of a divinely established authority. Now to move by reason and will is to command. Wherefore just as in virtue of the divinely established natural order the lower natural things need to be subject to the movement of the higher, so too in human affairs, in virtue of the order of natural and divine law, inferiors are bound to obey their superiors.

Reply Obj. 1. God left man in the hand of his own counsel, not as though it were lawful to him to do whatever he will, but because, unlike irrational creatures, he is not compelled by natural necessity to do what he ought to do but is left the free choice proceeding from his own counsel. And just as he has to proceed on his own counsel in doing other things, so too has he in the point of obeying his superiors. For Gregory says: "When we humbly give way to another's voice, we overcome ourselves in our own hearts." [2]

Reply Obj. 2. The will of God is the first rule whereby all rational wills are regulated; and to this rule one will approaches more than another, according to a divinely appointed order. Hence the will of the one man who issues a command may be as a second rule to the will of this other man who obeys him.

Reply Obj. 3. A thing may be deemed gratuitous in two ways. In one way on the part of the deed itself, because, to wit, one is not bound to do it; in another way on the part of the doer, because he does it of his own free will. Now a deed is rendered virtuous, praiseworthy, and meritorious chiefly according as it proceeds from the will. Wherefore although obedience be a duty, if one obey with a prompt will one's merit is not for that reason diminished, especially before God, Who sees not only the outward deed but also the inward will.

SECOND ARTICLE

WHETHER OBEDIENCE IS A SPECIAL VIRTUE?

We proceed thus to the Second Article:

Objection 1. It seems that obedience is not a special virtue. For disobedience is contrary to obedience. But disobedience is a general sin, because Ambrose says that "to sin is to disobey the divine law." [3] Therefore obedience is not a special virtue.

Obj. 2. Further, every special virtue is either theological or moral. But obedience is not a theological virtue, since it is not comprised under faith, hope, or charity. Nor is it a moral virtue, since it does not hold the mean between excess and deficiency, for the more obedient one is, the more is one praised. Therefore obedience is not a special virtue.

Obj. 3. Further, Gregory says that "obedience is the more meritorious and praiseworthy the less it holds its own." [4] But every special virtue is the more to be praised the more it holds its own, since virtue requires a man to exercise his will and choice, as stated in *Ethics* ii. 4. Therefore obedience is not a special virtue.

Obj. 4. Further, virtues differ in species according to their objects. Now the object of obedience would seem to be the command of a superior, of which, apparently, there are as many kinds as there are degrees of superiority. Therefore obedience is a general virtue, comprising many special virtues.

On the contrary, Obedience is reckoned by some to be a part of justice, as stated above. [5]

I answer that, A special virtue is assigned to all good deeds that have a special reason of praise; for it belongs properly to virtue to render a deed good. Now obedience to a superior is due in accordance with the divinely established order of things, as shown above (A. 1), and therefore it is a good, since good consists in mode, species, and order, as Augustine states. [6] Again, this act has a special aspect of praiseworthiness by reason of its object. For while subjects have many obligations toward their superiors, this one, that they are bound to obey their commands, stands out as special among the rest. Wherefore obedience is a special virtue,

and its specific object is a command tacit or express; because the
superior's will, however it become known, is a tacit precept, and
a man's obedience seems to be all the more prompt forasmuch as
by obeying he forestalls the express command as soon as he understands his superior's will.

Reply Obj. 1. Nothing prevents the one same material object
from admitting two special aspects to which two special virtues
correspond: thus a soldier, by defending his king's fortress, fulfills
both an act of fortitude, by facing the danger of death for a good
end, and an act of justice, by rendering due service to his lord.
Accordingly the aspect of precept, which obedience considers, occurs in acts of all virtues, but not in all acts of virtue, since not all
acts of virtue are a matter of precept, as stated above.[7] Moreover certain things are sometimes a matter of precept and pertain
to no other virtue, such things, for instance, as are not evil except
because they are forbidden. Wherefore if obedience be taken in its
proper sense as considering formally and intentionally the aspect
of precept, it will be a special virtue and disobedience a special sin;
because in this way it is requisite for obedience that one perform
an act of justice or of some other virtue with the intention of fulfilling a precept, and for disobedience that one treat the precept
with actual contempt. On the other hand if obedience be taken in
a wide sense for the performance of any action that may be a matter of precept, and disobedience for the omission of that action
through any intention whatever, then obedience will be a general
virtue, and disobedience a general sin.

Reply Obj. 2. Obedience is not a theological virtue, for its direct object is not God but the precept of any superior, whether expressed or inferred, namely, a simple word of the superior indicating his will, and which the obedient subject obeys promptly,
according to Titus iii. 1: "Admonish them to be subject to princes
and to obey at a word," etc.

It is, however, a moral virtue, since it is a part of justice, and it
observes the mean between excess and deficiency. Excess thereof
is measured in respect, not of quantity, but of other circumstances,
in so far as a man obeys either whom he ought not or in matters
wherein he ought not to obey, as we have stated above regarding

religion.[8] We may also reply that as in justice excess is in the person who retains another's property and deficiency in the person who does not receive his due, according to the Philosopher; [9] so too obedience observes the mean between excess on the part of him who fails to pay due obedience to his superior, since he exceeds in fulfilling his own will, and deficiency on the part of the superior, who does not receive obedience. Wherefore in this way obedience will be a mean between two forms of wickedness, as was stated above concerning justice (Q. 58, A. 10).

Reply Obj. 3. Obedience, like every virtue, requires the will to be prompt toward its proper object, but not toward that which is repugnant to it. Now the proper object of obedience is a precept, and this proceeds from another's will. Wherefore obedience makes a man's will prompt in fulfilling the will of another, the maker, namely, of the precept. If that which is prescribed to him is willed by him for its own sake apart from its being prescribed, as happens in agreeable matters, he tends toward it at once by his own will and seems to comply, not on account of the precept, but on account of his own will. But if that which is prescribed is nowise willed for its own sake, but considered in itself is repugnant to his own will, as happens in disagreeable matters, then it is quite evident that it is not fulfilled except on account of the precept. Hence Gregory says that "obedience perishes or diminishes when it holds its own in agreeable matters," [10] because, to wit, one's own will seems to tend principally, not to the accomplishment of the precept, but to the fulfillment of one's own desire; but that "it increases in disagreeable or difficult matters," because there one's own will tends to nothing beside the precept. Yet this must be understood as regards outward appearances; for on the other hand, according to the judgment of God, Who searches the heart, it may happen that even in agreeable matters obedience, while holding its own, is none the less praiseworthy, provided the will of him that obeys tend no less devotedly [11] to the fulfillment of the precept.

Reply Obj. 4. Reverence regards directly the person that excels; wherefore it admits of various species according to the various aspects of excellence. Obedience on the other hand regards the precept of the person that excels and therefore admits of only one aspect.

And since obedience is due to a person's precept on account of reverence to him, it follows that obedience to a man is of one species, though the causes from which it proceeds differ specifically.

THIRD ARTICLE

WHETHER OBEDIENCE IS THE GREATEST OF THE VIRTUES?

We proceed thus to the Third Article:

Objection 1. It seems that obedience is the greatest of the virtues. For it is written: "Obedience is better than sacrifices." [12] Now the offering of sacrifices belongs to religion, which is the greatest of all moral virtues, as shown above.[13] Therefore obedience is the greatest of all virtues.

Obj. 2. Further, Gregory says that "obedience is the only virtue that ingrafts virtues in the soul and protects them when ingrafted." [14] Now the cause is greater than the effect. Therefore obedience is greater than all the virtues.

Obj. 3. Further, Gregory says that "evil should never be done out of obedience; yet sometimes for the sake of obedience we should lay aside the good we are doing." [15] Now one does not lay aside a thing except for something better. Therefore obedience, for whose sake the good of other virtues is set aside, is better than other virtues.

On the contrary, Obedience deserves praise because it proceeds from charity; for Gregory says that "obedience should be practiced, not out of servile fear, but from a sense of charity, not through fear of punishment, but through love of justice." [16] Therefore charity is a greater virtue than obedience.

I answer that, Just as sin consists in man contemning God and adhering to mutable things, so the merit of a virtuous act consists in man contemning created goods and adhering to God as his end. Now the end is greater than that which is directed to the end. Therefore if a man contemns created goods in order that he may adhere to God, his virtue derives greater praise from his adhering to God than from his contemning earthly things. And so those, namely, the theological, virtues whereby he adheres to God in Himself are greater than the moral virtues whereby he holds in contempt some earthly thing in order to adhere to God.

Among the moral virtues, the greater the thing which a man contemns that he may adhere to God, the greater the virtue. Now there are three kinds of human goods that man may contemn for God's sake. The lowest of these are external goods, the goods of the body take the middle place, and the highest are the goods of the soul; and among these the chief, in a way, is the will, in so far as by his will man makes use of all other goods. Therefore, properly speaking, the virtue of obedience, whereby we contemn our own will for God's sake, is more praiseworthy than the other moral virtues, which contemn other goods for the sake of God.

Hence Gregory says that "obedience is rightly preferred to sacrifices, because by sacrifices another's body is slain, whereas by obedience we slay our own will." [17] Wherefore even any other acts of virtue are meritorious before God through being performed out of obedience to God's will. For were one to suffer even martyrdom or to give all one's goods to the poor, unless one directed these things to the fulfillment of the divine will, which pertains directly to obedience, they could not be meritorious; as neither would they be if they were done without charity, which cannot exist apart from obedience. For it is written: "He who saith that he knoweth God, and keepeth not His commandments, is a liar . . . but he that keepeth His word, in him in very deed the charity of God is perfected": [18] and this because friends have the same likes and dislikes.

Reply Obj. 1. Obedience proceeds from reverence, which pays worship and honor to a superior, and in this respect it is contained under different virtues, although considered in itself as regarding the aspect of precept, it is one special virtue. Accordingly in so far as it proceeds from reverence for a superior, it is contained, in a way, under observance; while in so far as it proceeds from reverence for one's parents, it is contained under piety; and in so far as it proceeds from reverence for God, it comes under religion and pertains to devotion, which is the principal act of religion. Wherefore from this point of view it is more praiseworthy to obey God than to offer sacrifice, as well as because "in a sacrifice we slay another's body, whereas by obedience we slay our own will," as Gregory says.[19] As to the special case in which Samuel spoke, it would have been better for Saul to obey God than to offer in sacrifice the fat animals of the Amalekites against the commandment of God.

Reply Obj. 2. All acts of virtue, in so far as they come under a precept, belong to obedience. Wherefore according as acts of virtue act causally or dispositively toward their generation and preservation, obedience is said to ingraft and protect all virtues. And yet it does not follow that obedience takes precedence of all virtues absolutely, for two reasons. First, because though an act of virtue come under a precept one may nevertheless perform that act of virtue without considering the aspect of precept. Consequently if there be any virtue whose object is naturally prior to the precept, that virtue is said to be naturally prior to obedience. Such a virtue is faith, whereby we come to know the sublime nature of divine authority, by reason of which the power to command is competent to God. Secondly, because infusion of grace and virtues may precede, even in point of time, all virtuous acts; and in this way obedience is not prior to all virtues, neither in point of time nor by nature.

Reply Obj. 3. There are two kinds of good. There is that to which we are bound of necessity, for instance, to love God, and so forth; and by no means may such a good be set aside on account of obedience. But there is another good to which man is not bound of necessity; and this good we ought sometimes to set aside for the sake of obedience to which we are bound of necessity, since we ought not to do good by falling into sin. Yet as Gregory remarks, "he who forbids his subjects any single good must needs allow them many others, lest the souls of those who obey perish utterly from starvation through being deprived of every good." [20] Thus the loss of one good may be compensated by obedience and other goods.

FOURTH ARTICLE

WHETHER GOD OUGHT TO BE OBEYED IN ALL THINGS?

We proceed thus to the Fourth Article:

Objection 1. It seems that God need not be obeyed in all things. For it is written that Our Lord after healing the two blind men commanded them, saying: " 'See that no man know this.' But they going out spread His fame abroad in all that country." [21] Yet they are not blamed for so doing. Therefore it seems that we are not bound to obey God in all things.

Obj. 2. Further, no one is bound to do anything contrary to virtue. Now we find that God commanded certain things contrary to virtue: thus He commanded Abraham to slay his innocent son,[22] and the Jews to steal the property of the Egyptians,[23] which things are contrary to justice; and Osee to take to himself a woman who was an adulteress,[24] and this is contrary to chastity. Therefore God is not to be obeyed in all things.

Obj. 3. Further, whoever obeys God conforms his will to the divine will even as to the thing willed. But we are not bound in all things to conform our will to the divine will as to the thing willed, as stated above.[25] Therefore man is not bound to obey God in all things.

On the contrary, It is written: "All things that the Lord hath spoken we will do, and we will be obedient." [26]

I answer that, As stated above (A. 1), he who obeys is moved by the command of the person he obeys, just as natural things are moved by their motive causes. Now just as God is the first mover of all things that are moved naturally, so too is He the first mover of all wills, as shown above.[27] Therefore just as all natural things are subject to the divine motion by a natural necessity, so too all wills, by a kind of necessity of justice, are bound to obey the divine command.

Reply Obj. 1. Our Lord in telling the blind men to conceal the miracle had no intention of binding them with the force of a divine precept, but, as Gregory says, "gave an example to His servants who follow Him, that they might wish to hide their virtue and yet that it should be proclaimed against their will, in order that others might profit by their example." [28]

Reply Obj. 2. Even as God does nothing contrary to nature (since "the nature of a thing is what God does therein," according to a gloss on Romans xi) and yet does certain things contrary to the wonted course of nature, so too God can command nothing contrary to virtue, since virtue and rectitude of human will consist chiefly in conformity with God's will and obedience to His command, although it be contrary to the wonted mode of virtue. Accordingly, then, the command given to Abraham to slay his innocent son was not contrary to justice, since God is the author of life and death. Nor again was it contrary to justice that He commanded the Jews to take things belonging to the Egyptians, because all things are His, and He gives them to whom He will. Nor was it contrary to chastity that Osee was commanded to take an adulteress, because God Himself is the ordainer of human generation, and the right manner of intercourse with woman is that which He appoints. Hence it is evident that the persons aforesaid did not sin, neither by obeying God nor by willing to obey Him.

Reply Obj. 3. Though man is not always bound to will what God wills, yet he is always bound to will what God wills him to will. This comes to man's knowledge chiefly through God's command, wherefore man is bound to obey God's commands in all things.

FIFTH ARTICLE

WHETHER SUBJECTS ARE BOUND TO OBEY THEIR SUPERIORS IN ALL THINGS?

We proceed thus to the Fifth Article:

Objection 1. It seems that subjects are bound to obey their superiors in all things. For the Apostle says: "Children, obey your parents in all things"; and farther on: "Servants, obey in all things your masters according to the flesh." [29] Therefore in like manner other subjects are bound to obey their superiors in all things.

Obj. 2. Further, superiors stand between God and their subjects, according to Deuteronomy v. 5: "I was the mediator and stood between the Lord and you at that time, to show you His words." Now there is no going from extreme to extreme, except through that which stands between. Therefore the commands of a superior must be esteemed the commands of God, wherefore the Apostle says: "You . . . received me as an angel of God, even as Christ Jesus"; [30] and: "When you had received of us the word of the hearing of God, you received it, not as the word of men, but, as it is indeed, the word of God." [31] Therefore as man is bound to obey God in all things, so is he bound to obey his superiors.

Obj. 3. Further, just as religious in making their profession take vows of chastity and poverty, so do they also vow obedience. Now a religious is bound to observe chastity and poverty in all things. Therefore he is also bound to obey in all things.

On the contrary, It is written: "We ought to obey God rather than men." [32] Now sometimes the things commanded by a superior are against God. Therefore superiors are not to be obeyed in all things.

I answer that, As stated above (AA. 1, 4), he who obeys is moved at the bidding of the person who commands him by a certain necessity of justice, even as a natural thing is moved through the power of its mover by a natural necessity. That a natural thing be not moved by its mover may happen in two ways. First on account of a hindrance arising from the stronger power of some other mover; thus wood is not burned by fire if a stronger force of water intervene. Secondly, through lack of order in the movable with regard to its mover, since, though it is subject to the latter's action in one respect, yet it is not subject thereto in every respect. Thus a humor is sometimes subject to the action of heat as regards being heated, but not as regards being dried up or consumed. In like manner there are two reasons for which a subject may not be bound to obey his superior in all things. First on account of the command of a higher power. For as a gloss says on Romans xiii. 2, "They that resist [a] the power, resist the ordinance of God.[33] If a commissioner issue an order, are you to comply if it is contrary to the bidding of the proconsul? Again if the proconsul command one

[a] Vulg.: He that resisteth.

thing and the emperor another, will you hesitate to disregard the former and serve the latter? Therefore if the emperor commands one thing and God another, you must disregard the former and obey God." Secondly, a subject is not bound to obey his superior if the latter command him to do something wherein he is not subject to him. For Seneca says: "It is wrong to suppose that slavery falls upon the whole man; for the better part of him is excepted. His body is subjected and assigned to his master, but his soul is his own." [34] Consequently in matters touching the internal movement of the will man is not bound to obey his fellow man, but God alone.

Nevertheless man is bound to obey his fellow man in things that have to be done externally by means of the body; and yet, since by nature all men are equal, he is not bound to obey another man in matters touching the nature of the body, for instance, in those relating to the support of his body or the begetting of his children. Wherefore servants are not bound to obey their masters, nor children their parents, in the question of contracting marriage or of remaining in the state of virginity or the like. But in matters concerning the disposal of actions and human affairs a subject is bound to obey his superior within the sphere of his authority; for instance, a soldier must obey his general in matters relating to war, a servant his master in matters touching the execution of the duties of his service, a son his father in matters relating to the conduct of his life and the care of the household, and so forth.

Reply Obj. 1. When the Apostle says "in all things," he refers to matters within the sphere of a father's or master's authority.

Reply Obj. 2. Man is subject to God simply as regards all things, both internal and external, wherefore he is bound to obey Him in all things. On the other hand inferiors are not subject to their superiors in all things, but only in certain things and in a particular way, in respect of which the superior stands between God and his subjects; whereas in respect of other matters the subject is immediately under God, by Whom he is taught either by the natural or by the written law.

Reply Obj. 3. Religious profess obedience as to the regular mode of life, in respect of which they are subject to their superiors; wherefore they are bound to obey in those matters only which may belong to the regular mode of life, and this obedience suffices for salvation. If they be willing to obey even in other matters, this will belong to the superabundance of perfection, provided, however, such things be not contrary to God or to the rule they profess, for obedience in this case would be unlawful.

Accordingly we may distinguish a threefold obedience: one, sufficient for salvation and consisting in obeying when one is bound to obey; secondly, perfect obedience, which obeys in all things lawful; thirdly, indiscreet obedience, which obeys even in matters unlawful.

SIXTH ARTICLE

WHETHER CHRISTIANS ARE BOUND TO OBEY THE SECULAR POWER?

We proceed thus to the Sixth Article:

Objection 1. It seems that Christians are not bound to obey the secular power. For a gloss on Matthew xvii. 25, "Then the children are free," says: "If in every kingdom the children of the king who holds sway over that kingdom are free, then the children of that King, under Whose sway are all kingdoms, should be free in every kingdom." Now Christians, by their faith in Christ, are made children of God, according to John i. 12: "He gave them power to be made the sons of God, to them that believe in His name." Therefore they are not bound to obey the secular power.

Obj. 2. Further, it is written: "You . . . are become dead to the law by the body of Christ," [35] and the law mentioned here is the divine law of the Old Testament. Now human law whereby men are subject to the secular power is of less account than the divine law of the Old Testament. Much more, therefore, since they have become members of Christ's body, are men freed from the law of subjection, whereby they were under the power of secular princes.

Obj. 3. Further, men are not bound to obey robbers, who oppress them with violence. Now Augustine says: "Without justice, what else is a kingdom but a huge robbery?" [36] Since therefore the authority of secular princes is frequently exercised with injustice or owes its origin to some unjust usurpation, it seems that Christians ought not to obey secular princes.

On the contrary, It is written: "Admonish them to be subject to princes and powers"; [37] and: "Be ye subject . . . to every human creature for God's sake, whether it be to the king as excelling or to governors as sent by him." [38]

I answer that, Faith in Christ is the origin and cause of justice, according to Romans iii. 22: "The justice of God by faith of Jesus Christ"; wherefore faith in Christ does not void the order of justice, but strengthens it. Now the order of justice requires that subjects obey their superiors, else the stability of human affairs would cease. Hence faith in Christ does not excuse the faithful from the obligation of obeying secular princes.

Reply Obj. 1. As stated above (A. 5), the subjection whereby one man is bound to another regards the body, not the soul, which retains its liberty. Now, in this state of life we are freed by the grace of Christ from defects of the soul, but not from defects of the body, as the Apostle declares by saying of himself that in his mind he served the law of God, but in his flesh the law of sin. [39] Wherefore those that are made children of God by grace are free from the spiritual bondage of sin, but not from the bodily bondage, whereby they are held bound to earthly masters, as a gloss observes on 1 Timothy vi. 1, "Whosoever are servants under the yoke," etc.

Reply Obj. 2. The Old Law was a figure of the New Testament, and therefore it had to cease on the advent of truth. And the comparison with human law does not stand, because thereby one man is subject to another. Yet man is bound by divine law to obey his fellow man.

Reply Obj. 3. Man is bound to obey secular princes in so far as this is required by the order of justice. Wherefore if the prince's authority is not just but usurped, or if he commands what is unjust, his subjects are not bound to obey him, except perhaps accidentally, in order to avoid scandal or danger.

ON KINGSHIP

(*De Regimine Principum*)

[Selections from Book One]

ON KINGSHIP

[Selections]

CHAPTER ONE

WHAT IS MEANT BY THE WORD "KING"

[3] In all things which are ordered toward an end wherein this or that course may be adopted, some directive principle is needed through which the due end may be reached by the most direct route. A ship, for example, which moves in different directions according to the impulse of the changing winds would never reach its destination were it not brought to port by the skill of the pilot. Now, man has an end to which his whole life and all his actions are ordered; for man is an intelligent agent, and it is clearly the part of an intelligent agent to act in view of an end. Men also adopt different methods in proceeding toward their proposed end, as the diversity of men's pursuits and actions clearly indicates. Consequently man needs some directive principle to guide him toward his end.

[4] To be sure, the light of reason is placed by nature in every man, to guide him in his acts toward his end. Wherefore, if man were intended to live alone, as many animals do, he would require no other guide to his end. Each man would be a king unto himself, under God, the highest King, inasmuch as he would direct himself in his acts by the light of reason given him from on high. Yet it is natural for man, more than for any other animal, to be a social and political animal,[1] to live in a group.[2]

[5] This is clearly a necessity of man's nature.[3] For all other animals, nature has prepared food, hair as a covering, teeth, horns, claws as means of defense, or at least speed in flight, while man alone was made without any natural provisions for

these things. Instead of all these, man was endowed with reason, by the use of which he could procure all these things for himself by the work of his hands.[4] Now, one man alone is not able to procure them all for himself, for one man could not sufficiently provide for life unassisted. It is therefore natural that man should live in the society of many.

[6] Moreover, all other animals are able to discern, by inborn skill, what is useful and what is injurious, even as the sheep naturally regards the wolf as his enemy. Some animals also recognize by natural skill certain medicinal herbs and other things necessary for their life. Man, on the contrary, has a natural knowledge of the things which are essential for his life only in a general fashion, inasmuch as he is able to attain knowledge of the particular things necessary for human life by reasoning from natural principles. But it is not possible for one man to arrive at a knowledge of all these things by his own individual reason. It is therefore necessary for man to live in a multitude so that each one may assist his fellows, and different men may be occupied in seeking, by their reason, to make different discoveries—one, for example, in medicine, one in this and another in that.

[7] This point is further and most plainly evidenced by the fact that the use of speech is a prerogative proper to man. By this means, one man is able fully to express his conceptions to others. Other animals, it is true, express their feelings to one another in a general way, as a dog may express anger by barking and other animals give vent to other feelings in various fashions. But man communicates with his kind more completely than any other animal known to be gregarious, such as the crane, the ant, or the bee.[5]—With this in mind, Solomon says: "It is better that there be two than one; for they have the advantage of their company."[6]

[8] If, then, it is natural for man to live in the society of many, it is necessary that there exist among men some means by which the group may be governed. For where there are many men together and each one is looking after his own interest, the multitude would be broken up and scattered unless there were also an agency to take care of what appertains to the common weal. In

like manner, the body of a man or any other animal would disintegrate unless there were a general ruling force within the body which watches over the common good of all members.—With this in mind, Solomon says: "Where there is no governor, the people shall fall." [7]

[9] Indeed it is reasonable that this should happen, for what is proper and what is common are not identical. [8] Things differ by what is proper to each; they are united by what they have in common. But diversity of effects is due to diversity of causes. Consequently, there must exist something which impels toward the common good of the many, over and above that which impels toward the particular good of each individual. Wherefore also in all things that are ordained toward one end, one thing is found to rule the rest. [9] Thus in the corporeal universe, by the first body, i.e., the celestial body, the other bodies are regulated according to the order of divine providence; and all bodies are ruled by a rational creature. [10] So, too, in the individual man, the soul rules the body; and among the parts of the soul, the irascible and the concupiscible parts are ruled by reason. [11] Likewise, among the members of a body, one, such as the heart or the head, is the principal and moves all the others. [12] Therefore in every multitude there must be some governing power.

[10] Now it happens in certain things which are ordained toward an end that one may proceed in a right way and also in a wrong way. So, too, in the government of a multitude there is a distinction between right and wrong. A thing is rightly directed when it is led toward a befitting end, wrongly when it is led toward an unbefitting end. [13] Now the end which befits a multitude of free men is different from that which befits a multitude of slaves, for the free man is one who exists for his own sake, while the slave, as such, exists for the sake of another. [14] If, therefore, a multitude of free men is ordered by the ruler toward the common good of the multitude, that rulership will be right and just, as is suitable to free men. If, on the other hand, a rulership aims, not at the common good of the multitude, but at the private good of the ruler, it will be an unjust and perverted rulership. The Lord, therefore, threatens such rulers, saying by the mouth of Ezechiel:

"Woe to the shepherds that feed themselves (seeking, that is, their own interest): should not the flocks be fed by the shepherd?"[15] Shepherds indeed should seek the good of their flocks, and every ruler, the good of the multitude subject to him.

[11] If an unjust government is carried on by one man alone,[16] who seeks his own benefit from his rule and not the good of the multitude subject to him, such a ruler is called a "tyrant"—a word derived from "strength"— because he oppresses by might instead of ruling by justice.[17] Thus among the ancients all powerful men were called tyrants. If an unjust government is carried on, not by one but by several, and if they be few, it is called an "oligarchy," that is, the rule of a few. This occurs when a few, who differ from the tyrant only by the fact that they are more than one, oppress the people by means of their wealth. If, finally, the bad government is carried on by the multitude, it is called a "democracy," i.e., control by the populace, which comes about when the plebeian people by force of numbers oppress the rich. In this way the whole people will be as one tyrant.

[12] In like manner we must divide just governments. If the government is administered by many, it is given the name common to all forms of government, viz., "polity," as for instance when a group of warriors exercise dominion over a city or province.[18] If it is administered by a few men of virtue, this kind of government is called an "aristocracy," i.e., noble governance, or governance by noble men, who for this reason are called the "Optimates."[19] And if a just government is in the hands of one man alone, he is properly called a "king." Wherefore the Lord says by the mouth of Ezechiel: "My servant, David, shall be king over them and all of them shall have one shepherd."[20]

[13] From this it is clearly shown that the idea of king implies that he be one man who is chief and that he be a shepherd seeking the common good of the multitude and not his own.

[14] Now since man must live in a group, because he is not sufficient unto himself to procure the necessities of life were he to remain solitary, it follows that a society will be the more perfect the more it is sufficient unto itself to procure the necessities of life.[21] There is, to some extent, sufficiency for life in one family

of one household, namely, in so far as pertains to the natural acts of nourishment and the begetting of offspring and other things of this kind. Self-sufficiency exists, furthermore, in one street [22] with regard to those things which belong to the trade of one guild. In a city, which is the perfect community, it exists with regard to all the necessities of life. Still more self-sufficiency is found in a province [23] because of the need of fighting together and of mutual help against enemies. Hence the man ruling a perfect community, i.e., a city or a province, is antonomastically [24] called the king. The ruler of a household is called father, not king, although he bears a certain resemblance to the king, for which reason kings are sometimes called the fathers of their peoples. [25]

[15] It is plain, therefore, from what has been said, that a king is one who rules the people of one city or province, and rules them for the common good. Wherefore Solomon says: "The king ruleth over all the land subject to him." [26]

CHAPTER TWO

WHETHER IT IS MORE EXPEDIENT FOR A CITY OR PROVINCE TO BE RULED BY ONE MAN OR BY MANY

[16] Having set forth these preliminary points we must now inquire what is better for a province or a city: whether to be ruled by one man or by many.

[17] This question may be considered first from the viewpoint of the purpose of government. The aim of any ruler should be directed toward securing the welfare of that which he undertakes to rule. The duty of the pilot, for instance, is to preserve his ship amidst the perils of the sea and to bring it unharmed to the port of safety. Now the welfare and safety of a multitude formed into a society lies in the preservation of its unity, which is called peace. If this is removed, the benefit of social life is lost and, moreover, the multitude in its disagreement becomes a burden to itself. The chief concern of the ruler of a multitude, therefore, is to procure

the unity of peace.[1] It is not even legitimate for him to deliberate whether he shall establish peace in the multitude subject to him, just as a physician does not deliberate whether he shall heal the sick man encharged to him,[2] for no one should deliberate about an end which he is obliged to seek, but only about the means to attain that end. Wherefore the Apostle, having commended the unity of the faithful people, says: "Be ye careful to keep the unity of the spirit in the bond of peace."[3] Thus, the more efficacious a government is in keeping the unity of peace, the more useful it will be. For we call that more useful which leads more directly to the end. Now it is manifest that what is itself one can more efficaciously bring about unity than several—just as the most efficacious cause of heat is that which is by its nature hot.[4] Therefore the rule of one man is more useful than the rule of many.

[18] Furthermore, it is evident that several persons could by no means preserve the stability of the community if they totally disagreed. For union is necessary among them if they are to rule at all; several men, for instance, could not pull a ship in one direction unless joined together in some fashion. Now several are said to be united according as they come closer to being one. So one man rules better than several who come near being one.[5]

[19] Again, whatever is in accord with nature is best, for in all things nature does what is best. Now every natural governance is governance by one.[a] In the multitude of bodily members there is one which is the principal mover, namely, the heart; and among the powers of the soul one power presides as chief, namely, the reason. Among bees there is one king bee,[b] and in the whole universe there is One God, Maker and Ruler of all things. And there is a reason for this. Every multitude is derived from unity. Wherefore, if artificial things are an imitation of natural things and a work of art is better according as it attains a closer likeness to what is in nature, it follows that it is best for a human multitude to be ruled by one person.[6]

[20] This is also evident from experience. For provinces or

a See above § 9; CG I, 42.
b In popular ancient and medieval opinion, the chief bee was considered to be a male. Aristotle, *Hist. Anim.* V, 21: 553a 25.

cities which are not ruled by one person are torn with dissensions and tossed about without peace, so that the complaint seems to be fulfilled which the Lord uttered through the Prophet: "Many pastors have destroyed my vineyard." [7] On the other hand, provinces and cities which are ruled under one king enjoy peace, flourish in justice, and delight in prosperity. Hence, the Lord by His prophets promises to His people as a great reward that He will give them one head and that "one Prince will be in the midst of them." [8]

CHAPTER THREE

THAT THE DOMINION OF A TYRANT IS THE WORST

[21] Just as the government of a king is the best, so the government of a tyrant is the worst.[1]

[22] For democracy stands in contrary opposition to polity, since both are governments carried on by many persons, as is clear from what has already been said; [a] while oligarchy is the opposite of aristocracy, since both are governments carried on by a few persons; and kingship is the opposite of tyranny, since both are carried on by one person. Now, as has been shown above,[b] monarchy is the best government. If, therefore, "it is the contrary of the best that is worst," [2] it follows that tyranny is the worst kind of government.

[23] Further, a united force is more efficacious in producing its effect than a force which is scattered or divided. Many persons together can pull a load which could not be pulled by each one taking his part separately and acting individually. Therefore, just as it is more useful for a force operating for a good to be more united, in order that it may work good more effectively, so a force operating for evil is more harmful when it is one than when it is divided. Now, the power of one who rules unjustly works to the detriment of the multitude, in that he diverts the common good

[a] Bk. I, §§ 11-12, p. 178.   [b] Bk. I, Ch. II, pp. 179 ff.

of the multitude to his own benefit. Therefore, for the same reason that, in a just government, the government is better in proportion as the ruling power is one—thus monarchy is better than aristocracy, and aristocracy better than polity—so the contrary will be true of an unjust government, namely, that the ruling power will be more harmful in proportion as it is more unitary. Consequently, tyranny is more harmful than oligarchy and oligarchy more harmful than democracy.

[24] Moreover, a government becomes unjust by the fact that the ruler, paying no heed to the common good, seeks his own private good. Wherefore the further he departs from the common good the more unjust will his government be. But there is a greater departure from the common good in an oligarchy, in which the advantage of a few is sought, than in a democracy, in which the advantage of many is sought; and there is a still greater departure from the common good in a tyranny, where the advantage of only one man is sought. For a large number is closer to the totality than a small number, and a small number than only one. Thus, the government of a tyrant is the most unjust.

[25] The same conclusion is made clear to those who consider the order of divine providence, which disposes everything in the best way. In all things, good ensues from one perfect cause, i.e., from the totality of the conditions favorable to the production of the effect, while evil results from any one partial defect.[3] There is beauty in a body when all its members are fittingly disposed; ugliness, on the other hand, arises when any one member is not fittingly disposed. Thus ugliness results in different ways from many causes, beauty in one way from one perfect cause. It is thus with all good and evil things, as if God so provided that good, arising from one cause, be stronger, and evil, arising from many causes, be weaker. It is expedient therefore that a just government be that of one man only in order that it may be stronger; however, if the government should turn away from justice, it is more expedient that it be a government by many, so that it may be weaker and the many may mutually hinder one another. Among unjust governments, therefore, democracy is the most tolerable, but the worst is tyranny.

[26] This same conclusion is also apparent if one considers the evils which come from tyrants. Since a tyrant, despising the common good, seeks his private interest, it follows that he will oppress his subjects in different ways according as he is dominated by different passions to acquire certain goods. The one who is enthralled by the passion of cupidity seizes the goods of his subjects; whence Solomon says: "A just king setteth up the land; a covetous man shall destroy it." [4] If he is dominated by the passion of anger, he sheds blood for nothing; whence it is said by Ezechiel: "Her princes in the midst of her are like wolves ravening the prey to shed blood." [5] Therefore this kind of government is to be avoided as the Wise man admonishes: "Keep thee far from the man who has the power to kill," [6] because, forsooth, he kills not for justice' sake but by his power, for the lust of his will. Thus there can be no safety. Everything is uncertain when there is a departure from justice. Nobody will be able firmly to state: This thing is such and such, when it depends upon the will of another, not to say upon his caprice. Nor does the tyrant merely oppress his subjects in corporal things but he also hinders their spiritual good. Those who seek more to use than to be of use to their subjects prevent all progress, suspecting all excellence in their subjects to be prejudicial to their own evil domination. For tyrants hold the good in greater suspicion than the wicked, and to them the valor of others is always fraught with danger.[c]

[27] So the above-mentioned [7] tyrants strive to prevent those of their subjects who have become virtuous from acquiring valor and high spirit in order that they may not want to cast off their iniquitous domination. They also see to it that there be no friendly relations among these so that they may not enjoy the benefits resulting from being on good terms with one another, for as long as one has no confidence in the other, no plot will be set up against the tyrant's domination. Wherefore they sow discords among the people, foster any that have arisen, and forbid anything which furthers

---

[c] This sentence occurs word for word in Sallust, *Bel. Cat.* VII, 2, where, however, it is said of kings. It is the sentence immediately preceding the one quoted below in § 31, p. 185. This plagiarism is most unusual in St. Thomas' writings.

society and co-operation among men, such as marriage, company at table, and anything of like character, through which familiarity and confidence are engendered among men. They moreover strive to prevent their subjects from becoming powerful and rich since, suspecting these to be as wicked as themselves, they fear their power and wealth; for the subjects might become harmful to them even as they are accustomed to use power and wealth to harm others. [8] Whence in the Book of Job it is said of the tyrant: "The sound of dread is always in his ears, and when there is peace (that is, when there is no one to harm him) he always suspects treason." [9]

[28] It thus results that when rulers, who ought to induce their subjects to virtue, [10] are wickedly jealous of the virtue of their subjects and hinder it as much as they can, few virtuous men are found under the rule of tyrants. For, according to Aristotle's sentence, brave men are found where brave men are honored. [11] And as Cicero says: "Those who are despised by everybody are disheartened and flourish but little." [12] It is also natural that men brought up in fear should become mean of spirit and discouraged in the face of any strenuous and manly task. This is shown by experience in provinces that have long been under tyrants. Hence the Apostle says to the Colossians: "Fathers, provoke not your children to indignation, lest they be discouraged." [13]

[29] So, considering these evil effects of tyranny, King Solomon says: "When the wicked reign, men are ruined," [14] because, forsooth, through the wickedness of tyrants, subjects fall away from the perfection of virtue. And again he says: "When the wicked shall bear rule the people shall mourn, as though led into slavery." [15] And again: "When the wicked rise up men shall hide themselves," [16] that they may escape the cruelty of the tyrant. It is no wonder, for a man governing without reason, according to the lust of his soul, in no way differs from the beast. Whence Solomon says: "As a roaring lion and a hungry bear, so is a wicked prince over the poor people." [17] Therefore men hide from tyrants as from cruel beasts, and it seems that to be subject to a tyrant is the same thing as to lie prostrate beneath a raging beast.

CHAPTER FOUR

WHY THE ROYAL DIGNITY IS RENDERED HATEFUL TO THE SUBJECTS

[30] Because both the best and the worst government are latent in monarchy, i.e. in the rule of one man, the royal dignity is rendered hateful to many people on account of the wickedness of tyrants. Some men, indeed, whilst they desire to be ruled by a king, fall under the cruelty of tyrants, and not a few rulers exercise tyranny under the cloak of royal dignity.

[31] A clear example of this is found in the Roman Republic. When the kings had been driven out by the Roman people, because they could not bear the royal, or rather tyrannical, arrogance, they instituted consuls and other magistrates by whom they began to be ruled and guided.[1] They changed the kingdom into an aristocracy, and, as Sallust relates: "The Roman city, once liberty was won, waxed incredibly strong and great in a remarkably short time."[2] For it frequently happens that men living under a king strive more sluggishly for the common good, inasmuch as they consider that what they devote to the common good they do not confer upon themselves but upon another, under whose power they see the common goods to be. But when they see that the common good is not under the power of one man, they do not attend to it as if it belonged to another, but each one attends to it as if it were his own.[a]

[32] Experience thus teaches that one city administered by rulers, changing annually, is sometimes able to do more than some kings having, perchance, two or three cities; and small services exacted by kings weigh more heavily than great burdens imposed by the community of citizens. This held good in the history of the Roman Republic. The plebs were enrolled in the army and were paid wages for military service.[3] Then when the common treasury was failing, private riches came forth for public uses, to such an extent that not even the senators retained any gold for themselves

[a] Cf. *S.* I-II, Q. 105, A. 1, pp. 86 ff.

save one ring and the one *bulla* (the insignia of their dignity).

[33] On the other hand, when the Romans were worn out by continual dissensions taking on the proportion of civil wars, and when by these wars the freedom for which they had greatly striven was snatched from their hands, they began to find themselves under the power of emperors who, from the beginning, were unwilling to be called kings, for the royal name was hateful to the Romans. Some emperors, it is true, faithfully cared for the common good in a kingly manner, and by their zeal the commonwealth was increased and preserved. But most of them became tyrants toward their subjects while indolent and vacillating before their enemies, and brought the Roman commonwealth to naught.[4]

[34] A similar process took place, also, among the Hebrew people. At first, while they were ruled by judges, they were ravished by their enemies on every hand, for each one "did what was good in his sight."[5] Yet when, at their own pressing, God gave them kings, they departed from the worship of the one God and were finally led into bondage, on account of the wickedness of their kings.[6]

[35] Danger thus lurks on either side. Either men are held by the fear of a tyrant and they miss the opportunity of having that very best government which is kingship, or they want a king and the kingly power turns into tyrannical wickedness.

CHAPTER FIVE

THAT IT IS A LESSER EVIL WHEN A MONARCHY TURNS INTO TYRANNY THAN WHEN AN ARISTOCRACY BECOMES CORRUPT

[36] When a choice is to be made between two things, from both of which danger impends, surely that one should be chosen from which the lesser evil follows. Now, lesser evil follows from the corruption of a monarchy (which is tyranny) than from the corruption of an aristocracy.

[37] Group government [polyarchy] most frequently breeds dissension. This dissension runs counter to the good of peace, which is the principal social good. A tyrant, on the other hand, does not destroy this good; rather he obstructs one or the other individual interest of his subjects—unless, of course, there be an excess of tyranny and the tyrant rages against the whole community. Monarchy is therefore to be preferred to polyarchy, although either form of government might become dangerous.

[38] Further, that from which great dangers may follow more frequently is, it would seem, the more to be avoided. Now, considerable dangers to the multitude follow more frequently from polyarchy than from monarchy. There is a greater chance that, where there are many rulers, one of them will abandon the intention of the common good than that it will be abandoned when there is but one ruler. When any one among several rulers turns aside from the pursuit of the common good, danger of internal strife threatens the group because, when the chiefs quarrel, dissension will follow in the people. When, on the other hand, one man is in command, he more often keeps to governing for the sake of the common good. Should he not do so, it does not immediately follow that he also proceeds to the total oppression of his subjects. This, of course, would be the excess of tyranny and the worst wickedness in government, as has been shown above.[a] The dangers, then, arising from a polyarchy are more to be guarded against than those arising from a monarchy.

[39] Moreover, in point of fact, a polyarchy deviates into tyranny not less but perhaps more frequently than a monarchy. When, on account of there being many rulers, dissensions arise in such a government, it often happens that the power of one preponderates and he then usurps the government of the multitude for himself. This indeed may be clearly seen from history. There has hardly ever been a polyarchy that did not end in tyranny. The best illustration of this fact is the history of the Roman Republic.

[a] Bk. I, Ch. III, pp. 181 ff. The statement in § 23: "tyranny is more harmful than oligarchy," is not contradictory to the thesis of the present chapter, as Endres, p. 266, affirms. The reasoning of Ch. III proceeds on the supposition of an absolute and total tyranny, which is here expressly set aside.

It was for a long time administered by the magistrates, but then animosities, dissensions, and civil wars arose, and it fell into the power of the most cruel tyrants. In general, if one carefully considers what has happened in the past and what is happening in the present,[1] he will discover that more men have held tyrannical sway in lands previously ruled by many rulers than in those ruled by one.[2]

[40] The strongest objection why monarchy, although it is "the best form of government," is not agreeable to the people is that, in fact, it may deviate into tyranny. Yet tyranny is wont to occur not less but more frequently on the basis of a polyarchy than on the basis of a monarchy. It follows that it is, in any case, more expedient to live under one king than under the rule of several men.[3]

CHAPTER SIX

HOW PROVISION MIGHT BE MADE THAT THE KING MAY NOT FALL INTO TYRANNY

[41] Therefore, since the rule of one man, which is the best, is to be preferred, and since it may happen that it be changed into a tyranny, which is the worst (all this is clear from what has been said), a scheme should be carefully worked out which would prevent the multitude ruled by a king from falling into the hands of a tyrant.

[42] First, it is necessary that the man who is raised up to be king by those whom it concerns should be of such condition that it is improbable that he should become a tyrant. Wherefore Daniel, commending the providence of God with respect to the institution of the king says: "The Lord hath sought him a man according to his own heart, and the Lord hath appointed him to be prince over his people."[1] Then, once the king is established, the government of the kingdom must be so arranged that opportunity to tyrannize is removed. At the same time his power should be so

tempered that he cannot easily fall into tyranny.[2] How these things may be done we must consider in what follows.

[43] Finally, provision must be made for facing the situation should the king stray into tyranny.[3]

[44] Indeed, if there be not an excess of tyranny it is more expedient to tolerate the milder tyranny for a while than, by acting against the tyrant, to become involved in many perils more grievous than the tyranny itself. For it may happen that those who act against the tyrant are unable to prevail and the tyrant then will rage the more. But should one be able to prevail against the tyrant, from this fact itself very grave dissensions among the people frequently ensue: the multitude may be broken up into factions either during their revolt against the tyrant or in process of the organization of the government, after the tyrant has been overthrown. Moreover, it sometimes happens that while the multitude is driving out the tyrant by the help of some man, the latter, having received the power, thereupon seizes the tyranny. Then, fearing to suffer from another what he did to his predecessor, he oppresses his subjects with an even more grievous slavery. This is wont to happen in tyranny, namely, that the second becomes more grievous than the one preceding, inasmuch as, without abandoning the previous oppressions, he himself thinks up fresh ones from the malice of his heart. Whence in Syracuse, at a time when everyone desired the death of Dionysius, a certain old woman kept constantly praying that he might be unharmed and that he might survive her. When the tyrant learned this he asked why she did it. Then she said: "When I was a girl we had a harsh tyrant and I wished for his death; when he was killed, there succeeded him one who was a little harsher. I was very eager to see the end of his dominion also, and we began to have a third ruler still more harsh—that was you. So if you should be taken away, a worse would succeed in your place." [4]

[45] If the excess of tyranny is unbearable, some have been of the opinion that it would be an act of virtue for strong men to slay the tyrant and to expose themselves to the danger of death in order to set the multitude free.[5] An example of this occurs even

in the Old Testament, for a certain Aioth slew Eglon, King of Moab, who was oppressing the people of God under harsh slavery, thrusting a dagger into his thigh; and he was made a judge of the people.[6]

[46] But this opinion is not in accord with apostolic teaching. For Peter admonishes us to be reverently subject to our masters, not only to the good and gentle but also the forward: "For if one who suffers unjustly bear his trouble for conscience' sake, this is grace." [7] Wherefore, when many emperors of the Romans tyrannically persecuted the faith of Christ, a great number both of the nobility and the common people were converted to the faith and were praised for patiently bearing death for Christ. They did not resist although they were armed, and this is plainly manifested in the case of the holy Theban legion.[8] Aioth, then, must be considered rather as having slain a foe than assassinated a ruler, however tyrannical, of the people. Hence in the Old Testament we also read that they who killed Joas, the King of Juda, who had fallen away from the worship of God, were slain and their children spared according to the precept of the law.[9]

[47] Should private persons attempt on their own private presumption to kill the rulers, even though tyrants, this would be dangerous for the multitude as well as for their rulers. This is because the wicked usually expose themselves to dangers of this kind more than the good, for the rule of a king, no less than that of a tyrant, is burdensome to them, since, according to the words of Solomon: "A wise king scattereth the wicked." [10] Consequently, by presumption of this kind, danger to the people from the loss of a good king would be more probable than relief through the removal of a tyrant.

[48] Furthermore, it seems that to proceed against the cruelty of tyrants is an action to be undertaken, not through the private presumption of a few, but rather by public authority.

[49] If to provide itself with a king belongs to the right of a given multitude, it is not unjust that the king be deposed or have his power restricted by that same multitude if, becoming a tyrant, he abuses the royal power. It must not be thought that such a multitude is acting unfaithfully in deposing the tyrant, even though

it had previously subjected itself to him in perpetuity, because he himself has deserved that the covenant with his subjects should not be kept, since, in ruling the multitude, he did not act faithfully as the office of a king demands. Thus did the Romans, who had accepted Tarquin the Proud as their king, cast him out from the kingship on account of his tyranny and the tyranny of his sons; and they set up in their place a lesser power, namely, the consular power.[11] Similarly Domitian, who had succeeded those most moderate emperors, Vespasian, his father, and Titus, his brother, was slain by the Roman senate when he exercised tyranny, and all his wicked deeds were justly and profitably declared null and void by a decree of the senate.[12] Thus it came about that Blessed John the Evangelist, the beloved disciple of God, who had been exiled to the island of Patmos by that very Domitian, was sent back to Ephesus by a decree of the senate.

[50] If, on the other hand, it pertains to the right of a higher authority to provide a king for a certain multitude, a remedy against the wickedness of a tyrant is to be looked for from him. Thus when Archelaus, who had already begun to reign in Judaea in the place of Herod, his father, was imitating his father's wickedness, a complaint against him having been laid before Caesar Augustus by the Jews, his power was at first diminished by depriving him of his title of king and by dividing one-half of his kingdom between his two brothers. Later, since he was not restrained from tyranny even by this means, Tiberius Caesar sent him into exile to Lugdunum, a city in Gaul.[13]

[51] Should no human aid whatsoever against a tyrant be forthcoming, recourse must be had to God, the King of all, Who is a helper in due time in tribulation.[14] For it lies in his power to turn the cruel heart of the tyrant to mildness.[15] According to Solomon: "The heart of the king is in the hand of the Lord, withersoever He will He shall turn it."[16] He it was who turned into mildness the cruelty of King Assuerus, who was preparing death for the Jews. He it was who so filled the cruel king Nabuchodonosor with piety that he became a proclaimer of the divine power.[17] "Therefore," he said, "I, Nabuchodonosor do now praise and magnify and glorify the King of Heaven; because all His works are true and

His ways judgments, and they that walk in pride He is able to abase." [18] Those tyrants, however, whom He deems unworthy of conversion He is able to put out of the way or to degrade, according to the words of the Wise Man: "God hath overturned the thrones of proud princes and hath set up the meek in their stead." [19] He it was who, seeing the affliction of his people in Egypt and hearing their cry, hurled Pharaoh, a tyrant over God's people, with all his army into the sea.[20] He it was who not only banished from his kingly throne the above-mentioned Nabuchodonosor because of his former pride, but also cast him from the fellowship of men and changed him into the likeness of a beast.[21] Indeed, his hand is not shortened that He cannot free his people from tyrants.[22] For by Isaias He promised to give his people rest from their labors and lashings and harsh slavery in which they had formerly served; [23] and by Ezechiel He says: "I will deliver my flock from their mouth," [24] i.e., from the mouth of shepherds who feed themselves.

[52] But to deserve to secure this benefit from God, the people must desist from sin, for it is by divine permission that wicked men receive power to rule as a punishment for sin,[25] as the Lord says by the Prophet Osee: "I will give thee a king in my wrath," [26] and it is said in Job that he "maketh a man that is a hypocrite to reign for the sins of the people." [27] Sin must therefore be done away with in order that the scourge of tyrants may cease.

CHAPTER SEVEN [a]

WHAT ADVANTAGES WHICH ARE RENDERED TO KINGS ARE LOST BY THE TYRANT

[76] It is to be added further, however, that the very temporal advantages for which tyrants abandon justice work to the greater profit of kings when they observe justice.

[77] First of all, among all worldly things there is nothing

[a] [Chapter Ten in the complete edition.]

which seems worthy to be preferred to friendship. Friendship unites good men and preserves and promotes virtue. Friendship is needed by all men in whatsoever occupations they engage. In prosperity it does not thrust itself unwanted upon us, nor does it desert us in adversity. It is what brings with it the greatest delight, to such an extent that all that pleases is changed to weariness when friends are absent, and all difficult things are made easy and as nothing by love. There is no tyrant so cruel that friendship does not bring him pleasure. When Dionysius, sometime tyrant of Syracuse, wanted to kill one of two friends, Damon and Pythias, the one who was to be killed asked leave to go home and set his affairs in order, and the other friend surrendered himself to the tyrant as security for his return. When the appointed day was approaching and he had not yet returned, everyone said that his hostage was a fool, but he declared he had no fear whatever regarding his friend's loyalty. The very hour when he was to be put to death, his friend returned. Admiring the courage of both, the tyrant remitted the sentence on account of the loyalty of their friendship, and asked in addition that they should receive him as a third member in their bond of friendship.[1]

[78] Yet, although tyrants desire this very benefit of friendship, they cannot obtain it, for when they seek their own good instead of the common good there is little or no communion between them and their subjects. Now all friendship is concluded upon the basis of something common among those who are to be friends, for we see that those are united in friendship who have in common either their natural origin, or some similarity in habits of life, or any kind of social interests.[2] Consequently there can be little or no friendship between tyrants and their subjects. When the latter are oppressed by tyrannical injustice and feel they are not loved but despised, they certainly do not conceive any love, for it is too great a virtue for the common man to love his enemies and to do good to his persecutors. Nor have tyrants any reason to complain of their subjects if they are not loved by them, since they do not act toward them in such a way that they ought to be loved by them. Good kings, on the contrary, are loved by many when they show that they love their subjects and are studiously intent on the

common welfare, and when their subjects can see that they derive many benefits from this zealous care. For to hate their friends and return evil for good to their benefactors—this, surely, would be too great a malice to ascribe fittingly to the generality of men.

[79] The consequence of this love is that the government of good kings is stable, because their subjects do not refuse to expose themselves to any danger whatsoever on behalf of such kings. An example of this is to be seen in Julius Caesar, who, as Suetonius relates, loved his soldiers to such an extent that when he heard that some of them were slaughtered, "he refused to cut either hair or beard until he had taken vengeance." [3] In this way, he made his soldiers most loyal to himself as well as most valiant, so that many, on being taken prisoner, refused to accept their lives when offered them on the condition that they serve against Caesar. Octavianus Augustus, also, who was most moderate in his use of power, was so loved by his subjects that some of them "on their deathbeds provided in their wills a thank offering to be paid by the immolation of animals, so grateful were they that the emperor's life outlasted their own." [4] Therefore it is no easy task to shake the government of a prince whom the people so unanimously love. This is why Solomon says: "The king that judgeth the poor in justice, his throne shall be established forever." [5]

[80] The government of tyrants, on the other hand, cannot last long because it is hateful to the multitude, and what is against the wishes of the multitude cannot be long preserved. For a man can hardly pass through this present life without suffering some adversities, and in the time of his adversity occasion cannot be lacking to rise against the tyrant; and when there is an opportunity there will not be lacking at least one of the multitude to use it. Then the people will fervently favor the insurgent, and what is attempted with the sympathy of the multitude will not easily fail of its effects. It can thus scarcely come to pass that the government of a tyrant will endure for a long time.

[81] This is very clear, too, if we consider the means by which a tyrannical government is upheld. It is not upheld by love, since there is little or no bond of friendship between the subject multitude and the tyrant, as is evident from what we have said. On the

other hand, tyrants cannot rely on the loyalty of their subjects, for such a degree of virtue is not found among the generality of men that they should be restrained by the virtue of fidelity from throwing off the yoke of unmerited servitude, if they are able to do so. Nor would it perhaps be a violation of fidelity at all, according to the opinion of many, to frustrate the wickedness of tyrants by any means whatsoever.[6] It remains, then, that the government of a tyrant is maintained by fear alone, and consequently they strive with all their might to be feared by their subjects. Fear, however, is a weak support. Those who are kept down by fear will rise against their rulers if the opportunity ever occurs when they can hope to do it with impunity, and they will rebel against their rulers all the more furiously the more they have been kept in subjection against their will by fear alone, just as water confined under pressure flows with greater impetus when it finds an outlet. That very fear itself is not without danger, because many become desperate from excessive fear, and despair of safety impels a man boldly to dare anything. Therefore the government of a tyrant cannot be of long duration.

NOTES

THE SUMMA THEOLOGICA, I-II

QUESTION 90

1 Rom. vii. 23.
2 *S.* I-II, Q. 57.
3 *Ibid.*, Q. 9, A. 1.
4 *Digest* i ff. 1.
5 *S.* I-II, Q. 17, A. 1.
6 *Ibid.*, Q. 1, A. 1 *ad* 3.
7 *Phys.* ii.
8 *S.* I-II, Q. 13, A. 3; Q. 76, A. 1.
9 *Eth.* vii. 3.
10 *S.* I-II, Q. 17, A. 1.
11 *Etym.* v. 3.
12 *Ibid.*, 21.
13 *S.* I-II, Q. 2, A. 7; Q. 3, A. 1.
14 *Eth.* v. 1.
15 Rom. ii. 14.
16 *Eth.* ii. 1.
17 *Etym.* v. 10.
18 *Eth.* x. 9.
19 *Codex* i. 7.
20 *Etym.* v. 3; ii. 10.

QUESTION 91

1 *De lib. arb.* i. 6.
2 *S.* I, Q. 22, Aa. 1, 2.
3 *De lib. arb.* i.
4 Ps. iv. 6.
5 *S.* I-II, Q. 10, A. 1.
6 *De lib. arb.* i.·6.
7 *Ibid.*
8 *De invent. rhet.* ii.
9 Ecclus. xv. 14.
10 *S.* I-II, Q. 14, A. 1.
11 Ps. cxviii. 33.
12 *S.* I-II, Q. 5, A. 5.
13 *De lib. arb.* i. 5, 6.
14 Heb. vii. 12.
15 *S.* I, Q. 30, A. 3.
16 Gal. iii. 24, 25.

17 Exod. iii. 8, 17.
18 Matth. iv. 17.
19 *Contra Faust.* iv.
20 *Contra Adimant.* xvii.
21 *Etym.* v.
22 Rom. vii. 23.

QUESTION 92

1 *S.* I-II, Q. 55, A. 4.
2 *Pol.* iii. 6.
3 *Eth.* ii. 1.
4 *Pol.* i.
5 *S.* I-II, Q. 63, A. 2.
6 *Ibid.*, A. 1.
7 *Conf.* iii.
8 *Pol.* iii. 2.
9 *Digest* i. 3.
10 *Contra duas epist. pelag.* ii.
11 *Etym.* v. 19.
12 *S.* I-II, Q. 18, A. 8.
13 I Cor. vii. 12.

QUESTION 93

1 *Qq.*, qu. 46.
2 *S.* I, Q. 34, A. 1.
3 *De vera relig.* xxx.
4 *De lib. arb.* i. 6.
5 *S.* I, Q. 14, A. 8.
6 *Ibid.*, Q. 103, A. 5.
7 *Ibid.*, Q. 15, A. 2.
8 *De Trin.* xv. 14.
9 *S.* I, Q. 16, A. 1.
10 I Cor. ii. 11.
11 *De lib. arb.* i. 6.
12 *De vera relig.* xxxi.
13 *De lib. arb.* i. 6.
14 *De vera relig.* xxxi.
15 Rom. viii. 7.
16 *De lib. arb.* i. 5.

17 Prov. viii. 15.
18 De lib. arb. i. 6.
19 De vera relig. xxxi.
20 Metaph. v. text. 6.
21 Prov. viii. 29.
22 S. I-II, Q. 1, A. 2.
23 S. I, Q. 22, A. 2.
24 Gal. v. 18.
25 Rom. viii. 7.
26 De lib. arb. i. 6.
27 De civ. Dei xix. 12.
28 De lib. arb. i. 15.
29 De catech. rud. xviii.
30 II Cor. iii. 17.
31 S. I-II, Q. 85, A. 2.

QUESTION 94

1 Eth. ii. 5.
2 D. F.: De fide orthod. iv. 22.
3 S. I, Q. 79, A. 12.
4 De bono conjug. xxi.
5 De Hebdom.
6 De fide orthod. iii. 4.
7 Ibid., ii. 30.
8 Dist. 1. [Decretum i. 1.]
9 Rom. x. 16.
10 Etym. v. 4.
11 De bello Gall. vi.
12 D.F. tr.: and among these it is proper to man to be inclined to act according to reason. Now the process of reason is from the common to the proper, as stated in *Phys.* i. The speculative reason, however, is differently situated in this matter, from the practical reason. For, since the speculative reason is busied chiefly with necessary things, which cannot be otherwise than they are, its proper conclusions, like the universal principles, contain the truth without fail. The practical reason, on the other hand, is busied with contingent matters, about which human actions are concerned; and consequently, although there is necessity in the general principles, the more we descend to matters of detail, the more frequently we encounter defects. Accordingly then in speculative matters truth is the same in all men, both as to principles and as to conclusions, although the truth is not known to all as regards the conclusions, but only as regards the principles which are called common notions. But in matters of action, truth or practical rectitude is not the same for all, as to matters of detail but only as to the general principles; and where there is the same rectitude in matters of detail, it is not equally known to all.

It is therefore evident that, as regards the general principles whether of speculative or of practical reason, truth or rectitude is the same for all, and is equally known by all. As to the proper conclusions of the speculative reason, the truth is the same for all, but is not equally known to all: thus it is true for all that the three angles of a triangle are together equal to two right angles, although it is not known to all. But as to the proper conclusions of the practical reason, neither is the truth or rectitude the same for all, nor, where it is the same, is it equally known by all. Thus it is right and true for all to act according to reason: and from this principle it follows as a proper conclusion, that goods entrusted to another should be restored to their owner. Now this is true for the majority of cases: but it may happen in a particular case that it would be injurious, and therefore unreasonable, to restore goods held in trust; for instance if they are claimed for the purpose of fighting against one's country. And this principle will be found to fail the more, according as we descend further into detail, *e.g.*, if one were to say that goods held in trust should be restored with such and such a guarantee, or in such and such a way; because the greater the number of conditions added, the greater the number of ways in which the principle may fail, so that it be not right to restore or not to restore.

Consequently we must say that the natural law, as to general principles, is the same for all, both as to rectitude and as to knowledge. But as to certain matters of detail, which are conclusions, as it were, of those general principles, it is the same for all in the majority of cases, both as to rectitude and as to knowledge; and yet in some few cases it may fail, both as to rectitude, by reason of certain obstacles (just as natures subject to generation and corruption fail in some few cases on account of some obstacle), and as to knowledge, since in some few cases the reason is perverted by passion, or evil habit, or an evil disposition of nature; thus formerly theft, although it is expressly contrary to the natural law, was not considered wrong among the Germans, as Julius Caesar relates (*De Bello Gall.* vi).

13 Gen. xxii. 2.
14 Exod. xii. 35.
15 Osee i. 2.
16 *Etym.* v. 4.
17 Dist. 5. [*Decretum* i. 5.]
18 *S.* I, Q. 105, A. 6 *ad* 1.
19 *Conf.* ii.
20 *S.* I-II, Q. 77, A. 2.
21 Rom. i.

QUESTION 95

1 *Eth.* v. 4.
2 *Etym.* v. 20.
3 *Pol.* i. 2.
4 *Rhet.* i. 1.
5 *Eth.* v. 7.
6 *Etym.* v. 4.

7 *Eth.* v. 7.
8 *Ibid.*
9 D.F.: *Digest* i. 3. 5.
10 *Rhetor.* ii.
11 *De lib. arb.* i. 5.
12 *Eth.* vi. 11.
13 *Etym.* v. 21.
14 *De offic.* vii. [*De offic.* i. 7.]
15 *Etym.* ii. 10.
16 D.F.: *Digest* xxv. 3.
17 *Etym.* v. 4 ff.
18 *Ibid.*, 9.
19 *Pol.* iii. 10.
20 *Etym.* v. 4 ff.

QUESTION 96

1 *Eth.* v. 7.
2 *Digest* i. 3. 2.
3 *Etym.* v. 21.
4 *De civ. Dei* ii. 21; xxii. 6.
5 *Eth.* v. 7.
6 *Metaph.* x. text. 4.
7 *Eth.* i. 3.
8 *Etym.* v. 20.
9 *Ibid.*, 21.
10 Prov. xxx. 33.
11 Matth. ix. 17.
12 *De lib. arb.* i. 5.
13 *Eth.* v. 1.
14 *S.* I-II, Q. 54, A. 2; Q. 60, A. 1; Q. 62, A. 2.
15 I Pet. ii. 19.
16 *De lib. arb.* i. 5.
17 Rom. xiii. 1, 2.
18 I Tim. i. 9.
19 D.F.: *Decretals*, causa 19, qu. 2. [*Decretum* ii. 19. 2. 2.]
20 Rom. viii. 14.
21 D.F.: *Digest* i. 3. 31.
22 Rom. xiii. 1.
23 *Ibid.*, ii. 14, 15.
24 *Extra, De constitutionibus,* cap. *Cum omnes.* [This refers to the *Decretals* of Gregory IX, Book I, tit. 2, c. 6.]
25 D.F.: Dionysius Cato, *Disticha de Moribus.* [Book I, preface.]

[26] Matth. xxiii. 3, 4.
[27] *De vera relig.* xxxi.
[28] Prov. viii. 15.
[29] *De Trinit.* iv.
[30] D.F.: *Digest* i. 3.

QUESTION 97

[1] *Eth.* v. 5.
[2] *De lib. arb.* i. 6.
[3] *Ibid.*
[4] Dist. 12. 5. [*Decretum* 12. 5.]
[5] D.F.: *Digest* i. 4.
[6] *Pol.* ii. 5.
[7] Ep. ad Casulan.
[8] *Synon.* ii. 16.
[9] *Etym.* v. 21.
[10] *Eth.* i. 2.
[11] Deut. i. 17.
[12] *Etym.* v. 3.
[13] I Cor. ix. 17.
[14] Luke xii. 42.

QUESTION 105

[1] *Pol.* iii. 4.
[2] Exod. xviii. 21.
[3] Num. xi. 16.
[4] Deut. i. 13.
[5] *Timaeus* ii. [Steph. 29.]
[6] Deut. xvii. 14, 15.
[7] III Kings xi. 29 ff.
[8] I Kings viii. 11.
[9] Num. xxiv. 5.
[10] *Pol.* iii. 5.
[11] Deut. i. 15.
[12] Exod. xviii. 21.
[13] Deut. i. 13.
[14] *Ibid.,* vii. 6.
[15] Num. xxvii. 16.
[16] Judges iii. 9, 10, 15.
[17] *Eth.* iv. 3.
[18] I Kings viii. 7.
[19] Deut. xvii. 14 ff.
[20] Osee xiii. 11.
[21] *Ibid.,* viii. 4.

THE SUMMA THEOLOGICA, II-II

QUESTION 42

[1] *Etym.* x.
[2] *S.* II-II, Q. 39, A. 1.
[3] II Cor. xii. 20.
[4] *S.* II-II, Q. 40, A. 1.
[5] II Cor. xii. 20.
[6] *De civ. Dei* ii. 21.
[7] *S.* II-II, Q. 41, A. 1.
[8] *Ibid.,* Q. 40, A. 1.
[9] *Pol.* iii. 5; *Eth.* viii. 10.

QUESTION 57

[1] D.F.: *Digest* i. 1. 1.
[2] *Etym.* v. 3.
[3] D.F.: *Eth.* vi. 8.
[4] *De mor. Eccl.* xv.
[5] *Etym.* v. 2.
[6] *Ibid.*
[7] *Eth.* v. 1.
[8] *Etym.* v. 1.
[9] *Eth.* v. 7.

[10] *Ibid.*
[11] Isa. x. 1.
[12] D.F.: *Digest.* i. 1. 1.
[13] *Pol.* i. 2.
[14] *Etym.* v. 4.
[15] *Ibid.*
[16] *Pol.* ii. 2.
[17] D.F.: *Digest* i. 1. 1.
[18] *Ibid.*
[19] *Pol.* i. 2.
[20] *De offic. min.* i. 24.
[21] *Eth.* v. 6.
[22] *Ibid.*
[23] D.F.: Cf. *Eth.* viii. 11.
[24] Ephes. v. 28.
[25] *Eth.* v. 6.

QUESTION 58

[1] D.F.: *Digest* i. 1. 10.
[2] *Eth.* v. 1.
[3] *De verit.* xii.
[4] *De mor. Eccl.* xv.

5 *Etym.* x.
6 *Eth.* ii. 4.
7 *Ibid.,* iii. 1.
8 *Ibid.,* v. 5.
9 *Tract. in Ioan.* xl.
10 *Eth.* v. 4.
11 *S.* II-II, Q. 25, A. 1.
12 Rom. iii. 22.
13 *De mor. Eccl.* xv.
14 *De offic.* i. 7.
15 *Eth.* v. 11.
16 *S.* I-II, Q. 113, A. 1.
17 Luke xvii. 10.
18 *De offic. min.* ii. 6.
19 *Metaph.* ix.
20 *Moral.* ii. 49.
21 D.F.: *Eth.* ii. 6.
22 *De offic.* i. 7.
23 Wis. viii. 7.
24 *Eth.* i. 13.
25 *De verit.* xii.
26 *S.* I, Q. 81, A. 2.
27 *Eth.* v. 1.
28 *Ibid.*
29 I John iii. 4.
30 *Eth.* v. 1.
31 *Ibid.*
32 *Ibid.*
33 *Pol.* iii. 2.
34 *Hom. in Matth.* xxv.
35 *Pol.* i. 1.
36 *Ibid.,* 2.
37 *Qq.,* qu. 61.
38 *Eth.* v. 2.
39 *Ibid.,* ii. 6.
40 *S.* I-II, Q. 61, Aa. 3, 4.
41 *Eth.* ii. 3.
42 D.F.: *S.* I-II, Q. 23, A. 4; Q. 31, A. 1; Q. 35, A. 1.
43 *Eth.* v. 1.
44 *S.* I-II, Q. 22, A. 3; Q. 59, A. 4.
45 *Eth.* vii. 11.
46 *Ibid.,* i. 8.
47 *Ibid.,* v. 5.
48 *Ibid.,* ii. 6.
49 *Ibid.*
50 *Ibid.,* ii. 6; v. 4.
51 D.F.: Didot ed., ix. 5. Cf. *Eth.* v. 4.

52 *De Trin.* xiv. 9.
53 *De offic.* i. 7.
54 *De offic. min.* i. 24.
55 *S.* II-II, Q. 80, A. 1.
56 *Eth.* v. 4.
57 *De offic.* i. 7.
58 *Eth.* v. 1.
59 *Rhet.* i. 9.

QUESTION 66

1 Luke xii. 18.
2 D.F.: *Hom. in Luc.* xii. 18.
3 *De Trin.* i. D.F.: *De Fide ad Grat.* i. 1.
4 Ps. viii. 8.
5 *S.* II-II, Q. 64, A. 1.
6 *Pol.* i. 3.
7 Gen. i. 26.
8 D.F.: *Serm.* 64 (81), *De tempore.*
9 D.F.: *Dist.* 47, canon *Sicut hi.* [The passage referred to is in the *Decretum* i. 47. 8.]
10 *De haeres.* 40.
11 I Tim. vi. 17, 18.
12 *Hom in Luc.* xii. 18.
13 Isa. iii. 9.
14 D.F.: *Serm.* 64 (81), *De tempore.*
15 D.F.: *Dist.* 47, canon *Sicut hi.* [*Decretum* i. 47. 8.]
16 *Etym.* x.
17 *S.* I-II, Q. 1, A. 3; Q. 18, A. 6.
18 *Etym.* x.
19 *Eth.* v. 2.
20 Ecclus. xv. 21.
21 Exod. xii. 35, 36.
22 D.F.: *Institutes* ii. 47.
23 Exod. xx. 15.
24 Wis. x. 19.
25 D.F.: *Digest* i. 8; *Institutes* ii. 1.
26 D.F.: *Institutes, loc. cit.,* 39; *Codex* x. 15.
27 Matth. xiii. 44.
28 D.F.: *Institutes, loc. cit.,* 47.
29 D.F.: *Digest* xli. 1. 9; *Institutes, loc. cit.,* 48.
30 *Serm.* 178. D.F.: Cf. also *Digest* xiv. 5.
31 Prov. vi. 30.

[32] *S.* II-II, Q. 59, A. 4; I-II, Q. 72, A. 5.
[33] Rom. ii. 2.
[34] *Tract.* 1, *super Ioan.*
[35] Exod. xxi. 16.
[36] *Extra, De furtis,* canon 3. [The *Decretals* of Gregory IX, Book V, tit. 18, c. 3.]
[37] *Eth.* ii. 6.
[38] *Contra mendac.* vii.
[39] D.F.: *Serm.* 64 (81), *De tempore.*
[40] D.F.: Dist. 47, can. *Sicut hi.* [Reference is to the *Decretum* i. 47. 8.]
[41] *De Patr.* 4. D.F.: *De Abraham* i. 3.
[42] *Ep. ad Vincent. Donat.* 93.
[43] *Serm.* 82, *De verb. Dom.* 19.
[44] *De civ. Dei* iv. 4.
[45] Ezech. xxii. 27.
[46] *S.* II-II, Q. 55, Aa. 4, 5.

QUESTION 77

[1] *Codex* iv. 44. 8, 15.
[1a] *De Trin.* xiii. 3.
[2] *Eth.* viii. 13.
[3] Matth. vii. 12.
[4] *De offic.* iii. 15.
[5] *Pol.* i. 3.
[6] D.F.: *Codex* iv. 44. 2, 8.
[7] *De Trin.* xiii. 3.

QUESTION 78

[1] Luke xix. 23.
[2] *Ibid.,* vi. 35.
[3] Exod. xxii. 25.
[4] *Eth.* v. 5; *Pol.* i. 3.
[5] Ezech. xviii. 8.
[6] D.F.: *Institutes* ii. 4.
[7] *Pol.* i. 3.
[8] Ezech. xviii. 17.
[9] *Eth.* iv. 1.
[10] Rom. xi. 16.
[11] *Extra, De usuris* in the Decretal, *Cum tu sicut asseris.* [Reference is to the *Decretals* of Gregory IX, Book V, tit. 79, c. 5.]
[12] Rom. i. 32.

[13] *S.* II-II, Q. 43, A. 2.
[14] *Eth.* v. 11.
[15] *Ibid.,* 5.
[16] Epistle 47.
[17] Jerem. xli. 8.

QUESTION 104

[1] Heb. xiii. 17.
[2] *Moral.* xxxv.
[3] *De Parad.* viii.
[4] *Moral.* xxxv.
[5] *S.* II-II, Q. 80.
[6] *De nat. boni* iii. D.F.: Cf. *S.* I, Q. 5, A. 5.
[7] *S.* I-II, Q. 94, A. 3.
[8] *S.* II-II, Q. 102, A. 2.
[9] *Eth.* v. 4.
[10] *Moral.* xxxv.
[11] D.F.: Cf. Q. 82, A. 2.
[12] I Kings xv. 22.
[13] *S.* II-II, Q. 81, A. 6.
[14] *Moral.* xxxv.
[15] *Ibid.*
[16] *Ibid.*
[17] *Ibid.*
[18] I John ii. 4, 5.
[19] *Moral.* xxxv.
[20] *Ibid.*
[21] Matth. ix. 30, 31.
[22] Gen. xxii.
[23] Exod. xi.
[24] Osee iii.
[25] *S.* I-II, Q. 19, A. 10.
[26] Exod. xxiv. 7.
[27] *S.* I-II, Q. 9, A. 6.
[28] *Moral.* xix.
[29] Coloss. iii. 20, 22.
[30] Gal. iv. 14.
[31] I Thess. ii. 13.
[32] Acts v. 29.
[33] D.F.: Cf. St. Augustine, *De verb. Dom.* viii.
[34] *De benef.* iii.
[35] Rom. vii. 4.
[36] *De civ. Dei* iv.
[37] Titus iii. 1.
[38] I Pet. ii. 13, 14.
[39] Rom. vii. 23.

ON KINGSHIP

CHAPTER ONE

[1] *Pol.* i. 2.

[2] *Hist. anim.* i. 1; *Eth.* i. 5; *ibid.,* ix. 9; *Pol.* i. 2. The Aristotelian formula is always that man is a *political* animal. Unless special reason suggested to Aquinas the exact textual reproduction of this Aristotelian principle, he generally prefers to say that man is a *social* animal (*De benef.* vii. 1. 7). The combination *social and political animal* is also found in *S.* I-II, Q. 72, A. 4; *In De interp.* i. 2.

[3] The source of the teaching in §§ 5-7 is not the Aristotelian *Politics* but Avicenna, *De anima* v. 1; cf. *C.I.* v. See also *In Eth. prologue* 4, where St. Thomas, following more closely the Aristotelian doctrine of *Pol.* i. 2, no longer believes the Avicennian reasoning to be capable of demonstrating the conclusion that man is a *political* animal. Avicenna's argument is used by Aquinas in IV *Sent.* 26. 1. 1; *Quodl.* vii. 17; *C.G.* iii. 85; and *ibid.,* 128, 129, 136, 147; *S.* I-II, Q. 95. A. 1 (see pp. 55-57).

[4] *De part. anim.* iv. 10. Cf. III *Sent.* 1. 2. sol. 1 ad 3; *C.I.* v; *Quodl.* vii. 17; *S.* II-II, Q. 187, A. 2 *c.* and *ad* 1.

[5] *Hist. anim.* i. 1.

[6] Eccles. iv. 9.

[7] Prov. xi. 14.

[8] Cf. *S.* I, Q. 96, A. 4.

[9] *Pol.* i. 5. *In Metaph. prologue; In I Tim.* ii. 3; *S.* I, Q. 96, A. 4.

[10] Cf. *C.G.* iii. 23, 78.

[11] *S.* I, Q. 81, A. 3 *ad* 2; I-II, Q. 9, A. 2 *ad* 3; Q. 17, A. 2 *ad* 2, A. 7 *c.* and often elsewhere.

[12] *Metaph.* iv. 1; *In Metaph.* v. 1.

[13] *Pol.* iii. 6; *Eth.* viii. 10. *In Eth.* viii. 10; *In Pol.* iii. 5.

[14] *Metaph.* i. 2.

[15] Ezech. xxxiv. 2.

[16] The classification of constitutions in §§ 11-12 is owed to Aristotle, *Pol.* iii. 7. The basis of number, however, on which this classification rests, is found inadequate by Aristotle himself, *ibid.* In later texts, St. Thomas gradually abandoned it; see *In Eth.* viii. 10; *S.* I-II, Q. 95, A. 4 (pp. 62 ff.); Q. 105, A. 1 (pp. 86 ff.); II-II, Q. 50, A. 1 *obj.* 1; Q. 61, A. 2; *In Pol.* iii. 6. St. Thomas ends up, just as Aristotle did, with a list of constitutions in which each finds its essential characteristic in a certain qualification on account of which political power is awarded: in monarchy and aristocracy, power is given on account of virtue; in oligarchy on account of riches; in democracy on account of liberty.

[17] *Etym.* ix. 19; *De civ. Dei* v. 19.

[18] The meaning of this proposition, which is doubtless intended to be a reproduction of *Pol.* iii. 7, is not clear. [The passage becomes clear, and faithful to Aristotle's text, if we refer it to another passage of the *Politics,* viz., 1265[b] 28, and to the commentary on it by St. Thomas (Bk. II, lectio 7), where he uses exactly the same words that are found here.

The meaning is this: one of the *just* forms of government (or rather forms of state) is what is called polity, in which the *many* rule. But a just form of state demands the possession of virtues on the part of the ruling body. And, unfortunately, the virtuous people are *few.* However, says Aristotle, there is one virtue which is found among the many and that is *bravery.* This virtue is politically used to constitute the armed forces needed by the state, first and foremost among which was the heavily armed infantry (the hoplites, rich enough to provide themselves ₁with the requisite armament). This is why Aristotle says this polity rests on the prevalence of "heavily armed soldiers." (*Politics, loc. cit.*) How highly Aristotle valued these hoplites is shown by what he says in a subsequent passage of the *Politics:* a state in which there are many laborers (Banausoi) and few hoplites cannot possibly be great. 1326ᵃ 23.]

[19] Cf. *Pro P. Sestio* 45, 36; *De offic.* ii. 23. 80.

[20] Ezech. xxvii. 24.

[21] *Pol.* i. 2; *In Pol.* i. 1. The Aristotelian doctrine is here adapted to medieval realities in almost the same fashion as in some other earlier writings of Aquinas: *In Matth.* xii. 2; *In Ioan.* xiv. 1. 3; *In I Cor.* xi. 4; *In Heb.* xi. 3. In the later writings, Aquinas (a) more clearly emphasized the fact that the Aristotelian city seeks the satisfaction of not only the material but also the moral needs of man: *In Eth. prologue* ii; *S.* I-II, Q. 90, A. 2. Moreover (b) he treats cities and kingdoms not as specifically different communities each having its own essential characteristics, but as formally equal and only materially, i.e., historically different realizations of the same idea of "perfect community." Proof of this is the use of the combination "city or kingdom" in *S.* II-II, Q. 47, A. 11; Q. 50, Aa. 1, 2.

[22] In Latin *vicus.* This is neither here nor in *Pol.* i. 1 the Aristotelian clan-village, but the street of the medieval town, called *vicus* (e.g., *Vicus Straminis*). In each street, St. Thomas says *In Pol.* i. 2, "one craft is exercised, in one the weaver's, in another the smith's." Modern towns

still preserve the memory of this medieval arrangement in street names such as Shoemaker Row, Cordwainer Street, Butter Row, etc.

[23] The word is of Roman imperial origin, cf. *Etym.* xiv. 2. 19; and it is also used in medieval Canon Law. In St. Albert's cosmography (*De nat. loc.* iii. 1 ff.; ix. 566 ff.) Italy "is a province" but it also "contains several provinces," viz., Calabria, Apulia, Romana, Emilia, Tuscia, Lombardia. Likewise, Spain is a province and "has several provinces and kingdoms." See St. Thomas' use of the word in II *Sent.* 10. 1. 3 *ad* 3; IV *Sent.* 24. 3. 2. *sol.* 3; *S.* II-II, Q. 40, A. 1. Nothing is very definite about this notion except that, at any rate, a province is part of a greater and more comprehensive whole. The word is therefore characteristic of a properly medieval type of political thinking which still retains the memory of the Roman Empire. It was soon to be cast out of the political vocabulary; see *De pot. reg. et pap.* i. 1.

[24] "Antonomasia" is the figure of speech by which a generic predicate is used to designate an individual because it belongs to this individual in an eminent degree; e.g., Rome is *the* city (*S.* II-II, Q. 125, A. 2); divine truth is *the* truth (*C.G.* i. 1.).

[25] *Eth.* viii. 12; *In Eth.* viii. 10.

[26] Eccles. v. 8.

CHAPTER TWO

[1] *C.G.* i. 42; iv. 76; *S.* I, Q. 103, A. 3. This idea is characteristic of Hellenistic political philosophy, according to which the main function of the King-Saviour is considered to be the establishment of order and peace. Cf. P. Wendland, *Die hellenistisch-römische Kultur*, pp. 143 ff. Also *De civ. Dei* xix. 12 ff.; *De div. nom.* xi.

[2] *Eth.* iii. 5; *In Eth.* iii. 8; *C.G.* iii.

146; *In Matth.* xii. 2. In thus tracing back to Aristotle the idea that peace is the chief social good, St. Thomas was misled by the fact that the Latin text of the *Ethics* translated the Greek *eunomia* (good laws well obeyed) by *peace.*

3 Ephes. iv. 3.

4 *C.G.* iv. 76; *S.* I, Q. 103, A. 3.

5 *In Eth.* viii. 10.

6 *Phys.* ii. 2.

7 Jerem. xii. 10.

8 Ezech. xxxiv. 24; Jerem. xxx. 21.

CHAPTER THREE

1 *Eth.* viii. 12; *In Eth.* viii. 10.

2 *Eth.* viii. 12.

3 *De div. nom.* iv. 30; *R.P.* iii. 22.

4 Prov. xxix. 4.

5 Ezech. xxii. 27.

6 Ecclus. ix. 18.

7 In Latin: *praedicti tyranni.* § 27 is a reproduction of Aristotle's account of the traditional tyrant's policy of repression, "many of whose characteristics are supposed to have been instituted by Periander of Corinth; but many may also be derived from the Persian government" (*Pol.* v. 11). It is perhaps not unreasonable to think of the possibility that St. Thomas' original carried a mention of Periander and the Persian tyrants. On this supposition it would be easier to explain the surprising reference to names or persons which have not been mentioned.

8 Although there is no doubt about the fact that *Pol.* v. 11 is the source of this section, yet the text cannot be shown to depend literally on this source. Cf. Susemihl, ed., *Aristotelis Politicorum libri octo cum vetusta translatione Guilelmi de Moerbeka,* pp. 573-579. A disturbing feature of this paraphrase is that the author makes it a point of the tyrant's policy to "forbid marriage." No trace of such a prohibition is to be found

in Aristotle's account or its medieval version. St. Thomas is usually very accurate even in the most trifling details of his quotations.

9 Job xv. 21.

10 *Eth.* ii. 1; *In Eth.* ii. 1; *S.* I-II, Q. 95, A. 1, pp. 55 ff.

11 *Eth.* iii. 11; *In Eth.* iii. 16.

12 *Tusc. disp.* 1, 2, 4.

13 Coloss. iii. 21.

14 Prov. xxviii. 12.

15 *Ibid.,* xxix. 2.

16 *Ibid.,* xxviii. 28.

17 *Ibid.,* 15.

CHAPTER FOUR

1 *De civ. Dei* v. 12; *Bel. Cat.* vi. 7.

2 *Ibid.*

3 This and the subsequent propositions are taken from *De civ. Dei* iii. 19 (Livy xxvi. 36). The golden *bulla* is an ornament of the noble or rich Roman youth, consisting of a lenticular plate which was worn hanging upon the breast: Pauly-Wissowa III. 1048.

4 Cf. *De civ. Dei* v. 12.

5 I Kings iii. 18.

6 *Ibid.,* xii. 12, 13.

CHAPTER FIVE

1 Cf. *Pol.* v. 12.

2 St. Thomas may here be thinking of the Italian city-republics, where an originally oligarchic constitution was often superseded by the one-man rule and the despotism of a faction-chief, i.e., a Podestà or a Captain (head of either the *popolo* or the militia). Ezzelino, the Podestà of Padua, who exiled the Dominican Bishop Bartolomeo di Breganza, was Aquinas' contemporary. See *Cambridge Medieval History* IV, pp. 178 ff., 875 ff.

3 On St. Thomas' whole doctrine of the superiority of kingship see Gilson, *Thomisme,* pp. 455 ff.

CHAPTER SIX

[1] I Kings xiii. 14.

[2] Cf. *S*. I-II, Q. 105, A. 1, pp. 86 ff. Carlyle (*A History of Mediaeval Political Theory in the West*, vol. V, p. 94) correctly observes that, if these remarks had been completed, it would have been under terms similar to those on which in the *Summa, loc. cit.,* a mixed constitution is recommended. For a different interpretation see McIlwain, *The Growth of Political Thought in the West*, pp. 330 ff.

[3] A similar problem is discussed in II *Sent.* 44. 2. 2, and *S*. II-II, Q. 42, A. 2 *ad* 3; cf. also *S*. II-II, Q. 64, A. 3. For the history of this problem see Carlyle *loc. cit.*, vol. I, pp. 147 ff., 161 ff., vol. III, pp. 115 ff. The considerations of the present chapter should also be read against the background of the history of the Italian Communes in the thirteenth century; see *Cambridge Medieval History* VI, pp. 179 ff.

[4] *Val. Max. Fact.* vi. 2. Ext. 2 (*Spec. Hist.* iii. 73).

[5] Cf. *Policrat.* viii. 18, 20.

[6] Judges iii. 14 ff. See *Policrat.* viii. 20.

[7] I Pet. ii. 18, 19.

[8] *Acta Sanctorum Septembris,* vol. VI, 308 ff.

[9] IV Kings xiv. 5, 6.

[10] Prov. xx. 26.

[11] *Chron.* ii; *De civ. Dei* v. 12.

[12] *Chron.* ii; *De vir. illus.* i. 9. See also *De civ. Dei.* v. 21.

[13] *De bello Iud.* ii. 80 ff., 93, 111. Archelaus, however, was not exiled to Lugdunum (Lyons) by Tiberius, but to "Vienna (Vienne), a town in Gaul" by Augustus (*Ibid.,* 111; Chron. ii; Peter Comestor, *Historia Scholastica, In Ev.* xxiv; *Spec. Hist.* vi. 103). St. Thomas was probably misled by the *Glossa Ordinaria, In Matth.* ii. 22. The above statement, however, is somewhat puzzling in view of what Aquinas has said in *Catena Aurea; In Matth.* ii. 10, and in the commentary to St. Matthew ii. 4.

[14] Ps. ix. 10.

[15] Cf. Esther xv. 11.

[16] Prov. xxi. 1.

[17] See Esther.

[18] Dan. iv. 34.

[19] Ecclus. x. 17.

[20] Exod. xiv. 23-28.

[21] Dan. iv. 30.

[22] Isa. lix. 1.

[23] *Ibid.,* xiv. 3.

[24] Ezech. xxxiv. 10.

[25] *Moral.* l. 25, 16; *Sentent.* iii. 48. 11; II *Sent.* 33. 1. 2 *ad* 5; *S*. II-II, Q. 108, A. 4 *ad* 1.

[26] Osee xiii. 11.

[27] Job xxxiv. 30.

CHAPTER SEVEN

[1] *Val. Max. Fact.* iv. 7. Ext. 1; *Spec. Doctr.* v. 84.

[2] Cf. *Eth.* viii. 12; *In Eth.* viii. 12; III *Sent.* 29. 6; *De Perf.* xiii; *S*. II-II, Q. 23, A. 5, *et al.*

[3] *Div. Iul.* 67.

[4] *Div. Aug.* 59.

[5] Prov. xxix. 14.

[6] For instance Manegold of Lautenbach, *Ad Gebhardum Liber,* p. 365; See McIlwain, *op. cit.,* p. 210. For other authors see Carlyle, *op. cit.,* vol. III, pp. 130 ff. See above § 49, pp. 190 ff.

LIST OF ABBREVIATED TITLES

De anim.
   Avicenna, *De anima*
Bel. Cat.
   Sallust, *Bellum Catilinae*
De bello Gall.
   Caesar, *De bello Gallico*
De bello Iud.
   Flavius Iosephus, *De bello Iudaeico*
De benef.
   Seneca, *De beneficiis*
De bono conjug.
   Augustine, *De bono conjugali*
De catech. rud.
   Augustine, *De catechizandis rudibus*
C.G.
   St. Thomas, *Summa contra gentiles*
Chron.
   Eusebius, *Chronicon*
C.I.
   St. Thomas, *Contra impugnantes Dei cultum et religionem*
De civ. Dei
   Augustine, *De civitate Dei*
Coloss.
   St. Paul's Epistle to the Colossians
Conf.
   Augustine, *Confessions*
Contra Adimant.
   Augustine, *Contra Adimantum Manichaei discipulum*
Contra duas epist. pelag.
   Augustine, *Contra duas epistolas pelagianorum ad Bonifacium Papam*
Contra Faust.
   Augustine, *Contra Faustum Manichaeum*
Contra mendac.
   Augustine, *Contra mendacium liber ad Consentium*
Cor.
   St. Paul's Epistle to the Corinthians

Dan.
   The Book of Daniel
Decretals
   The *Decretals* of Gregory IX
Decretum
   Gratian, *Decretum magistri Gratiani*
Deut.
   Deuteronomy
Div. Aug.
   Suetonius, *Vitae XII Caesarum:* "Divus Augustus"
Div. Iul.
   Suetonius, *Vitae XII Caesarum:* "Divus Iulius"
De div. nom.
   Dionysius the Pseudo-Areopagite, *De divinis nominibus*
Eccles.
   Ecclesiastes
Ecclus.
   Ecclesiasticus
Ep. ad Casulan.
   Augustine, Epistola ad Casulanum (36)
Ep. ad Vincent. Donat.
   Augustine, Epistola ad Vincentium Donatistam (93)
Ephes.
   St. Paul's Epistle to the Ephesians
Eth.
   Aristotle, *Nicomachean Ethics*
In Eth.
   St. Thomas' commentary on the *Nichomachean Ethics*
Etym.
   Isidore, *Etymologiae*
Exod.
   Exodus
Ezech.
   Prophecy of Ezechiel
De fide ad Grat.
   Ambrose, *De fide ad Gratianum*
De fide orthod.
   Damascene, *De fide orthodoxa*

Gal.
St. Paul's Epistle to the Galatians

Gen.
Genesis

De haeres.
Augustine, *De haeresibus*

Heb.
St. Paul's Epistle to the Hebrews

De Hebdom.
Boethius, *De Hebdomadibus*

Hist.
Polybius, *Historiarum libri qui supersunt*

Hist. anim.
Aristotle, *Historia animalium*

Hom. in Luc.
Basil's Homily on St. Luke's Gospel

Hom. in Matth.
Chrysostom's Homily on St. Matthew's Gospel

In De interp.
St. Thomas' commentary on Aristotle's *De interpretatione*

De invent. rhet.
Cicero, *De inventione rhetorica*

Isa.
Prophecy of Isaias

Jerem.
Prophecy of Jeremias

De lib. arb.
Augustine, *De libero arbitrio*

Matth.
Gospel of St. Matthew

Metaph.
Aristotle, *Metaphysics*

In Metaph.
St. Thomas' commentary on *Metaphysics*

De mor.
Dionysius Cato, *Disticha de moribus ad filium*

De mor. Eccl.
Augustine, *De moribus Ecclesiae Catholicae et de moribus Manichaeorum*

Moral.
Gregory I, *Moralia*

De nat. boni
Augustine, *De natura boni contra Manichaeos*

De nat. loc.
Albert the Great, *De natura locorum*

Num.
Numbers

De offic.
Cicero, *De officiis*

De offic. min.
Ambrose, *De officiis ministrorum*

De Parad.
Ambrose, *De Paradiso*

De part. anim.
Aristotle, *De partibus animalium*

De Patr.
Ambrose, *De Abraham*

De perf.
St. Thomas, *De perfectione vitae spiritualis*

Pet.
Epistle of St. Peter

Phys.
Aristotle, *Physics*

Pol.
Aristotle, *Politics*

In Pol.
St. Thomas' commentary on *Politics*

Policrat.
John of Salisbury, *Policraticus*

De pot. reg. et pap.
John of Paris, *De potestate regia et papali*

Pro P. Sestio
Cicero, *Orations:* "Pro Publio Sestio"

Prov.
The Book of Proverbs

Ps.
The Book of Psalms

Qq.
Augustine, *De diversis quaestionibus lxxxiii*

Quodl.
St. Thòmas, *Quaestiones quodlibetales*

De repub.
   Cicero, *De republica*
Rhet.
   Aristotle, *Rhetoric*
Rhetor.
   Cicero, *De rhetorica ad Herennium*
Rom.
   St. Paul's Epistle to the Romans
R.P.
   St. Thomas, *De regimine principum*
   (*On Kingship*)
S.
   St. Thomas, *The Summa Theo-*
   logica
Sent.
   St. Thomas' commentary on the
   Sentences of Peter Lombard
Sentent.
   Isidore, *Sententiae*
Spec. doctr.
   Vincent of Beauvais, *Speculum*
   doctrinale
Spec. hist.
   Vincent of Beauvais, *Speculum*
   historiale
Suppl.
   St. Thomas, Supplement to the
   Summa Theologica
Synon.
   Isidore, *Synonima*

Thess.
   St. Paul's Epistle to the Thessa-
   lonians
Tim.
   St. Paul's Epistle to Timothy
Tract. in Ioan.
   Augustine, *In Ioannis Evangelium*
   tractatus
De Trin.
   Augustine, *De Trinitate*
De Trinit.
   Hilary, *De Trinitate*
Tusc. disp.
   Cicero, *Tusculanae disputationes*
Val. Max. Fact.
   Valerius Maximus, *Factorum et*
   dictorum memorabilium exempla
De vera relig.
   Augustine, *De vera religione*
De verit.
   Anselm of Canterbury, *Dialogus*
   de veritate
De vir. illus.
   St. Jerome, *De viris illustribus*
Vulg.
   The Vulgate
Wis.
   The Book of Wisdom
Zach.
   Prophecy of Zacharias

GLOSSARY [1]

accident: Something which does not have ontological consistency and which therefore needs to inhere in something else, as upon a foundation. It is opposed to *substance*. Examples of accidents are: weight (quantity), virtue (quality), paternity (relationship) which cannot exist without something to support them. The support of an accident is called a "subject." St. Thomas, following Aristotle, accounts for nine accidents, which, added to *substance,* constitute the Ten Predicaments or Categories.

administratively: This word, used in the text to translate the Latin *administrative,* means *subordinately,* that is, performed by a *minister,* who is a servant.

apprehension: Man's action depends on two faculties: one by which he *learns* about the existence of an external object; the other by which he is *attracted* (or repelled) by this object. The former is the *apprehensive* faculty, the latter is the *appetitive.*

art: Human activity directed to the modification of external matter is said to be engaged in a *factio* (cutting, building, melting, etc.); but when this activity remains within the doer, it is called *actio* (in the restricted sense of the word). Examples of *actio* are feeling, willing, etc. The rational regulation of a *factio* is *art. Art* is contrasted with *nature* in that the latter is a principle of change within the thing itself: a seed grows *naturally* into a tree because the seed contains within itself the principle of germination. But in the case of *art* the principle of change is external to the thing: a stone becomes a statue not because of something it possesses but because of an action external to it. This distinction is still kept alive by our use of *artificial* vs. *natural.*

difference (*differentia*): It is the relation of otherness between things that, from another point of view, are identical. This identity may be a generic one (as between one kind of animal and another). The character that distinguishes one species from others within the same genus is called the *differentia specifica.* So, e.g., *man* is constituted within the genus *animal* by the differentia of rationality. Popularly this was described by saying that the *differentia* is the knife that carves a species out of the genus.

[1] This is not a list of formal definitions. It is a list of suggestions intended to facilitate an initial study of the text of St. Thomas.

element: This is anything *from which* something is *originally* made. In a bronze statue, bronze is not an element, because bronze itself is made out of something simpler (earth, etc.). An element moreover has a *form* and is thus constituted into a species, a fact which differentiates it from formless primal matter. And finally an element is inherent in the things it constitutes, which differentiates it from a principle. In physics the four elements were earth, water, air, and fire, to which ether (the quintessence) is added.

end (*finis*): It is that for the sake of which something else is done. The end is the first and foremost principle of causality, for, according to Aristotle, not only does man act finalistically (teleologically) but nature as well. The only cause not controlled by teleology is *chance*. And yet even here it plays its part because, though the ploughman who stumbles upon a buried pot of gold does not *intend* to find it (he is not actuated by *that* end), yet if we are to speak at all of fortune, the thing accidentally discovered must be such as to be able to be envisaged as an end by the human will (it must be such that, were its existence known, would be desirable. The end is the first moment in the endeavor and the last in the achievement; e.g., recovery of health, the thought of which *begins* the series of: deliberation, visit to the physician, entrance into the hospital, etc., is the *last* moment of the process. Since the *end* is what our will strives after, its meaning coincides with what we call "the *good*."

essentially: This word is frequently used in the text in the strict sense of "according to essence or nature"; not in the common sense which the word has acquired colloquially, whereby it means "not completely but almost so."

fomes: An inclination in man, due not to human nature as instituted by God, but to nature as corrupted by original sin. It consists in a proclivity to sensuality in disregard of the dictates of reason.

form: It is that by which a thing is what it is: John is a man, i.e., an animal with a *rational* soul, and this rational soul is his *form*. Form is the principle of being; by itself it constitutes a thing in *act;* form is to act as matter is to potency.

habit: This word is sometimes used to designate one of the Ten Predicaments. It then has the meaning we find in the phrase: "The *habit* does not make the monk." It also has the post-predicamental meaning and signifies then the opposite of *privation*. Finally, it can designate one of the varieties of the accident *quality*. In this sense it has a meaning close to ours when we say "Virtue is a habit," or, "Walking becomes a habit in a well-trained child." St. Thomas uses the word *habitudo* to mean *relationship*.

honest: "Honesty" (*honestas*) does not regularly have the restricted meaning which the word has acquired. It is broadly equivalent to "moral virtue." *Honestum* is contrasted to "useful" and "pleasurable." What is honest is desired for its own sake by the rational appetite, as opposed to that which is desired for its use or, by the appetitive faculty, for pleasure.

injury: The Latin word *iniuria* is translated in the text by "injury." We must recall however that *iniuria* is the opposite of "justice," so that the colloquial meaning of "injury" does not fit.

intention: In addition to the ordinary meaning this word still possesses in the volitional sphere, it had another one which was once very common in the field of apprehension. The representation of an external thing, as it exists in human consciousness, was called an *intentio*. The adverb *intentionaliter* was, therefore, regularly contrasted with the adverb *realiter*. Logic is an *intentional* science, botany a *real* one.

ius: This word has given rise to confusion. Like *droit, Recht, diritto*, etc., *ius* has two aspects: viz., that of a regulating *norm*, and that of a *faculty* to a claim. Today the first is called "objective," the latter "subjective" *ius*. In English we have two different words for these two aspects: *ius* as *norm* is "law"; as a *faculty* it is "right." Confusion arises when the subjective term "right" is used to translate *ius, droit, Recht*, in the objective sense of "law." St. Thomas seldom uses *ius* in its subjective sense.

judicial: This term has a narrow technical significance: *iudicialia* are those precepts given by God for the purpose of regulating man's action toward other men which became obsolete at the coming of Christ.

legal: This term has a special sense as a modifier of "justice." It applies to the enjoinment of certain moral acts (bravery, temperance, etc.) the performance of which is deemed politically indispensable. When the state, for example, commands a man to face death on the battlefield, it issues an order which is indeed *just,* but it is so by a kind of *political* justice, which, according to the Aristotelian usage, is called "legal" justice.

motion: The word *motus* has more meanings than our term "motion." St. Thomas speaks of spiritual and of natural *motus,* and of the latter he frequently considers three varieties: qualitative, e.g., change of color; quantitative, e.g., change of weight; and local, e.g., change of place, which is the sense in which we still use the word.

order: A *multiplicity* of diverse individuals acting together for the attainment of an end of common interest to them all must be made into a *unit*. This unification is obtained by assigning to the properly endowed and accurately prepared individuals the performance of those tasks necessary for the attainment of the desired end. This hierarchy of indispensable posts graded up to the highest is called an "ordo." The term covers both the form of the array and the resulting organization. A good example of "ordo" is an army, arrayed from the lowest private up to the commanding general. What keeps it together is order, which subsequently comes to mean a command which, in turn, is not a mere arbitrary injunction but rather the norm imposed by the very nature of the organization. The purely formal side of order is obvious when we consider, for example, that an army seized by panic loses its capacity to defend itself and the life of its components. But as soon as order is re-established these same soldiers, in the same numbers and with the same weapons, pass from destructive confusion to victory.

politic: St. Thomas, following Aristotle, gives to this the meaning of "non-despotic," derived from the word *politia* when used in the sense of the *good* popular government (a popular government which rules not for the good of the lower classes alone, but for the benefit of the entire community).

positive: In addition to the meanings which this word has as the opposite of *negative* and *privative,* it also has that of *non-natural.* This is a very old usage and originates with the Greek Sophists who dwelt on the distinction between that which is abiding (by nature) and that which is transient (by convention). The latter term eventually came to be "thesis," which was easily translated into Latin as "positio."

potency: In addition to other well-known meanings, "potency"—as passivity—was used in the sense which is still found today when we speak of a thing as *potential* and not *actual.* The seed is the tree (in potency). A country, *potentially* invincible, may *actually* be very vulnerable. Closely connected with this significance is the meaning which the word has in psychological parlance: the power of seeing, of hearing, etc. As long as we live we *can* always see but we *do not* see at every instant of our life; we must have the *potentia,* the *power* to see at all times; this potency becomes an act at the apparition of the appropriate object (color).

principally: The adjective *principal* does not render the corresponding Latin one. *Principally* often means something quite different from *chiefly:* it does not indicate that something which is affirmed of a thing could, in a lesser degree, be affirmed of others; but rather that these other things must be traced back to it. If we say that snow is principally constituted by water, it does not mean that there is another minor element in it, but that water is the one thing from which snow comes.

principle: This is the source or cause of being ("nature is the *principle* of motion, etc."); it is also the source of intelligibility ("not every *principle* of knowing is a *principle* of being"). It is a proposition posited at the start of a discourse, which, within the given system, cannot be further deduced from anything anterior to it, and which therefore is accepted without further discussion. (This is the sense in which it is used by St. Thomas in the treatment of natural law; in this sense it is usually called *primum principium*.) It is a basic constituent: e.g., "The *principles* of natural things are these: matter, form, privation." A principle is more comprehensive than *cause,* and cause in turn more so than *element.* The point is the *principium* of the line, but not its cause. It must be recalled that cause among Aristotelians is fourfold: the material cause, the formal, the efficient, and the final. What we today call *cause* corresponds to the efficient cause.

property: (*proprium*). The accident *proprium* is the one which is possessed by every individual of a species and by no one outside of that species; e.g., the property of a magnet is the power to attract iron. From Aristotle down through medieval times, the *proprium* ascribed to man was "risible," because every man can smile, and no other being can. Intellectuality is *not* man's "property" because angels also have it.

reason (*ratio*) This word is often used in a restricted sense, in opposition to intellect (*intellectus*). It then signifies the discursive, ratiocinative process in contrast to the immediate, intuitive grasp of the intellect. It is *dianoetic* and the intellect is *noetic.*

simply: This word is used in the texts above to translate *simpliciter*. We must remember however that *simpliciter* is a quasi-synonym of "absolutely" and is used in contrast with the term "relatively" (*secundum quid*).

subject: In the logical sphere it is that concept of which something must be predicated and which cannot itself be a predicate. In its ontological sense it is correlative to accident; the support of an accident, be that support another and more basic accident, or, ultimately, the substance, is called *subject;* e.g., the subject of color is the surface of a body. In view of this usage we are confronted with the passages in which the Latin word *subjective* must be translated as "objectively." Both the logical and the ontological meaning must be kept in mind in interpreting the Aristotelian definition of substance as "that which is not in a subject nor is predicated of a subject." The first part excludes *accident* which is in a subject; the second part excludes the universal, or second substance, i.e., species or genus. For in a proposition of which John Doe is the predicate no subject (other than John Doe himself) can be placed; therefore John Doe is a substance.

suppositum: This term denotes an individual *subsisting* in any given species or nature: John Doe is a *suppositum* in the species "man"; Fido, in the species "dog." The natures of created things are individuated by matter which is *subjected* to the nature of the species. *Individuum, suppositum,* and *person* are closely connected. Any single nature, to whatever genus it might belong, can be called "individual"; when restricted to the category of substance it is a "suppositum"; further narrowed to rational substance it becomes "person." Any person is a suppositum, and any suppositum is an individual. But the converse is not true. "Hypostasis," likewise, means "person." The word originally signified essence or physis (nature). But as a result of the Trinitarian controversies over substance and persons, and of those over the nature of Christ, the word "hypostasis" lost its original significance and came to be used in the sense of person.